Diagnosing and Treating Complex Trauma

The term complex trauma refers to a broad range of symptoms resulting from exposure to prolonged or repeated severely traumatizing events. This broad spectrum of psychological symptoms complicates the formulation of an all-encompassing explicit definition, which in turn complicates the creation of specific treatment guidelines. In *Diagnosing and Treating Complex Trauma*, Trudy Mooren and Martijn Stöfsel explore the concept of complex trauma with reference to severely traumatized people including refugees, asylum seekers, war veterans, people with severe occupational trauma and childhood trauma, and others who have dealt with severe violence.

The book introduces a layered model for diagnosing and treating complex trauma in four parts. Part I introduces the concept of complex trauma, its historical development, and the various theories about trauma. The authors introduce a layered model that describes the symptoms of complex trauma, and conclude with a discussion on the three-phase model. Part II describes the diagnostic options available that make use of a layered model of complex trauma. Part III discusses the treatment of complex trauma using the three-phase model as an umbrella model that encompasses the entire treatment. Chapters cover a multitude of stabilization techniques crucial to the treatment of every client group regardless of the therapeutic expectations. This part also contains an overview of the general and specific trauma processing techniques. The last chapter in this part covers the third phase of the treatment: integration. Part IV addresses the characteristics of different groups of clients who are affected by complex trauma, the components that affect their treatment, and the suggested qualities required of a therapist to deal with each group. The book concludes with a chapter discussing the consequences for therapists providing treatment to people afflicted by complex trauma.

Developed from the authors' own clinical experiences, *Diagnosing and Treating Complex Trauma* is a key guide and reference for healthcare professionals working with severely traumatized adults, including psychologists, psychotherapists, psychiatrists, social-psychiatric nurses, and case managers.

Trudy Mooren, PhD, is a clinical psychologist and senior researcher in Foundation Centrum '45, the national institute for specialised diagnostics and treatment of psychotraumatic problems in the Netherlands. She is a licensed CBT, EMDR, and family therapist and publishes in the field of complex trauma.

Martijn Stöfsel, MSc, is a clinical psychologist at Sinai Centrum, a Jewish specialized institute for the treatment of posttraumatic stress disorder and comorbidity. He also runs a private practice for psychotherapy and is a lecturer and supervisor at the Dutch Society for CBT (VGcT). He publishes in the field of complex trauma.

Diagnosing and Treating Complex Trauma

Trudy Mooren and Martijn Stöfsel

Routledge
Taylor & Francis Group
LONDON AND NEW YORK

First published in the Netherlands 2010
by Bohn Stafleu van Loghum
Het Spoor 2, 3994 AK Houten, Netherlands

First published in English 2015
by Routledge
27 Church Road, Hove, East Sussex, BN3 2FA

and by Routledge
711 Third Avenue, New York, NY 10017

Routledge is an imprint of the Taylor & Francis Group, an informa business

Published by arrangement of Bohn Stafleu van Loghum, part of Springer Media.

British Library Cataloguing in Publication Data

A catalogue record for this book is available from the British Library

Library of Congress Cataloging-in-Publication Data

Mooren, Trudy, 1965– author.
[Complex trauma. English]
Diagnosing and treating complex trauma / Trudy Mooren and Martijn Stöfsel.
p. ; cm.
Author's names reversed on the Dutch edition.
I. Stöfsel, Martijn, author. II. Title. [DNLM: 1. Stress Disorders, Post-Traumatic—diagnosis. 2. Psychotherapy—methods. 3. Stress Disorders, Post-Traumatic—therapy. WM 172.5]
RC552.P67
616.85'21—dc23
2014010432

ISBN: 978-0-415-82113-1 (hbk)
ISBN: 978-0-415-82114-8 (pbk)
ISBN: 978-1-315-77980-5 (ebk)

Typeset in Times
by Apex CoVantage, LLC

Contents

Preface

The term complex trauma refers to a broad pallet of symptoms resulting from exposure to prolonged or repeated severely traumatizing events. This broad spectrum of psychological symptoms complicates the formulation of an all-encompassing explicit definition, which complicated rendering specific treatment guidelines. For this reason, this book includes descriptions of our clinical *practice-based* experiences in combination with existing *evidence-based* guidelines to demonstrate how this eclectic treatment strategy has proven to be successful. After an introduction and a formulation of a working definition of the concept of complex trauma, this book provides an extensive overview of all the specific interventions we implement to treat complex trauma. Our eclectic, integrative strategy of treatment is garnered from many techniques which are generally familiar to most therapists; some are perhaps less familiar. We are trained cognitive behavioural therapists. Cognitive behavioural therapeutic methods are predominantly represented in the interventions and techniques described.

This book focuses on the treatment of severely traumatized people such as: Second World War victims, refugees and asylum seekers, veterans, people with severe occupational-related trauma (fire brigade, police, train personnel), people with problems resulting from early childhood traumatization (which includes a special group of post-war or second-generation children), and others who have dealt with severe violence.

The material in this book is based on our experiences acquired at the organizations where we perform treatment, namely: Foundation Centrum '45, and the Sinai Centrum.

Foundation Centrum '45 is the national institute for specialized assessment and treatment of people with complex psychotrauma symptoms. It performs scientific research focused on knowledge and expertise in psychotraumatology, which it disseminates through training and education programmes. Foundation Centrum '45 is a top referent institute in the Netherlands and is a partner of Arq Psychotrauma Expert Group, a supportive holding for institutes and organizations in the field of psychotrauma and the consequences of traumatic events.

The Sinai Centrum is a specialized institute for the treatment of posttraumatic stress disorder and comorbidity. The Sinai Centrum is the only Jewish centre for psychotrauma expertise in Europe. Its experience with treating Jewish victims of the Second World War has, throughout the decades, evolved into more generalizable expertise to help various target groups – regardless of background or religion. These groups include war-stricken people, asylum seekers, refugees, young veterans, victims of physical abuse, sexual violence, and victims of abuse during childhood. In addition to reducing symptoms of traumatic experiences, treatment also aims to help people regain control over their lives.

The impetus for this book originated while providing courses included in the training programme for health psychologists in the Netherlands. It was there that we were confronted with the great need for a description of the concrete treatment options available that can be adopted for treating complex trauma. Despite the focus on our sometimes Netherlands-specific experiences, we hope this book will be helpful to our colleagues who treat complex trauma elsewhere in the world. The translation of the book faced us with several challenges regarding the generalizability or our experience acquired over the years. We have maintained our Dutch perspective on how we deal with trauma, but refrained from being too specific about components that are explicitly Dutch. Nevertheless, we trust that our international colleagues will be able to identify with all of the facets addressed in this book and that it will facilitate generalization to their own cultural contexts, as well as to those of their clients.

In order to bring about a clearer overview of complex trauma, we divided this book into four main parts.

Part I explores the concept of complex trauma, its historical development, and the various theories about trauma. We introduce a layered model that describes the symptoms of complex trauma, and conclude with a discussion on the three-phase model (stabilization, processing, and integration).

Part II describes the diagnostic options available that make use of a layered model of complex trauma. The development of a case conceptualization and a treatment plan based on the three-phase model is explained. We designed a four-quadrant diagram that demonstrates how the client's life phase at the time of the trauma and their general degree of social integration can affect the treatment options applicable to their situation.

Part III is the core of the book. It discusses the treatment of complex trauma using the three-phase model as an umbrella model that encompasses the entire treatment. A number of chapters in this part discuss a multitude of stabilization techniques crucial to the treatment of every client group regardless of the therapeutic expectations. In addition, the criteria needed for the transition from the stabilization accomplished in phase 1 to phase 2, the therapeutic processing phase, are also discussed. This part also contains an overview of the general and specific trauma processing techniques. The last chapter in this part covers the third phase of the treatment: integration.

Part IV addresses the characteristics of different groups of clients who are often affected by complex trauma, the components that affect their treatment, and the suggested qualities required of a therapist to deal with each group. The last chapter describes the consequences for the therapists who provide treatment to people afflicted by complex trauma.

This book is intended for people in the mental healthcare field who work with severely traumatized adults: psychologists, psychotherapists, psychiatrists, social-psychiatric nurses, and case managers. It can also be used as a reference by others working in the field who are involved with severely traumatized people in other, non-psychotherapeutic ways. The book can function as a text book, but also as a reference for experienced therapists.

The image of a chestnut on the book cover symbolizes the core of the problem of complex trauma: a round, smooth, vulnerable core that is strongly protected by a prickly shell; which – with overly intense confrontations – bursts open to reveal the hidden vulnerability.

We use the word 'client' because it is the term commonly used in the healthcare sector. We use the word 'therapist' because it is the most general term to cover the different professional groups for whom this book is intended. As mentioned in the initial paragraphs of this preface, many of the Netherlands-specific references have been generalized to a broader audience. However, we only have our own empirical experience to draw from, which naturally implies that our examples – all of which have been redacted to maintain the confidentiality of our clients – will include a select population of all the groups mentioned. In other words, our experience with war veterans is with Dutch soldiers, although not exclusively as you will see; our country may not host the same refugees that yours does or vice versa; and of course, there is the frequently inherent limitation that comes with everyone's historical context being geographically determined. Our references to diagnostic instruments used may not apply to your situation. Although the Netherlands has its own original questionnaires and surveys, it is often the case that our psychodiagnostic instruments have been translated from English into Dutch, which are then subjected to standard psychometric normative procedures before applicability can be considered reliable. As evidenced in our piece on dealing with clients with other countries of origin, neither the English nor the Dutch versions of these instruments may be suitable. We suggest you survey the applicability of the instruments used within your scope of practice and we hope that, at a minimum, you are able to acquire a compass direction towards the solutions specific to your needs.

The description of our daily work with severely traumatized clients has brought us tremendous satisfaction. This effective and constructive collaboration took a great deal of time, and we would also like to thank those who assisted in its actualization: Piet van Dijk, Ivo van der Velden, Saskia van Broeckhuysen, Jackie June ter Heide, and Jeroen Knipscheer. The boards of both Centrum '45 and Sinai Centrum are greatly acknowledged for their support. Yulma Perk, editor at Bohn Stafleu van Loghum, supported the initiative for this book and introduced us to James Caulfield who translated this book from Dutch into English. He made great efforts to grasp the meaning of the Dutch-specific components which were critically questioned for their cross-cultural validity. He did a great job. We appreciate very much the exchanges we had during the process of translation and rewriting. Susannah Frearson and Joanne Forshaw, co-editor and senior editor at Routledge, assisted us throughout the writing process.

We are deeply grateful to these people for their time and contributions.

Trudy Mooren and Martijn Stöfsel
October 2013

Part I

Definition and treatment models

Chapter 1

Complex trauma defined

Complex trauma is a term commonly used to describe the problems of severely traumatized people. The concept, however, has not been properly defined, yet no other term adequately covers all the problems that typically result from multiple interpersonal events of violence (Chu, 2011; Courtois & Ford, 2013). The *Diagnostic and Statistical Manual of Mental Disorders* (DSM-IV-TR) (American Psychiatric Association, 2000), for instance, refers to posttraumatic stress disorder (PTSD), but its diagnostic criteria fail to adequately describe the effects of experiencing multiple repeated traumatizations. The new edition (DSM-5; APA, 2013) encompasses an additional category to describe negative alterations in cognitions and mood but is far from complete in describing the more complex symptoms observed in most severe clients. The World Health Organisation (WHO) while preparing the *International Classification of Diseases* (ICD-11) suggests including both PTSD and complex PTSD as describers of trauma-related features (Cloitre et al., 2013). Thus, for want of a better word, in this book we will use the term 'complex trauma' to cover the full spectrum of reactions and symptoms resulting from exposure to multiple or repeated traumatic childhood or adulthood events and including both the shocking events themselves and their psychological and social repercussions.

Although most people manage to cope with the effects of complex trauma and carry on with their lives as normal, some people experience complex traumatizations and develop severe problems, which, as mentioned above, we will refer to as complex trauma. This introductory chapter explores the concept of complex trauma.

1.1. Disruptive experiences

This section discusses a few typical features of the events that precede the development of complex trauma.

1.1.1. Chronic and multiple exposure

People who suffer from complex trauma have been exposed to prolonged, multiple events of a violent nature. Examples are incest, sexual abuse, maltreatment, torture, captivity, and war. In some cases people with complex trauma have been exposed to extremely severe forms of violence and terror, such as witnessing the torture or death of another person.

In the 1970s, a South American man was picked up by the military police of his country, tortured and severely maltreated. Among other things, the police hung him by his arms tied behind his back, administered electrical shocks to his body and extinguished cigarette butts on his back; the man was even raped on one occasion. Held in captivity for 18 months under extremely adverse conditions, he witnessed how cellmates who had been physically tortured ultimately succumbed to their injuries.

After seeking refuge in the Netherlands, he married, had children, and seemed to be coping well. In recent years, however, most especially as his children have gradually left home, he has been suffering from intrusive images and nightmares about events of the past and is now seeking help.

1.1.2. Interpersonal violence

Sexual abuse, physical abuse, torture, captivity, and domestic violence are examples of severe violence inflicted on people by other people. Such interpersonal violence has a greater negative impact than violence caused by nature. Violent acts of nature are experienced as a whim of fate or as caused by a higher power because they are not preceded by conscious human acts. Interpersonal violence, however, always leads to slight to severe mistrust of others.

A Bosnian woman raised in a family atmosphere of affective neglect fled with her family from Serbian violence during the Balkan War. After two men from the family that sheltered them raped her, she sought help from a therapist for PTSD. During the consultation, she was observed not to be forthcoming but to be rather detached and reticent.

1.1.3. Limited (or no) support

Most victims of complex trauma have, at best, a limited support system available to them during or after a traumatic event, mainly due to the severe disruption caused by a war and the quantity of people who have had to flee or emigrate. This leaves little, if any, support for people who are severely victimized, as people, in general, are operating in survival mode.

Victims of incest, sexual abuse, physical abuse, and domestic violence often do not seek support because the perpetrators are known to them or they may be bound by feelings of loyalty. Families in these situations tend to socially distance themselves and frequently limit their reaction to the maltreatment by coping in fearful silence while secretly bearing the weight of this knowledge.

Soldiers at war often have experiences that are so alienating and shocking that they are unable to talk about them after returning home, with family and friends simply failing to understand what they have been through. The alienation experienced during deployment thus often continues after they return home.

> A man who had served in Lebanon for years sought help because of feelings of social isolation that led to his marriage ending in divorce. For years he had felt that his wife did not understand him and he had never dared to tell her about his traumatic experiences, such as seeing a ten-year-old boy shot right in front of him as they were talking to each other and seeing people burning alive while trapped inside a jeep that was struck by a missile. He had also felt powerless using outdated equipment to carry out what he perceived to be an impossible mission: establish peace, but do not intervene.

1.1.4. Differing impact depending on life stage

A person's development will be influenced differently depending on the life stage when the overwhelming events take place. A distinction can be drawn between three broad exposure groups, depending on the period over which a person is exposed to trauma.

1.1.5. Childhood exposure

People in this group undergo overwhelming events early in life that have a strong negative effect on their development of stress sensitivity, personality, identity, and autonomy. Such events, which often involve maltreatment and sexual abuse, are accompanied by personality disorders, including dissociative disorders (Van der Hart et al., 2006). Also belonging to this category is the post-war generation of children who grow up in the shadow of a conflict, raised by at least one parent who had directly experienced a war. The experience of war often damages parenting ability, leaving children in eventual need of help. Families in these circumstances commonly show a great deal of stress, a lack of intimacy and warmth, and high levels of anxiety.

1.1.6. Adult exposure

This group of clients had a stable childhood, but has since witnessed traumatic events. Examples are war veterans and most refugees. War veterans are usually young adults aged between 18 and 20 years at the time of their first mission. Many refugees from war-stricken countries are also in this category. The traumatic experiences of refugees in their country of origin are further exacerbated by stressful experiences in their host country.

1.1.7. Childhood and adult exposure

People who have experienced domestic violence, maltreatment, or sexual abuse as children usually develop a vulnerable personality structure and are at greater risk of developing a psychological disorder if exposed to a shocking event later in life. Negative early childhood experiences have been shown to be a strong predictor of the severity of PTSD symptoms that may develop later in life.

1.2. History of complex trauma

Clinicians and scientists have long been concerned with the effects of violence and shocking events on the human mind. Important historical events and social movements, moreover, have affected how they view the effects of severely overwhelming experiences. Historical events that gained the attention of scientists were full-scale wars such as the American Civil War, the First World War, the Second World War (including the Holocaust), the Vietnam War, the Balkan Wars, and the recent conflicts in Iraq and Afghanistan. As for social movements, these include the women's movement, migration flows, and changing attitudes to children's rights. Even though shocking events have led to violence and the disruption of life since time immemorial, relatively speaking, scientific research on the effects of such disruptive life events is still in its nascence.

1.2.1. A brief history of PTSD

Different terms were used in the nineteenth century to describe severe physical and emotional reactions resulting from overwhelming events; for instance, *railway spine* was the diagnosis for symptoms occurring after a train accident, and *traumatic neurosis* referred to injuries to the head (Kleber & Brom, 1992). Originally the physical damage was thought to cause the symptoms, but Pierre Janet was the first to point to the psychological processes that were at work after the event. Van der Hart et al. (2000), who thoroughly reviewed Janet's work, describe the processes of dissociation, memory fragmentation, and emotional fragmentation. The assumption was that traumatic experiences fragmented one's consciousness, with the detachment of overwhelming emotions from consciousness serving as a coping mechanism that enabled the person to continue functioning. The therapeutic processing of deeply overwhelming experiences included the reintegration of unprocessed traumatic memories with normal consciousness.

The First World War confronted society with the severely emotionally and physically damaged soldiers who had suffered the horrors of the trenches. Their complaints were ascribed to *shellshock*, the term used to initially describe the physical damage caused by explosions, bombardments, and shrapnel. Gradually, however, psychological explanations for the intense emotional problems experienced by soldiers began to take form. Pat Barker's *Regeneration* trilogy (1991), about the work of the psychiatrist Dr William Rivers and his colleagues, is illustrative of how trauma was conceptualized during the First World War (Shepard, 2000).

The Second World War confronted the world with such extreme horrors that new terms – such as *concentration camp syndrome*, *survivor syndrome*, and *KZ syndrome* (where the KZ refers to *Konzentrationslager*) – were coined to describe the consequences for psychological functioning caused by these traumas (Enning, 2009; Jongedijk et al., 1995). Soldiers experiencing traumatic reactions after the Second World War were considered to be suffering from *combat fatigue*, with terms such as *traumatic neurosis*, *gross stress reaction*, and *adjustment reaction* commonly used by the general public (Kleber & Brom, 1992). This was the first time the link between overwhelming experiences and stress was made.

In his exposition titled *Stress Response Syndromes: PTSD, Grief and Adjustment Disorders*, Horowitz (1997) makes explicit use of the new stress paradigm. Horowitz's fundamental notion is that traumatized persons experience more stress than they can cope with or think they can cope with, calling this an issue of *appraisal*. Two fundamental tendencies help to normalize the overburden of stress, namely, reexperiencing and avoidance. Although notions regarding an individual's capacity for resilience and endurance (*stimulus barriers*) had been addressed by Freud, they have recently gained new momentum because of the meaningfulness of the cognitive component included by Horowitz.

Dutch authors (Bastiaans, 1974; Blijham, 1984; Cohen, 1969; Hustinx, 1973; Musaph, 1973) have regularly addressed stress reactions in Holocaust survivors and in other groups of war-stricken people using various terms such as *KZ syndrome*, *concentration camp syndrome* and *existential emotional stress syndrome* while emphasizing the existential dimension of the violence. This dimension particularly affects a person's ability to enter into and maintain relationships, and to give meaning to the violent events and to life in general; survivors also experience *survivor's guilt*, which is guilt associated with surviving when others died.

The historical event that very well may have had the greatest bearing on defining PTSD as we know it today was the Vietnam soldiers' homecoming to the USA. In retrospect, recovery was not so much a matter of dealing with what happened *there* during the war and its consequences but of facing up to the growing lack of social support at *home* for returning servicemen and servicewomen. By the end of the 1960s, US society was completely opposed to the deployment of soldiers to Vietnam, and returning soldiers could not count on much support; at times they were even publicly shamed.

PTSD, however, would have never been included in the American Psychiatric Association's *Diagnostic and Statistical Manual of Mental Disorders* (DSM) had it not been for the pressure exerted by the women's movement in general, including feminists, who demanded that victims of sexual violence and abuse – often young – be given the attention they needed (Herman, 1992).

1.2.2. PTSD

PTSD (Appendix 1) has carved out a place of its own in the DSM since the publication of DSM-III in 1980. It is the only diagnosis to have situational circumstances included as a criterion (that is, the criterion is external to the person). This has led to tremendous debate regarding the definition of and criteria for PTSD in subsequent versions of the DSM, as it is very difficult to reach consensus on which severe symptoms – reexperiencing the trauma, avoidance behaviour, and the hypervigilance – are required for a diagnosis of PTSD (APA, 2000).

A diagnosis of PTSD is only made when the traumatic events are intrusive or reexperienced, when the associated stimuli are persistently avoided, and when there are symptoms of increased arousal (hyperarousal or hypervigilance) that were not present prior to the event. Examples of intrusions are recurrent nightmares about the trauma, flashbacks, and intrusive, uncontrollable memories. People who suffer from intrusions preferably avoid them because the memories are associated with distressing emotions and traumatic sensory experiences. Avoidance reactions (cognitive avoidance, restricted range of affect, and amnesia) may eventually become pervasive to the point of causing complete isolation. Increased arousal symptoms include reactions that reflect persistent hypervigilance and heightened sensitivity to potential danger, such as reduced concentration, exaggerated startle response, and irritability (APA, 2000).

The growing understanding of PTSD led to awareness that individual differences in psychological vulnerability are key determinants for developing PTSD. Researchers initially assumed that PTSD was only caused by the event itself: anyone who experienced a particular type of traumatic event would develop PTSD. However, experience has shown us that individuals differ greatly in how they react to similar events, which has made it necessary to identify risk factors and vulnerability factors that affect the development of PTSD (McNally, 2001).

Acute stress disorder (ASD) was later incorporated into DSM-IV (and included in DSM-5; APA, 2013), as a diagnosis made when PTSD symptoms (in particular, dissociation) manifest themselves within a month after the traumatic event has taken place.

> A veteran soldier who served in Srebrenica as a paramedic sought help for nightmares and intrusions. He was highly alert and appeared to be constantly on guard. The smallest occurrence could trigger an excessively aggressive response from him. He avoided anything that reminded him of his mission. He had thrown all of his papers from this period and his military uniform into the bottom of a wardrobe and he avoided anything on TV that had to do with war, especially the Balkan War. He especially steered clear of all programmes about football, even though he used to be a big fan, as football pitches evoked feelings of extreme fear and panic. He also refused to kick a ball around with the children in the neighbourhood, because football made him think of the field near the compound where women separated from the men were held captive by the Serbian militia.

1.2.3. Prevalence

Many studies have been conducted to investigate different aspects of PTSD. Epidemiology research (Kessler et al., 1995) has shown that as many as 60.7 per cent of men and 51.2 per cent of women in the USA have experienced a traumatic event at some time in their lives. According to De Vries and Olff (2009), around 80 per cent of the Dutch population has experienced at least one traumatic experience in their lives and 7.4 per cent of this group have at one time or another been diagnosed with PTSD. Many people experience more than one overwhelming event during their lives (Breslau et al., 1999; Classen et al., 2005), although only around 5 per cent of men and 10.4 per cent of women develop PTSD, with women tending to develop PTSD at a higher rate than men (De Vries & Olff, 2009). Breslau (1998) estimated that the PTSD prevalence following a traumatic event is approximately 10 to 15 per cent.

Various studies on different refugee populations indicate that the prevalence of PTSD and of related psychological disorders varies enormously, with rates ranging anywhere between 5 and nearly 80 per cent (Fazel et al., 2005). Since no standard method for collecting data was used in these studies, direct comparisons are difficult. The time elapsed between the occurrence of an overwhelming episode and data collection also varied greatly. Finally, the populations varied greatly, ranging from clients requiring mental healthcare to representative samples from the general population.

Studies with war veterans have shown that, when clinical interviews are used, PTSD prevalence is approximately 4 per cent (Engelhard et al., 2007). Note that clinical interviews are the preferred measurement method, even though they are more labour intensive, because self-report inventories tend to over-estimate prevalence.

For a Dutch population, Draijer (1988) found that childhood sexual violence was more prevalent than had initially been assumed; that study found 15.6 per cent and 24.4 per cent reported one or more incidents of sexual abuse committed by family members and non-family members, respectively.

1.2.4. The legitimacy of PTSD

Since its inclusion in the DSM in 1980, transmitting expectations of greater diagnostic clarity, PTSD has been widely researched and has been extensively reported in many publications. PTSD societies can be found at local, regional and international levels (for instance, the European Society for Traumatic Stress Studies and the International Society for Traumatic Stress Studies), treatment guidelines have been drawn up and treatment methodologies have been developed and tested. The fact that a clinical framework for PTSD exists means that occupational doctors have a tool to assess disability for pension and insurance purposes. There is, however, also some discord regarding PTSD, with several authors arguing that listing PTSD as the only trauma-specific diagnosis leads to the exclusion of a number of symptoms that have been encountered in some traumatized victims.

1.2.5. Criticism

Diagnosis of PTSD is mainly based on the experiences of US clinicians with victims of multiple violence, particularly Vietnam War veterans and women with a history of sexual abuse. The introduction of the diagnosis brought them recognition and vindication, as their trauma symptoms were now regarded as normal reactions to abnormal events. The focus was thus shifted away from possible vulnerabilities in the personality towards the events themselves. This shift, however, neglected to examine the role that vulnerabilities in the personality may have (Withuis, 2009). Nevertheless, it was the accumulated clinical experience with victims of multiple and prolonged violence which yielded the information necessary to adjust the diagnostics. PTSD as it has been defined was considered to be too simplistic a representation of what has since proved to include more key symptoms.

Some ten years after official inclusion of PTSD in the DSM, the American psychiatrist Lenore Terr asked for a more thorough differentiation between traumatic events (Terr, 1991). Terr had been involved in the care and treatment of school children held hostage in a school bus for several days, and, drawing on this experience, distinguished between type I and type II traumatic events. Type I events refer to the experience of a single, brief shocking event, whereas type II events refer to prolonged and multiple traumatization. While type I events place a person at greater risk of developing PTSD, the symptomatology of type II events is more complicated and multifaceted. This differentiation led to the distinction between *simple trauma* and *complex trauma*.

With regard to refugees, it has been argued that in view of the persistent and ongoing stressful circumstances in which refugees typically find themselves even after the identified traumatic event, the use of the word *post* in the term posttraumatic stress disorder is a misnomer (Summerfield, 1999). Refugees typically live through a prolonged process of seeking asylum and living collectively in a refugee centre, while experiencing constant uncertainty regarding acceptance into the host country and their future in general. Even though PTSD has frequently been used to describe the problems of refugees, it is argued that its guidelines are insufficient for the treatment of symptoms that refugees experience.

There has also been criticism with regard to the confusing meaning of the term *trauma* as associated with posttraumatic stress. Trauma may refer either to the traumatic event itself or to the consequences of the traumatic event (the wound). It would seem sensible, however, to reserve the concept of trauma for the multitude of reactions that result when people undergo shocking or deeply overwhelming experiences – especially as *wound* is also the Greek etymological meaning of the word *trauma*.

For the DSM versions that succeeded DSM-III, Criterion A, which describes the exposure to the traumatic event, was also a point of debate in the interest of bringing about a crystallized conceptualization of PTSD. Attempts were made to establish a definition that was as objectifiable as possible. On the one hand, it had to be specific enough to exclude other stress-provoking events, yet, on the other hand, it had to be generalizable enough to include the entire spectrum of conceivable traumatic events. In later editions since DSM-III, Criterion A was elaborated upon by including subjective responses such as horror and helplessness.

One problem remained unsolved, however: the severity of a psychotrauma is not only determined by the event itself, but also by the survivor's individual vulnerability. This means that similar extremely shocking experiences do not always induce the same reactions in everybody. Individual differences can, in fact, be enormous, and what is extremely traumatizing for one person may be minimally so for another. The interaction between personality traits and environmental features is therefore an essential factor in eliciting PTSD.

The fact that most people prove to be fairly capable of returning to a state of healthy functioning after exposure to violence or powerlessness provokes the question: what is it that protects such people from this specific psychological damage? A criticism of the PTSD diagnosis is, in fact, that too much emphasis is placed on pathology, when it is people's resilience that has something to teach us. Interventions should be based on the *essence of resilience* that emerges in survivors largely unaffected by exposure to a traumatic event.

The question that remains is whether PTSD is separable from any other conditions. If it is, can it be treated independently from other disorders or is there significant comorbidity?

1.2.6. PTSD comorbidity with other psychological disorders

PTSD is frequently accompanied by other conditions. Indeed, it is fairly rare for PTSD to manifest itself in people who have a serious psychological trauma without there being a concomitant disorder. As a case in point, the comorbidity of PTSD with depression is very high, with approximately 80 per cent of people with PTSD also having depression. This can be partially explained by avoidance behaviour and the negative symptoms of depression (loss of appetite, anhedonia, and loss of energy) overlapping with negative cognitions ('It will all come to nothing', 'There's no hope for me', or 'I'll never get out of this'). There is, thus, something of a conceptual resemblance between a mood disorder and an anxiety disorder.

PTSD is also frequently accompanied by addiction problems, attention deficit hyperactivity disorder, psychosomatic disorders resulting from the physiological symptoms of stress, and, to a lesser degree, anxiety disorders (social phobia and panic disorder with agoraphobia). It is common for dissociative and psychotic symptomology to develop in people with a history that includes exposure to severe violence such as torture or sexual abuse, or bearing witness to executions. It is sometimes difficult to identify the difference between a hallucination and a flashback. In addition, interpersonal problems are often seen in these people's relationships, social networks and work situations.

1.2.7. PTSD comorbidity with personality disorders

Exposure to severe interpersonal violence often leads to existential problems, the loss of a sense of meaning in life, and interpersonal relationship problems.

These, in turn, can lead to personality problems, as there seems to be a correlation between personality problems and complex psychotrauma. On the one hand, traumatic experiences can be harmful for the development of a normal personality; on the other hand, a vulnerable personality may be a precipitating factor for the development of psychotraumatic symptoms.

In general, personality is thought to be the result of a complex interplay between biological predispositions (temperament) and learning experiences (social learning) (Livesley, 2003; Millon & Everly, 1985). Learning through experience occurs in the context of how individuals deal with the demands of their immediate environment and their relationship with themselves. This concept forms the foundation for the general diagnostic criteria for personality disorders established in DSM-IV. Moreover, the difference between a normal personality and a disordered personality is not qualitative but *quantitative* (Allen, 2013; Livesley, 2003; Stuyling de Lange et al., 2009).

In actual practice, it is not always feasible to diagnose personality problems in people with psychotrauma because the premorbid personality is difficult to assess. With refugees – but also with war veterans in whom the disruptive entanglements took place a number of years ago – it is difficult to assess whether the problems are ascribable to the situation or the personality structure (*state* or *trait*). The DSM does not offer many options to address this issue, beyond what usually happens in many cases, namely, by diagnosing the problem as a *personality disorder not otherwise specified*. It is not only theoretically important to have an effective understanding of the correlation between severe interpersonal traumatization and changes in personality, there are also major practical repercussions inherent in this correlation. Benefit claims for war veterans and the plausibility of being accepted as a refugee, for example, depend upon an accurate diagnosis.

Personality disorders have long been considered to remain fairly stable over time and to be therapy-resistant. Relatively recent large multi-site studies, however, have significantly altered this rather antiquated notion, as they have shown how various interventions can be effective in alleviating the associated problems. This is why the relationship between personality and lifetime experience has become a relevant subject worthy of investigation. Psychotrauma has been proved to play a major role in the aetiology of a number of problems. A case in point is the relationship between traumatic experiences during early childhood and severe disorders of affect-regulation such as borderline personality disorder – a dynamic that has been demonstrated repeatedly. Narcissistic and antisocial personality disorders have also been attributed to early childhood traumatic experience.

Generally speaking, changes in personal identity or interpersonal skills can manifest themselves in different ways: in cognitions, in behaviour, in social functioning, and in emotions (Livesley, 2007). To an increasing degree, cognitions have recently become a focus of interest (Stuyling de Lange et al., 2009). In particular, so-called *core cognitions* have been attributed with an essential role in the maintenance of complex trauma symptoms (Beck, Emery & Greenberg, 2005; Ehlers & Clark, 2000). Either implicitly or explicitly, influencing the core cognitions will always need to be a treatment goal.

1.2.8. PTSD comorbidity with other problems

Clients who report a complex range of trauma complaints and symptoms also have a high incidence of physical complaints. People who have been tortured often have pain specific to the parts of the body that were targets of torture. The traces of torture are not always visible in the form of scars and this makes it difficult for them to feel validated with regard to their physical problems. Refugees who seek help after many years have often felt distressed, as they experience physical complaints that are partially attributable to prolonged stress and fatigue.

1.3. Trauma models

The PTSD diagnosis has proved to be inadequate in describing complex traumatization. Several suggestions have been made to more adequately describe the multiple consequences of disruptive experiences: (1) complex trauma, complex PTSD, or disorders of extreme stress not otherwise specified (DESNOS); (2) developmental trauma disorder (DTD); and (3) enduring personality change after catastrophic experiences (EPCACE). Each is described in turn below, as an aid to developing a pragmatic working definition of complex trauma.

1.3.1. Complex trauma, complex PTSD, or DESNOS

The October 2005 issue of the *Journal of Traumatic Stress* published a special section on complex trauma to discuss the need for 'more rigorous research on treatment efficacy, effectiveness, and safety' (Kilpatrick, 2005; Van der Kolk et al., 2005). More than a decade previously, Herman (1992) had already proposed incorporating complex trauma with PTSD in a diagnosis of *complex posttraumatic stress disorder* (C-PTSD). C-PTSD is defined as a syndrome with 27 symptoms, clustered in seven domains whose common theme is inadequate self-regulation. These symptoms consistently reflect alterations of the situation of before the shocking events (Ford et al., 2006; Jongedijk et al., 1995; Luxenberg et al., 2001):

- Alterations in regulation of affect and impulses, evident as greater affect lability and poor aggression regulation, self-mutilation, suicidal ideations, problems with the regulation of sexual needs, and risky behaviours.
- Alterations in attention and consciousness, including amnesia, temporary dissociative episodes, and depersonalization.
- Alterations in self-perception referring to feelings of helplessness, guilt, and shame, belief that the damage is permanent or that no one can understand the damage, and the trivialization or minimization of the experiences.
- Alterations in perceptions of the perpetrator, idealization of the perpetrator, or an excessive preoccupation with feelings of revenge.
- Alterations in relations with others, leading to feelings of mistrust of others and social isolation, repetitive revictimization during unpleasant events in the here-and-now, or even victimizing other people.

- Somatization, involving a range of symptoms such as gastrointestinal complaints, chronic pain, cardiopulmonary symptoms, symptoms of conversion disorder, and sexual symptoms.
- Alterations in systems of meaning, including a sense of hopelessness and pessimism with regard to the future, a loss of firm convictions such as the belief that life has meaning, and important changes in ethical or religious beliefs.

Further analysis of complex PTSD criteria has resulted in a diagnosis called DESNOS (not included in DSM-5 (see Appendix 2)). Since the introduction of the concept of DESNOS, an instrument called Structured Interview of Disorders of Extreme Stress (SIDES) has been developed (Pelcovitz et al., 1997) along with a subsequent revised version (SIDES-R) (Scoboria et al., 2008). The incidence of DESNOS in the general population turns out to be rare, at 1 to 3 per cent for the USA. It appears to be particularly correlated with interpersonal violence and childhood traumatization.

The DESNOS criteria were investigated in the DSM-IV Field Trial for PTSD (Van der Kolk et al., 1996a; Van der Kolk et al., 1996b). An important outcome is that DESNOS rarely occurs without PTSD. This was the reason for not including DESNOS as a separate diagnostic category, but rather as an entity associated with PTSD. Furthermore, it turns out that early trauma, chronic trauma, and trauma that is more interpersonal trauma lead to PTSD more frequently than does trauma occurring later in life. The risk of developing DESNOS thus decreases dramatically for people who experience trauma when they are older than 25 years (Ford et al., 2006).

The validity of DESNOS has not been fully addressed; varying reports on consensus with regard to the criteria exist. Researchers in Australia found disappointing reliability when the diagnosis was applied to a group of clients (Beltran & Silove, 1999). Ford and colleagues (2006), however, found the clusters of symptoms in a number of studies to be vividly reflective of the criteria.

In the DSM-5 that has appeared recently (APA, 2013) an additional cluster of features (negative alterations in cognition and mood due to the traumatic events) was added to deal with the cognitive changes victims reveal (Appendix 5). Complex trauma, DESNOS or developmental trauma disorder (DTD) were not included however.

1.3.2. Developmental trauma disorder

Van der Kolk (2005) developed a theoretical framework called DTD to diagnose complaints and symptoms of children and adolescents exposed to multiple acts of interpersonal violence. DTD is a variant of DESNOS, which Van der Kolk regards as a classification system for complex trauma symptoms in adults. Just as with DESNOS, self-regulation occupies a central place in the DTD framework (see Appendix 3 for diagnostic criteria).

1.3.3. Enduring personality change after catastrophic experiences

The International Classification of Diseases (ICD-10) (WHO, 2007) has included a specific description of EPCACE since 1993 (see Appendix 4). This disorder is characterized by a hostile and distrustful attitude towards the world, social isolation, feelings of emptiness or hopelessness, a chronic sense of threat, and alienation. Posttraumatic stress disorder may precede this personality change. EPCACE has also been used to describe the personality change that occurs after concentration camp experiences, prolonged exposure to life-threatening situations (for instance, terrorism), long-term captivity under a real threat of death, torture, and catastrophes.

1.4. A working definition of complex trauma

Complex trauma comprises a coherent cluster of traumatic reactions to extremely overwhelming – predominantly multiple and chronic – acts of violence. It includes problems associated with emotion regulation, attention and concentration, identity, trust, and functioning within relationships. Comorbidity is the rule rather than the exception. As for differential diagnostics, the main challenge is to draw a distinction between complex PTSD, borderline personality disorder, and dissociative identity disorder.

The essence of the symptomology of complex trauma is the trauma symptoms associated with PTSD combined with alterations in cognition, affect, personality, and relationships. The symptoms are often accompanied by an overall sense of malaise, which means that complex trauma lies somewhere at the juncture between trauma and personality disorders.

As stated above, three attempts – DESNOS, DTD, and EPCACE – have been made to systematically classify complex trauma. None has led to a stable diagnostic construct, yet the term complex trauma is often adopted in practice. Based on the clinical experience reported to date and the above systematic descriptions, we provide a practice-based working definition of complex trauma which we will use throughout the rest of this book. This working definition is mainly based on the ICD-10 concept of EPCACE and the model of personality development reported by Livesley (Livesley, 2007; Stuyling de Lange et al., 2009).

Livesley's model defines personality as the outcome of interactions between biological predispositions (temperament) and learning experiences (social learning) (Millon & Everly, 1985; Sprey, 2002). Personality development is regarded as a dynamic, layered, and lifelong process. A distinction is drawn between five components: genetic predisposition, internal concepts (core cognitions and cognitive schemas), emotional regulation, observable behaviour, and environmental factors. Social support or therapy aims to address these five components in the reverse order of this sequence, beginning with environmental factors and observable behaviour, continuing with emotional regulation, and concluding with internal concepts.

Combining Livesley's personality model with the ICD-10 definition of EPCACE yields our working definition of complex trauma.

Working definition of complex trauma:

- Experienced multiple and/or prolonged severe traumatization.
- Definitive and persistent alterations in a person's perception of one's relationship with and thoughts over the social surroundings and oneself; having a permanent sense of being altered or being different than others (alienation).
- Cognitive alterations characterized by a permanently hostile or mistrusting attitude towards the world, and an excessive feeling of guilt.
- Hypervigilance and alertness, heightened irritability, reexperiences, and nightmares. This is often accompanied by destructive forms of suppression of these feelings with numbing substances or alcohol.
- A fundamentally depressed mood and/or feeling of emptiness and/or hopelessness.
- Social withdrawal or constant tension in social contacts.
- Diverse symptoms that give the impression of general malaise and unhappiness, including physical symptoms, usually after prolonged tension.
- Intense problems with daily personal functioning, severe personal distress and having a negative effect on one's social surroundings.

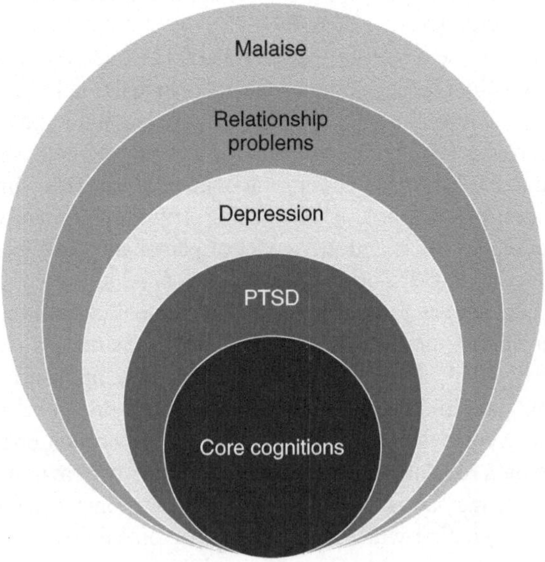

Figure 1.1 Complex trauma components

We aim for this working definition to be pragmatic and do not regard it as yet another attempt – like DESNOS, DTD, and EPCACE – to systematically define or investigate complex trauma. The various components of this working definition are depicted in Figure 1.1 which shows the various components or symptoms as a hierarchy that reflects the extent to which they can be influenced: the outermost and innermost layers contain the most easily and the least easily influenced components, respectively. Because core cognitions are central to complex trauma, we have clustered traditional PTSD symptoms such as reexperiencing, avoidance, and alertness together in the innermost layer; depression and problems with the social environment and relationships are located in the intermediate layer; and the outermost layer constitutes a variety of symptoms that result from deep-seated complaints that we include under the name *malaise*.

We will be using this model throughout this book to present diagnostic and treatment options for complex trauma. The next chapter describes theoretical insights regarding the treatment of psychotrauma.

Chapter 2

Treatment models

In the first chapter we explained that complex trauma can result from exposure to multiple, repetitive, and interpersonal violence that puts the victim at risk for a wide variety of problems, among them, posttraumatic stress disorder (PTSD). In this chapter we discuss the current basic principles underlying the treatment of (complex) psychotrauma. Rather than offer an exhaustive exposition on the topic, the aim here is to signal significant trends. Psychotrauma has been a topic of keen interest for as long as psychology has existed. The evidence garnered from the treatment of simple psychotrauma should not be dismissed in any strategy for dealing with multiple problems.

The first section of this chapter discusses general theories regarding trauma treatments. The second section discusses the therapeutic methods found to be effective as a strategy for treating complex trauma problems. Section three describes useful planning principles for the treatment of complex trauma and reviews existing guidelines based on evidence collected for the different methods. The three-phase model for the treatment of complex trauma, discussed at the end of the chapter, is widely used by clinical practitioners despite being less directly based on evidence. Essential to this treatment method is the fundamental assumption that the ability to regulate emotions and the ability to tolerate or stabilize any dysregulation is crucial to treatment.

2.1. General treatment theories

This section discusses the most common precepts that may play a role in the treatment of psychotrauma after multiple overwhelming experiences.

2.1.1. Learning theory

Learning theory and behavioural psychology have greatly influenced the treatment of posttraumatic symptoms. The learning theory model is based on learning experiences. A traumatic event teaches a person that in a specific situation a specific stimulus leads to a harmful response (that is, an unconditioned stimulus leads to a conditioned response, UCS-CR) – classical and operant conditioning principles at work. An example might be exposure to a traumatic event when the perpetrator was wearing a ski mask leading to the person associating a ski mask with the responses experienced during the trauma. Hence, seeing a ski mask in another situation will automatically lead to an anxiety response, followed by a behavioural response which will always include an element of avoidance. Avoidance of situations involving a ski mask is calming because intense anxiety is prevented; this is, however, merely a temporary solution.

An effective therapeutic process relies on techniques that gradually reduce the need for avoidance, so that ultimately the client can tolerate images representing the traumatic event. A small proportion of people exposed to trauma feel so much anxiety in confronting such images that the avoidance behaviour is maintained. In such people, the amount of cues or triggers that elicit anxiety over time are more likely to increase rather than decrease, causing the avoidance behaviour to increase and impeding the person's normal functioning. The technique implemented during treatment with learning theory or behavioural psychology is *exposure*, which involves exposing the client to the feared stimuli in a safe and structured therapeutic environment.

2.1.2. Cognitive theory

The treatment of psychotrauma has benefitted greatly from the integration of the cognitive component with the learning theory model. A great deal of the evidence underpinning current guidelines for psychotrauma treatment originates from this combined approach. The premise of the cognitive component is that when a person responds to a stimulus (trigger), a memory is called up (that is, an unconditioned stimulus leads to an unconditioned response, UCS-CR) that evokes an emotional response (anxiety, anger, shame) or a behavioural response (fight, flight, freeze), which is not necessarily determined by the memory of the specific event or by what is actually happening at the time of the response. Experiences from the past thus colour perceptions of current circumstances to a significant degree. Most people take this for granted most of the time, but many clients are barely conscious of how this operates in the context of their trauma.

A second development regarding the cognitive approach to psychotrauma was Janoff-Bulman's (1992) emphasis on how people operate on the basis of assumptive worlds. Although these worlds are illusory, in everyday life they have extremely practical uses. Examples are how almost everyone thinks they are an above-average car driver and how most people tend to have positive expectations regarding the future. Traumatized people, however, have gone through experiences that have left them feeling powerless. Their confrontation with powerlessness, disruption, and unpleasant consequences has threatened the integrity of their fundamental cognitive assumptions – for instance, that 'people can be trusted'. Fundamental cognitive assumptions are core beliefs that affect individual perceptions, experiences, and behaviour to a strong degree. If these assumptions turn out to no longer hold true, either they must be adjusted in some way, or the explanations behind the occurrence of the circumstances must be adjusted. A familiar example is that a sexual assault or rape was 'provoked' by the victim being scantily clothed or walking alone in the dark. Cognitive attribution processes determine whether basic cognitions are maintained or adjusted. In general, people are cognitively conservative, meaning that they do not change deep-seated beliefs so easily and will seek to make adjustments externally.

Cognitive themes that commonly affect traumatized people are victimhood, inferiority, powerlessness, control, and justice. The main cognitive theme, victimhood, raises the issue that if a traumatic event is not somehow processed, the person will remain embroiled in an inescapable mindset of being a constant victim of the traumatic event. They also sometimes generalize this mindset of victimhood to other areas of life ('There's no hope for me'). Cognitions regarding victimhood are often accompanied by cognitions about inferiority. When the traumatic events took place, the person was powerless and had no control over the circumstances, and the cognitions that were founded in the traumatic situation will persist as long as the traumatic events have not been processed. These cognitions are also often generalized to other domains of life, and the thoughts of powerlessness are also occasionally expressed in the form of powerless aggression ('Why always me?'). Since, in general, a traumatic event involves unjust treatment of someone, a logical consequence of this is active cognitions relating to a sense of injustice. Such active cognitions and feelings of injustice can easily be evoked in the here-and-now (an unjustified situation), and this, in turn, leads to an intense reaction ('It always happens to the same people', 'The perpetrators always get away with it', 'I always have to pay the price'). These thoughts are also expressed in all sorts of negative cognitions regarding self-worth and inferiority that actually perpetuate the traumatic event and maintain the feeling of insignificance ('I'm not permitted to be who I am', 'I cannot be who I want to be', 'I don't count, I'm worthless'). A victim of a traumatic event often perceives the world as a constant source of potential danger and being convinced of this leads to increased stress or agitation. It also leads to interactions with others from an attitude of basic mistrust ('I don't trust anyone', 'They aren't thinking about what's good for me', 'They'll get me if I'm not careful').

Finally, thoughts of guilt and shame often arise. Some people find it humiliating to admit they need any help at all, let alone psychiatric help. Many refugees consider psychiatry to be stigmatizing and a sign of failure, or fear that people will think that they are mentally ill ('If anyone finds out that I come here, they will think I'm crazy'). A person's ability to function is also impaired by survivor's guilt: a feeling of guilt for having survived when other people have died or are still imprisoned.

2.1.3. Theories of memory

One particular cognitive model, which has had a huge impact on the treatment of psychotrauma, theorizes that PTSD develops from what is called an anxiety network in which all types of associations that distort other information take root within a structure of sensorial memories (Foa & Kozak, 1986; Foa et al., 2013). These fear structures contain inaccurate ideas of associations between elements in daily reality. These associations have been based on experiences earlier. For instance, 'Nobody is to be trusted'. The development of mental networks around core experiences accounts for individual differences in traumatic reactions.

In another cognitive model, also based on information processing, psychotrauma is posited to occur when the storage of memories is impaired (Brewin et al., 1996), as this prevents events from being stored in the autobiographical memory. Information needs to be properly processed for it to be stored and made accessible for voluntary retrieval.

A treatment called Eye Movement Desensitization and Reprocessing (EMDR) is based on a variant of cognitive information processing theories that make explicit use of memory processes. In a person with psychotrauma, unprocessed information has not been integrated into the memory of experiences of the self, stored in long-term memory. In other words, specific sensory information (with representations of various traumatic sensory stimuli) has not yet been incorporated into the person's biography. Therapeutically it is important for the person to confront and deal with this information stored as an isolated network of memories. The working mechanisms of EMDR are currently being investigated (Engelhard et al., 2010). It is presumed that the exchange between the left and right halves of the body plays a role when isolated unprocessed memories are integrated. Even though little evidence of this has been found so far, something similar happens in natural situations, such as with eye movement during REM sleep.

2.1.4. Cognitive theories integrated with learning theory

The integration of cognitive theory and learning theory principles offers a solid basis for treating stress symptoms that arise after the experience of deeply overwhelming events. This approach is effective in breaking through persistently recurring tendencies to avoid exposure to anxiety-provoking stimuli, while equipping the client with the ability to give new meaning to the traumatic event. Since how trauma is experienced is unique, each person has to formulate the meaning of the experience now and in the future. The meaning – the UCS-UCR representation – is embedded because the interaction between confrontation and avoidance (temporary relief) has been distorted, and this keeps memories unprocessed and unintegrated.

Recent retrospective studies (see for an overview Foa et al., 2013) have clearly demonstrated that treatments consisting of learning theory (exposure) combined with cognitive interventions (cognitive restructuring) are more effective than either treatment administered on its own. This has been demonstrated, moreover, for different populations of victims, such as people traumatized at an early age, war veterans, and victims of rape.

2.1.5. Existential theory

Insights on psychotrauma garnered from a more existential perspective partially overlap those from the perspective on cognitive core beliefs. Core beliefs are felt to have been infringed (often seen with refugees) or distorted (as happens in children who are damaged at an early age). Complex psychotrauma in this context means that the meaning of life has been altered and there is a loss of identity (one is no longer who one was). The sense of continuity – with regard to beliefs, expectations, norms, and values – is disrupted by the traumatic events (Ebert & Dyck, 2004; Frankl, 2004; Lifton, 1979).

2.1.6. Object relations theory

In recent years object relations theory has been receiving more attention with regard to development psychopathology, including early childhood trauma (Fonagy & Target, 2003). Violence and the absence of safety in the home obstruct the development of an appropriate, healthy attachment relationship between parent and child, as the basic conditions for healthy identity development are not met. Children raised under such circumstances do not know what feeling safe is, and develop distorted mental representations of people and of the world around them. This undermines all sorts of developmental tasks such as exploration, autonomy, creativity, and assertiveness. The development of mental representations based on interactions in the daily living environment is crucial for these concepts; hence, parents who behave inconsistently, unpredictably, or unsafely (physical abuse, neglect, overindulgence) do not adequately meet the needs of their children and affect their children's perspective on the world. In terms of cognitive development, this affects the development of schemas (see 2.2.2).

2.1.7. System theory

Disruption of a person's course of life is usually not the only consequence of complex trauma. Often, collective structures are disrupted; with many refugees, for instance, entire societies are disrupted by war and conflict. Escape and migration break up social networks (families, villages, whole communities). Soldiers return from the front to familiar social surroundings, but they and their social circle have both become accustomed to their absence. The reunion therefore requires a new adaptation of the family. People who were traumatized as children in their family of origin often have misplaced loyalties towards their parents who were not always capable of taking care of them properly, and this splits the family.

System theory assumes that cohesion and balance are sought and maintained. Traumatic experiences often lead to imbalance and disruption in the system. The goal of treatment is to correct the balance within the system (Figley & Kiser, 2013; Nickerson et al., 2011; Walsh, 2006).

2.1.8. Narrative school of thought

The essence of narrative techniques is that the traumatic episode is embedded in the client's life as their story, or narrative. With narrative techniques, the client – with or without the structure or help offered by a therapist – relates their story. This can result in very extensive writing projects in the form of memoirs and autobiographies.

One such narrative technique is testimony therapy, developed in South America when psychologists discovered that writing testimonies for lawyers had a cleansing effect on the health of traumatized clients (Cienfuegos & Monelli, 1983). The disrupted events play a central role, yet are embedded in the – usually – good times in their lives prior to the disruptive events and the circumstances that follow (Mooren & Van Dijk, 2004). Variants and combinations of methods were subsequently developed, such as Narrative Exposure Therapy (NET) and Brief Eclectic Psychotherapy for Psychotrauma (BEPP). The 'structured writing' takes place using Interapy: the client's structured writing task is to describe their traumatic event explicitly and in detail (Lange et al., 2003). The effective element in narrative techniques is the initiation of integrative processes in the client: the trauma is no longer an isolated incident, but becomes part of the entirety of the client's life.

2.1.9. Dissociation

Pierre Janet, whose work was rediscovered by Van der Hart et al. (2000), described a structure model whereby psychotrauma can cause fragmentation of the consciousness and the self. Dissociation makes fragmentation possible and maintains the split in the ego. Nonetheless, dissociation, and, in particular, dissociative identity disorder, have become somewhat controversial elements in the discussion regarding recovered memories.

Dissociation is a mechanism that splits the human mind to protect the person from the expression of emotions that are too intense to deal with. Understandably, dissociative phenomena manifest themselves in the mind when a person is exposed to trauma, an experience that involves intense emotions. Dissociation is usually triggered by the occurrence of the traumatic experience as a mechanism to repress its severity and pain. It allows people to continue focusing on survival. This is why fragments of traumatic memories may be inaccessible or associated with a lack of emotion in some people. The protection is so strong that processing of the memories is hindered. Dissociation can manifest itself in the following ways:

- Amnesia or the inability to remember important personal information, usually of a traumatic or stress-inducing nature
- Fugue, that is, suddenly and unexpectedly going on a trip, away from home or the usual work place, unable to remember one's own past
- Depersonalization, a persistent or recurring experience of the feeling of being alienated from one's own social surroundings
- Dissociative identity disorder, whereby at least two mutually independent, distinct identities or personality states exist within one person.

Dissociative symptoms are part of traumatic stress responses and vary in severity and duration. The symptoms, specifically for amnesia and, to a lesser degree, for depersonalization, arise with every trauma. These symptoms arise because feelings from the past are somehow overwhelming and obstruct someone's ability to function.

The most severe variant of dissociation is dissociative identity disorder (DID). It occurs infrequently, however, and tends to be reported in relation to severe early childhood abuse. An iatrogenic aspect also potentially plays a role. For further information about DID and associated disorders, see Van der Hart et al. (2006).

2.1.10. Resilience, resistance, and posttraumatic stress growth

In the 1980s, publications from the United Kingdom discussed the protective factors against symptoms that arise after stressful experiences. From the developmental psychopathology domain, resilience gained attention, which makes sense because how else can the fact that most children exposed to similar harmful events do not develop symptoms be explained? The focus of research shifted from a concentration on clinical samples to samples drawn from the general population, enabling knowledge to be gained from people with fewer or no symptoms. Resilience, or the ability to respond to stress with adaptive behaviour, became an important point of discussion. In general, it is facilitated by factors that contribute to a healthy interpretation of meaning (Bonanno, 2004; Mooren et al., 2009; Schok, 2009; Walsh, 2006). Communication, social support, and recognition, in particular, contribute to developing an adaptive capacity in response to stress.

Calhoun and Tedeschi (1999) reported that harmful consequences are not necessarily inevitable following traumatic stress. In the course of their development, people can also grow by confronting the overwhelming event. A sign of posttraumatic growth is a statement such as 'It wasn't my choice to go through this, but it has made me wiser'.

2.1.11. Neurophysiological stress responses

Knowledge of neurophysiological processes that play a role in psychotrauma is accumulating at a rapid rate. Two physiological sub-systems regulate human response to stress, one operating at the basic level within the nervous system, and the other operating within the endocrine system. The sympathetic nervous system (SNS) – that is, the involuntary nervous system – is responsible for mobilizing the body's short-term fight or flight response. The long-term response is the responsibility of the endocrinal or hormonal hypothalamus-pituitary-adrenal (HPA) axis (see Friedman (2003) and Sapolsky (1998) for a succinct overview).

In the SNS, the amygdala, located deep inside the brain, plays a predominant role. This group of nuclei generate an immediate response to a perceived threat. Neurotransmitters such as adrenaline and noradrenaline are released to facilitate the necessary responses in the brain, heart, gastrointestinal system, and circulatory system, enabling the body to respond quickly.

The hormonal HPA axis functions somewhat more gradually, although, like the SNS, it is also activated immediately. The hypothalamus, located centrally in the brain close to the amygdala and the pituitary gland, secretes a hormone called the corticotrophin-releasing factor; this, in turn, signals the pituitary gland to secrete adrenocorticotropic hormone, which makes sure that more of the cortisol hormone is produced. Cortisol is called the stress hormone because its level elevates sharply as a normal human response to stress. Among its other functions, cortisol increases the blood glucose level and decreases immune processes.

The neurotransmitter serotonin also plays a role in both the SNS and the HPA axis by helping to mediate their activity. This neurotransmitter is important because the well-known selective serotonin reuptake inhibitors (SSRIs) are often dispensed as part of the treatment of PTSD. SSRIs, like other antidepressants, inhibit excessive reuptake, and hence waste, of serotonin. Thus, more serotonin remains available, which makes more activation, more reflection, and more extensive executive functioning possible.

Technological advances in recent decades have contributed much knowledge regarding the negative consequences of chronic stress on the development of the brain. Use of techniques such as magnetic resonance imaging has shown that the volume of the hippocampus, crucial for information processing, is smaller in clients with PTSD than in people without PTSD. This smaller volume diminishes the ability to learn and use memory.

Significant dysregulation of the neurological and hormonal systems occurs with incidental stress, and particularly with chronic stress. Neurotransmitter systems – noradrenergic, serotonergic, and dopaminergic – become ultrasensitive to changes in the immediate environment. The HPA axis is overactive also (Güzelcan & Olff, 2005). This is often noticeable in soldiers, who seem to remain dysregulated even years after returning from war; they may suffer from heightened irritability, poor concentration and impaired memory, are constantly hypervigilant, and give the impression that they continuously anticipate danger.

Finally, it has been reported that traumas can predict later onset of psychological disorders such as depression and social anxiety; traumatic events such as emotional abuse, neglect, physical abuse, and sexual violence are particularly predictive (Elzinga et al., 2010; Liu et al., 2009). Central regulation systems remain dysregulated despite the malleability of the brain. Severe and persistent stress is harmful at whatever age it is incurred.

2.2. Treatment methodologies

This section addresses a number of treatment options derived from the theories already described. These are further elaborated upon in the chapters that cover phase 2 treatment options.

2.2.1. Cognitive behavioural therapy

The treatment methods most extensively tested and verified for effectiveness are from the cognitive behavioural therapy school of thought. The result of many studies (Cloitre, 2009; Ehlers et al., 2010) indicate that the preferred method of treatment – over and above supportive counselling or stress-reducing methods – is exposure to traumatizing memories combined with the readjustment (challenging, cognitive restructuring) of thoughts and assumptions (core beliefs). Alteration of the client's interpretation of the meaning of the trauma is regarded as one of the effective components of treatment, requiring confrontation with and breaking through the client's avoidance behaviour.

EMDR, a method that renders the need for repetitive discussion of a client's traumatic memories less necessary, is a structured treatment that is carried out in the following approximate sequence of stages:

- Determine the target experience, the accompanying feeling, the related negative cognition and the complementary positive cognition that is to be developed.
- Focus attention on the traumatic memory while alternating stimulation from the right brain to the left brain.
- Install positive cognitions and carry out a body scan to detect residual sources of tension.

There is considerable evidence for the effectiveness of EMDR administered to different groups of people who have experienced violence.

Treatment methods that use exposure techniques are mostly implemented in the form of narration or storytelling. NET was developed to treat traumatized refugees – more specifically, refugees who had fled from conflict areas. The intention of the therapy is to help with the creation of a narrative that enables the clients to place the disruptive events (war and flight) in the context of their lives overall, while also allowing space for positive life experiences. On a line symbolizing the course of their lives, clients place stones to represent disruptive experiences and flowers to represent positive experiences. This method fosters the organization of memories and appeals to the healthy aspects of the client's identity. BEPP combines narrative techniques with writing therapy through the creation of an autobiography, with closure for the therapeutic processing of traumatic memories achieved using some form of ritual, for instance, composing a farewell letter or creating a document to symbolize closure. Clients usually find working with narrative methods to be a pleasant experience, as they offer autonomy and control; the narrative is also an exceptional and interesting source of information that is processed and integrated into therapy, with results in the sense of the client being validated (Bohlmeijer et al., 2007; Olthof & Vermetten, 1994).

2.2.2. Schema therapy

Schema therapy (ST) uses the concept of schemas taken from cognitive science (Young, 2005; Young et al., 2003). Just as with the dialectical behavioural therapy and mentalization-based therapy methods discussed below, ST has proven to be effective in dealing with complex personality disorders (Giesen-Bloo et al., 2006). ST is based on the existence of cognitive schemas that strongly influence behaviour. Schemas are mental representations of earlier acquired experiences, emotions, and beliefs (acquired from one's culture or family), generally easily accessible or evoked in reaction to stimuli from the immediate environment. Complex trauma situations that occur at an early age generate cognitive schemas that, at the time of the traumatization, enable the person to cope with or survive the traumatic events. When that coping mechanism is no longer necessary, however, the cognitive schemas may prove to be an obstacle to normal healthy functioning. Altering these schemas involves cognitive readjustment, the identification and management of weak spots, practising with behaviour alternatives, and the therapeutic processing of trauma memories.

2.2.3. Dialectical behavioural therapy

Dialectical behavioural therapy (DBT) has been very influential for the treatment of people with severe borderline personality problems (Linehan, 1993). The goal of DBT is for the client to acquire various skills that will help improve responses to problems as best as possible. Through the use of a variety of techniques, clients are first taught to identify their own behaviour, thoughts, and emotions, and are then taught how to regulate them. The treatment is administered as part of individual psychotherapy in combination with skills training sessions, preferably in groups.

2.2.4. Mentalization-based therapy

Just like DBT and ST, Mentalization-based therapy (MBT) (Allen et al., 2008; Bateman & Fonagy, 2004) has proven to be an effective treatment for clients who have personality problems, such as poor affect-regulation and impulsivity. The basic premise is that the client has not properly developed attachment relationships over time, so interventions focus on enhancing the capacity for empathy, reciprocation, and autonomy; in other words, clients learn to mentalize. Being able to place oneself in another person's shoes and being able to self-reflect are necessary conditions for developing and maintaining meaningful social interactions. Connecting with the clients from their own perspectives is fundamental to this form of therapy. This premise of a tailor-made basis also makes it possible to work with clients who are from different target groups.

2.2.5. Other methods

Other treatments for trauma use modern media such as the Internet for writing therapy, earthquake simulators to implement exposure techniques (Salcioglu et al., 2007), and virtual reality computer programs to evoke memories of deployment to Iraq or Afghanistan (Reger & Gahm, 2009). So far only a few randomized studies of these interventions have been conducted. One study on the results of a virtual reality program for soldiers who had been in Iraq or Afghanistan showed good results in terms of reducing symptoms. A mere 20 per cent of the veterans who were given access to the program chose to participate, however, as most found it too confrontational (Cukor et al., 2009).

2.3. Treatment planning principles

This section first addresses the multidisciplinary guidelines for the treatment of psychotrauma and then discusses the three-phase model that orders and structures the treatment of complex trauma.

2.3.1. Multidisciplinary guidelines for complex trauma

Several guidelines are available for the treatment of (simple) psychotrauma, for example, that of the National Institute of Clinical Excellence (2005), Taylor (2006), and another by Foa and colleagues (2009). In the Netherlands, the Trimbos Institute has published the Dutch Multidisciplinary Guidelines for Anxiety Disorders (2013). There are also a growing number of retrospective studies that report on the effect sizes of selected studies. In general, these guidelines are more relevant to less complex PTSD, so the question remains whether or not they are relevant to complex trauma.

The Trimbos Institute's publication, for example, does not include any recommendations for the treatment of complex trauma, although it does allude to it, indicating that psychotherapy currently has relatively little impact on the treatment of chronic PTSD. It also proposes that interventions such as cognitive behavioural therapy and EMDR should always be included in a broader, usually phased, treatment programme, except in cases of *pure* PTSD resulting from type 1 trauma.

The Dutch Multidisciplinary Guidelines for Personality Disorders (2008) from the Trimbos Institute does not mention complex trauma either. Complex trauma is, after all, not classified as a personality disorder in DSM-IV. There are, however, recommendations for dealing with PTSD and personality problems in the context of PTSD comorbidity with personality disorders. It concludes by stating that there is very little research on the treatment of PTSD concomitant with a personality disorder. This leads to the following recommendation: 'Focusing exclusively on PTSD is not advisable in the case of severe personality pathology, particularly with Cluster A or Cluster B personality disorders. In those cases, it is recommended to implement an integrated approach that not only treats PTSD, but also places the focus of the treatment on the personality disorder'. This implies that when severe personality problems complicate traumatic stress (complex trauma), the recommendation is to first attend to the stabilizing factors. The personality disorders cause too much psychological instability to allow for treatment of a dysregulated trauma process. That means that if it is indicated, stabilization of function (phase 1) must be achieved prior to starting with confrontation (phase 2).

2.3.2. *The three-phase model*

The treatment of complex trauma requires a model that broadly structures and organizes treatment while addressing the complexities of an individual's particular circumstances. The model should not be overly specific; as such a model would fail to encompass the multifaceted symptomology associated with complex trauma. The three-phase model developed by Herman (1992), Van der Hart, and Nijenhuis (Van der Hart & Nijenhuis, 2003; Van der Hart & Nijenhuis, 2007) is a pragmatic complex trauma treatment model that does not rely on any one specific school of treatment, a fact which enables it to provide a broader range of support. According to this model, interventions are successively focused on stabilization, symptom reduction, traumatic memory treatment, personality integration, and redefinition of a perspective for the future.

Three-phase model

1. Stabilization of functioning and symptom reduction.
2. Treatment of traumatic memories.
3. Personality integration and perspective on the future.

Although its effectiveness has not been proven by randomized controlled studies and no objective criteria exist to guide the transition from one phase to another, therapists who have used it in clinical practice have reached broad consensus on how to use the model. Part three of this book describes some of the treatment interventions that follow the three-phase model, discusses how it can be implemented in practice, and suggests criteria to follow for the transition from one phase to another.

Part II

Diagnostics and indication assessment

Chapter 3

Psychodiagnostics

Proper assessment of presenting symptoms is the essential primary task when treating complex trauma. It is advisable that the therapist and the client use the initial treatment phase to jointly formulate a theory regarding cohesive interrelation of the symptoms with the client's circumstances and traumatic experiences. This case conceptualization lays a solid foundation for future interventions.

Psychodiagnostics involves the therapist deciding on suitable methods and instruments for assessing the client's complaints and symptoms in a valid and effective manner. The therapist should also consider which instruments are suitable for clients who have immigrated to a host country.

The chapter begins by laying out the different presenting problems and symptoms that accompany complex trauma. This symptomatology is categorized in distinct layers represented in Figure 3.1 that affect the choice of diagnostic instruments and are discussed separately. Finally, the tests and interview schedules commonly used for assessing trauma-related problems are discussed in terms of their validity and reliability.

This chapter also addresses the tests that have been developed for immigrants, including refugees; many of these instruments have limitations. One such instrument is the Structured Interview for Disorders of Extreme Stress (SIDES). Also discussed is the applicability of the Minnesota Multiphasic Personality Inventory (MMPI) for complex trauma, often used to determine a person's capacity for self-regulation and affect-regulation, which are two mechanisms of complex trauma.

3.1. Instrument selection

Psychodiagnostic assessment focuses on establishing a proper indication for treatment. After clinical assessment, tests are administered to provide further insight into clients' problems and capacities. It is even becoming common to administer a standard battery of tests to enable comparisons within homogenous groups. Administering tests periodically also reveals changes in diagnostic components during a course of treatment and alerts the therapist to the need to make adaptations to fluctuating needs.

Nonetheless, determining a suitable battery of tests is a complicated and uncertain matter, given not only the vague definition of complex trauma but also the accompanying broad pallet of symptoms. The choice ultimately may depend on which symptoms the diagnostician prioritizes. It is therefore advisable to carefully consider the client's capacity and resilience and, on that basis, to assemble a range of tests based on the client's presenting problem and the therapist's hypothesis. The fundamental psychodiagnostic objectives of these tests are to create a treatment indication, develop a treatment plan, and if possible, monitor treatment progress.

Diagnostic assessment has specific objectives for specific problems. Although different problems may be interrelated in some way, they must be prioritized for treatment. Livesley's personality model (Livesley, 2007; Stuyling de Lange et al., 2009) – used in Chapter 1 to help determine a working definition of complex trauma – describes a framework to effectively prioritize the interrelatedness of problems. Livesley's model can help structure diagnostics for clients with complex trauma symptoms since it defines personality as the outcome of interactions between biological dispositions (temperament) and the learning experiences (social learning) (Millon & Everly, 1985) that teach people how to deal with the demands of their immediate environment and how to relate to themselves. The assumption that a personality is a dynamic, layered, and lifelong process must also be taken into consideration when formulating diagnostics and treatment.

Livesley's personality model distinguishes between five components that collectively shape personality: genetic predisposition, internal concepts (core cognitions and cognitive schemas), emotional regulation, observable behaviour, and environmental factors. As mentioned in Chapter 1, social support and therapy both address the last four of these components in reverse order, that is, environmental factors and observable behaviour, then emotional regulation, and finally internal concepts. This model corresponds to a working definition of complex trauma, which encompasses the following: core cognitions; posttraumatic stress disorder (PTSD); depression; relationship problems; and, finally, malaise, a non-specific term for a range of complaints that result from the identified problem domain.

The diagnostic instruments described in this chapter, categorized according to the layers of trauma-related problems represented in Figure 3.1, are used to inventory (in this order) general symptoms, social functioning, depression, PTSD reactions, and core cognitions. This sequence is used on the assumption that core cognitions influence the manifestation of PTSD symptoms to a significant degree.

The psychodiagnostic tests described below comply with minimum psychometric properties, have adequate to good validity and reliability, and are sufficiently sensitive and specific.

3.1.1. General symptom inventories

Self-report inventories are commonly used when making standard assessments. The Symptom Checklist (SCL-90) (Derogatis et al., 1973) – which has been adapted by Arrindell and Ettema (1986) for use in the Netherlands – is perhaps the most widely used inventory. Also commonly used are the Brief Symptom

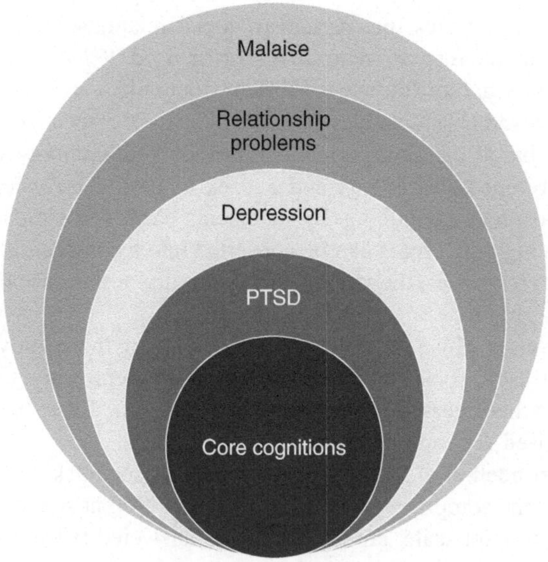

Figure 3.1 Layered components of complex trauma

Inventory (BSI) and the Hopkins Symptom Checklist (HSCL), both derived from the SCL-90 (Mollica et al., 1987).

The SCL-90 is the most extensive inventory available, covering, as the name indicates, 90 items that assess symptoms the degree to which it has troubled a client in the previous seven days. The symptoms are categorized in eight domains of functioning: agoraphobia, anxiety, depression, summarization, sleep disturbance, cognitive deficits, hostility, and interpersonal sensitivity. The overall outcome provides an impression of the client's psychoneuroticism (sense of discomfort). The psychometric properties of the SCL-90 have been examined extensively and are good, and test norms are available for different populations and age groups.

Different inventories are used for general assessments. For quality of life, the World Health Organization's Quality of Life (WHOQOL) is the most popular instrument, although the Quality of Life Scale (QOLS) is also commonly administered. WHOQOL, which inventories the domains of functioning and improvement in the quality of life notwithstanding symptoms, exists in a short form, called the WHOQOL-BREF, consisting of 26 items that address physical health, mental well-being, social relationships, and environmental factors (WHO, 2004). The WHOQOL-BREF is available on the Internet.

The Pennebaker Inventory of Limbic Languidness (PILL) (Pennebaker, 1982) is often used to inventory specific physical symptoms. This inventory, which has good reliability, comprises 54 items aimed at identifying physical symptoms. The PILL is also available on the Internet.

3.1.2. Social relationships and interactions

The self-report inventories that pertain to social relationships and interactions addressed here are the Interpersonal Checklist-Revised (ICL-R), the Interpersonal Circle (IPC), the Scale for Interpersonal Behaviour (SIB), and the Social Support List Interactions and Discrepancies (SSL-I and SSL-D, respectively).

The ICL-R, based on Leary's interaction theory (commonly called Leary's Rose), was developed by LaForge and Suczek in 1955. The checklist has eight interactional positions containing 16 statements each, for a total of 128 statements. Even though the scores can be converted into a convincing looking graph to help interpret responses, the validity and reliability of this checklist have yet to be confirmed as good.

The IPC, developed by Kiesler (1983), has been more thoroughly examined for its ability to measure social interactions. This instrument is somewhat long and integrates four other interaction inventories including the Interpersonal Checklist prior to the revised version.

The SIB (Arrindell et al., 1984), which measures social skills in people from the age of 14 years, comprises 50 items describing different situations. The items, answered on a 5-point scale, are presented and answered twice, the first time to measure the amount of distress evoked by a certain situation, and the second time to measure the frequency of that situation so as to estimate the probability of a specific behaviour. Adding up the scores results in outcomes on four subscales: displaying negative feelings (negative assertion), expressing and dealing with personal limitations, initiating assertiveness, and praising others and receiving the compliments and praise of others (positive assertion). Based on the total score, respondents are categorized as assertive, anxious, sub-assertive, or indifferent.

The SSL-I and SSL-D, with good psychometric properties, were developed at the University of Groningen (Van Sonderen, 1993) and administered to diverse groups in the Netherlands. They can be used to compare groups with gender and age differences. The statistically reliable subscales for these instruments are daily emotional interactions, emotional support for problems, esteem, and social issues (companionship). The SSL-I has 34 items about different forms of social support, and seven additional items that measure negative interactions. The respondent's perceptions are measured by starting each question with 'Does it ever happen to you that . . .' with the respondent indicating how often the situation occurs. Discrepancies between the perception of social support and desired social support are compared using SSL-D.

3.1.3. Depression

The general screening of presenting symptoms may also indicate that depression symptoms need to be more thoroughly investigated. Examples of instruments that examine depression are the Beck Depression Inventory (BDI, BDI-II) (Beck et al., 1961) and the Hamilton Rating Scale for Depression (HRSD) (Hamilton, 1960).

The BDI-II (Beck et al., 1996), developed to assess symptoms in accordance with the criteria in the Diagnostic and Statistical Manual of Mental Disorders

(DSM-IV), is the result of 35 years of accumulated psychometric data and clinical experience. The BDI-II which measures affective and somatic symptoms, comprises 21 statements about symptoms, with the respondent choosing statements that best describe how they felt in the previous seven days. Responses are expressed as a total score that indicates the general severity of depression. The BDI-II has two subscales: affective (8 items) and somatic symptoms (13 items). Reliability is good, whereas validity tends to fluctuate.

The HRSD assesses the severity of depression symptoms through a semi-structured interview comprising 17, 21, or 24 items. Of these items, 17 can be answered on either a 3-point scale (0 to 2) or a 5-point scale (0 to 4). A person can score a maximum of 52 points on the original list of 21 items.

3.1.4. PTSD

Commonly used inventories in the Dutch language are the Self-Rating Inventory for Posttraumatic Stress Disorder (SRIP) (Hovens et al., 2000) and the Impact of Event Scale (IES) (Brom & Kleber, 1985). The latter was translated into Dutch from the original English version (Horowitz et al., 1979) and validated for a Dutch population. The difference between these two self-report instruments is that the IES, unlike the SRIP, explicitly connects items to the shocking events.

The SRIP has 22 items to estimate the severity of PTSD symptoms. Norm groups are available and the psychometric properties have been investigated and are excellent. The original IES comprises 15 items and has been administered to a wide range of people after shocking events. Responses are based on the degree to which items were relevant during the seven days prior to administration. Item content focuses on a specific overwhelming event. The 15 items are part of two subscales – reexperiencing and avoidance – which represent the key issues for clients. The revised edition (IES-R) contains seven additional items that examine a third PTSD domain of heightened irritability. It is not entirely clear if the IES is an indicator of the severity of the symptoms or a process indicator for integrating memories of overwhelming events. Use of IES is limited by the fact that norm groups have not yet been compiled and published.

A third self-report inventory is the Harvard Trauma Questionnaire (HTQ), developed originally by Richard Mollica for use with South East Asian refugees in the USA (Mollica et al., 1992). The inventory has since been translated into many languages and is widely used for refugees with diverse backgrounds. Used in the Netherlands is a modified translation adapted by Kleijn and colleagues (2001) consisting of three parts. The first part of this instrument asks clients to draw a distinction between the traumas they have experienced, witnessed, and heard about. The second part of the instrument examines the severity of the PTSD symptoms in the previous seven days. The third part consists of additional items that are considered to be typical of the psychosocial symptoms that refugees often present with (items that involve dissociation or loss of trust). It is important to perform a systematic study on how people respond to items – and in particular, the items added in the third part about the meaning of one's life – because it can be presumed (the topic has not yet been researched) that refugees from different cultural backgrounds experience them differently.

The gold standard for establishing a PTSD diagnosis is the semi-structured clinical interview called the Clinician-Administered PTSD Scale (CAPS) (Blake et al., 1990), used to survey the prevalence as well as the severity of each PTSD symptom separately. CAPS, adapted for a Dutch population by Hovens and colleagues (Hovens et al., 2005), has been appraised as having very positive psychometric properties (Weathers et al., 2001).

3.1.5. Dissociation

The Dissociative Experiences Scale (DES) (Bernstein & Putnam, 1986) is frequently used to detect dissociative symptoms in traumatized people, as its psychometric properties are good. A disadvantage of this scale is that outcomes tend to be distributed unevenly; in other words, certain symptoms fail to or infrequently occur in the general population, making scores very low. Another scale used is the Structured Clinical Interview for DSM-III-R Dissociative Disorders (SCID-D); although more time-consuming and intensive, it is more thorough than an inventory (Boon & Draijer, 2007).

3.1.6. Core cognitions

A variety of inventories are available to assess crucial and trauma-related cognitive assumptions. Key cognitions of traumatic experiences are often measured using the World Assumption Scale (Janoff-Bulman, 1989). The inventory has three domains and eight subscales that address beliefs about the self, the immediate social environment, and life in general. The items address – in a non-confrontational way – the respondents' perception of being unlucky or lucky, about their sense of control over life, and if they are trustful or mistrustful towards others. Normative data have not yet been compiled.

Mooren and Kleber developed the *Zingevingslijst* (in English: the meaningful experience survey) (Mooren & Kleber, 2001; Mooren et al., 2009; Schok, 2009) for refugees to the Netherlands from Bosnia-Herzegovina and Dutch soldiers returning home after deployment. Items used to design this instrument were derived from statements war-stricken refugees made in their attempts to regain cognitive control during treatment, from items in the Sense of Coherence Scale by Antonovsky et al. (1998), and ideas on meaning in life by Debats (1996). It assesses meaningfulness with the following scales: finding causal explanations, trust and mistrust, posttraumatic stress growth, expressed in terms of hope and new goals in life, attitudes about the war, and the importance of religion. An example of an item is: 'Since the war, I only trust myself, I try not to expect too much from other people.' Reliability is good, particularly of the first three subscales (Mooren et al., 2009).

A third core cognition inventory is the Young Schema Questionnaire (YSQ) (Young et al., 2003), adapted and validated for the Dutch population by Rijkeboer (2005). The effectiveness of the YSQ, used in schema-focused cognitive therapy, has been demonstrated in a large-scale multi-site study of clients with borderline personality disorders (Giesen-Bloo et al., 2006). The YSQ inventories how much a client identifies with statements that belong in 16–18 distinct cognitive schemas. Examples of these cognitive schemas or weak spots are abandonment/instability, emotional deprivation, failure to achieve, social isolation/alienation, and self-sacrifice.

Finally, also frequently used is the Posttraumatic Cognitions Inventory (PTCI) (Foa et al., 1999), which comprises three subscales: negative cognitions about the self, negative cognitions about the world, and self-blame.

3.1.7. Personality structure

The mental healthcare sector often uses the MMPI to appraise a client's structural situational possibilities for stress management. Different methods for interpreting outcomes are available, all largely in agreement with each other. Eurelings-Bontekoe and Snellen (2003) describe dynamic profile interpretation using a combination of the Dutch short-form MMPI and the MMPI. This profile interpretation is founded on personality theory and distinguishes between stable personality traits (extraversion, vulnerability) and more situational facets (summarization, physical complaints). This model generally has broad clinical applicability, and the empirical support for trauma clients shows promise. Another method described by Derksen is oftentimes used for analyses of responses (Derksen et al., 1996).

Completion of the MMPI or the MMPI-2 requires patience as they have 567 true/false questions. They are typically administered using a computer and programs are available that display the response data in graphs. The validity scale profiles, the main clinical scales, and the content scales are used the most. The profile created by the validity scales shows whether the test has been completed in a valid manner. It can thus demonstrate if there is presenting behaviour that can be an indicator of, for example, the structural manner of how someone deals with stress. The main clinical scales – which can only be interpreted if the test has been completed in a valid manner – give an image of the typical way the respondent deals with stress. According to the dynamic profile interpretation, a neurotic ('largely healthy'), borderline or psychotic dynamic follows. This classification is dependent on the relationship between the ability to control impulses and controlled expression given to general stress. The context of a structural, personal style of dealing with stress provides meaning to the presence of alienation, aggression, isolation, panic, or depression.

Two supplementary content scales (PS (after author Schlenger) and PK (after author Keane)) address psychotrauma; however, these have not been found to be sufficiently sensitive to signal any PTSD symptoms. In general, although clients with psychotrauma symptoms score high on both of these subscales, high scores are not good predictors of PTSD or trauma-related problems.

We mention the MMPI here because it is widely used to analyze structural vulnerability. People differ in the degree to which they are sensitive to the pressure of their immediate environment. The MMPI is able to reveal stress sensitivity and strategies for detecting and reducing tension.

3.1.8. Complex trauma

Specific instruments have been developed to measure complex trauma. Pelcovitz and colleagues (2000) developed the SIDES, which has 37 items that make up the seven subscales that measure disorders of extreme stress not otherwise specified (DESNOS): altered affect-regulation, dissociation, summarization, altered perception of perpetrators, altered self-perception, altered relationships with others, and altered systems of beliefs. Each item is appraised using a 4-point scale representing normal presentation to severe symptom presentation. The SIDES is administered repeatedly, especially when dealing with early childhood trauma, and particularly if the client has had symptoms in the past (Pelcovitz et al., 2000).

Scoboria and colleagues (2008) tested the factor structure of a revised version of the SIDES (SIDES-R). The SIDES-R items were changed but the subscales remained the same, resulting in five factors: demoralization, somatic dysregulation, anger dysregulation, risk/self-harm, and altered sexuality. These factors are usually strongly associated with early childhood sexual trauma. The use of this interview seems sound because it is reliable and the competitive, convergent, and discriminant validity from the SIDES study were proven. However, for the time being, the factors that determine a DESNOS diagnosis differ in each study and in each population studied (Scoboria et al., 2008).

Overall, therefore, a truly consistent instrument is still not available and the question remains whether, in fact, the development of such an instrument is even possible. We think not, preferring to believe that the answer lies in the applicability of a combination of the psychometrically sound instruments already available, aided by supplementary, specific sub-questions.

3.2. Psychodiagnostic assessment of immigrants

Psychodiagnostics for clients who have immigrated to a country with a different language and culture is challenging. Administering the more commonly used instruments for this population has several limitations, the first of which is that there are hardly any normative data available. The possibility of obtaining normative data for each cultural group is also limited, because an immigrant would perceive the items in an instrument very differently from the average native of the same age, given that their perceptions depend on cultural background. Comparison with existing norms – as is done with achievement tests – raises the question as to what exactly the outcome would indicate, whether it is language proficiency or the measurement of a diagnostic symptom.

Various screening inventories for psychotrauma and its consequences are available in different languages, for example, the HTQ and the HSCL, specifically developed for use on South East Asian refugees in the USA. However, these need to undergo supplemental validity analyses before construct validity can be considered good.

The Structured Interview for DSM Personality Disorders (SIDP-IV) has been developed as a semi-structured interview for the assessment of personality disorders. In the Netherlands, it is particularly used with clients from different cultural backgrounds. The SIDP-IV, based on DSM criteria, assesses ten different domains of life: activities and interests, work, interpersonal relationships, social contacts, emotions, observations, self-perceptions, view of others, stress and anger, and social conformity. The fact that the interview questions are arranged in themes makes administration comfortable. The interview uses the five-year rule to operationalize Criterion D of DSM general diagnostic criteria. All questions are answered on a 4-point scale that indicates incidence and produces two scores for each diagnosis established by the SIDP-IV: a dichotomous score to determine whether the criteria for a diagnosis have been met, and a dimensional score that indicates the severity of the diagnosis.

Chapter 4

Treatment design

In Chapter 2 the three-phase model was advocated as the most suitable template for the treatment of complex trauma, whereas Chapter 3 explored complex trauma diagnostics. This chapter integrates both issues: how the diagnosis of complex trauma leads to a treatment plan based on the three-phase model.

4.1. Intake

Intake generally comprises three phases. The first phase is a global screening phase during which a primary diagnosis is determined based on an informed referral. An introductory interview with the therapist then follows. Sometimes a second therapist does the intake if there is a lengthy intake and indication procedure. Information about the client's diagnosis, medical history and the presenting problem are obtained during intake. Chapter 3 has already addressed the topic of psychodiagnostics, so this chapter will focus on the client's medical history and presenting problem and will also consider the collaborative relationship between client and therapist.

4.1.1. Medical history

The client's life story and background, the cause of the presenting problem, and the development of symptoms are explored in one or more sessions. Clients vary greatly in the extent to which they are willing to discuss painful experiences. Some resolutely refuse to speak about them in the early stages of treatment, whereas others are prepared to share their stories in detail. The therapist has to gauge the extent to which a client is capable of talking about the trauma. It is not necessary to obtain the details of the traumatic events during the initial phase of the treatment, as a general appraisal of the client's situation takes priority. The client's ability to disclose information determines how accurate that appraisal is. It is advisable to reassure the client beforehand that this phase only requires general information to be shared. This also avoids wrong expectations being cultivated by clients who do not yet feel ready to share the details of their stories.

The rest of the intake sessions are carried out in accordance with local healthcare guidelines. This usually involves gathering information on the client's demographics (employment status, marital status, financial situation, education, etc.), symptoms and presenting problems, history with health services, sources of support and how the client deals with stress (including use of substances).

The services of an interpreter by way of telephone or in person are used if needed. The topic of engaging an interpreter in the therapeutic process is addressed in Chapter 14.

4.1.2. Collaboration

Intake provides both parties with the opportunity to get acquainted and to obtain an impression of each other, with the client and therapist both verifying and adjusting their mutual expectations. The sessions also provide the therapist with a preliminary impression of the client's interpersonal behaviour and the clients have the opportunity to confirm whether they are where they should be and whether they will be understood and validated. This means that the therapist must listen closely, and, above all, maintain a respectful attitude towards the client. Interpersonal violence has damaged traumatized people's trust in others and, therefore, these clients – and even more so than clients with other problems – will assess their therapist's trustworthiness to see if they can reveal their vulnerability.

Of course, even as they respect the client's vulnerabilities, therapists also need to gather information, and this can create an atmosphere of tension. That is why it is important to be clear about the goals of the early sessions and to provide specific information regarding practical aspects of the preliminary phase. Examples of what needs to be clarified are whether the intaker will also be the therapist, if the client will have to discuss the traumatic experiences in detail, and what the client can expect from the organization or intake procedure.

It is also possible for the client to have posttraumatic stress disorder (PTSD) reactions such as reexperiencing or dissociation during these sessions, so it is important that the intaker be prepared for such reactions, and able to recognize and respond to them appropriately. Grounding techniques are available to deal with this (see Section 7.5).

4.1.3. Presenting problem

It is important to clarify the presenting problem, as, after all, this is where the greatest distress lies and determines what the client wants to change. The motivation for change is derived directly from the distress. Therapeutic activities, and also their success, can only be achieved from what the client wants to change. There is a certain danger that therapists – experienced as well as inexperienced – develop their own assumptions about the client's problems, draw conclusions too quickly, and formulate theories accordingly. This disconnect between what is offered and the client's presenting problem places treatment effectiveness at risk, most especially regarding complex problems in clients who have a poor overview of their problems and whose therapist also has difficulty understanding the problems. The difficulty here lies in the fact that the client may have an ambiguous presenting problem. So, in addition to establishing a safe therapeutic relationship, another initial goal of the treatment is to formulate a clear presenting problem.

Intake protocols usually devote just one session to obtaining a complete impression of the complex problems that form the basis for determining the treatment indication. A few sessions after treatment has started, a discrepancy almost inevitably develops between the client's actual distress and the presenting problem that was formulated in the intake report. For many clients one session is not conducive to developing a sufficient amount of trust to disclose the actual issues that require treatment. Traumatized clients, who are often mistrusting of others in general, will not openly reveal all their vulnerabilities to an unfamiliar therapist in just one session. Hence, when starting treatment, a therapist needs to devote time to getting acquainted with the client's problems, first, to establish a trusting relationship, and second, to see clearly where the client's distress lies and what the presenting problems are.

Severely traumatized clients have problems embedded in different layers. Distress is caused by problems with adapting to new situations, tensions with the client's family and friends, problems with work and finances, etc. If trust is as yet not fully developed, the client will usually reveal a less threatening problem from a superficial layer of problems, rather than reveal vulnerable issues, which will require some time. The presenting problems may also change over the course of the treatment, which is why the therapist needs to make interim evaluations of the treatment and interim reviews of any potential shift in the presenting problems.

Another motivation for interim reviews is when the therapist questions the pertinence of the presenting problem, giving rise to one of two possible situations. The first is when a client's current mental state makes treatment of a presenting problem unrealistic.

> A woman with borderline personality disorder reports that she would like to 'work on her sexual abuse'. In her youth she was severely sexually abused and emotionally neglected by her father who, in turn, had been traumatized in a concentration camp. Her current mental state is emotionally unstable, she inflicts self-harm, she has practically no social contacts and her personal financial situation is in turmoil.

The priority here is to first stabilize the situation. Only then can work begin on therapeutically processing the sexual abuse. Tact will be required from the therapist in order to avoid any potential disappointment that may lead to the treatment being ended prematurely if the client feels that the presenting problem is not addressed immediately.

A second example is almost the exact opposite: the client had a presenting problem that could only be addressed after some therapeutic processing of the trauma had already taken place, but the client was reluctant to do this processing.

> A veteran who was exposed to different traumatic experiences when serving in the Bosnian War driving cargo states, as his presenting problem, that he wants to deal with his children in a normal way without getting angry at them so quickly. One of his experiences was driving in a fast-moving convoy with orders from the commander not to slow down because of the danger of an ambush, but while driving at full speed, the convoy ran over some children. He said he had absolutely no desire to talk about his traumatic experiences.

The therapist had to explain to the client that successful treatment of his presenting problem would require him to work on his traumatic experiences. By the same token, this required the therapist to motivate the client in a way that did not discourage him from continuing the treatment.

The therapist's ultimate goal of dealing with the client's presenting problem means that the client needs to see his presenting problem clearly reflected in the treatment plan formulated by the therapist.

4.2. Case conceptualization

As with all treatments – irrespective of the originating theoretical school – it is important to formulate a hypothesis about the aetiology of the client's problems and how they are maintained. Formulating such a hypothesis is more difficult for complex problems, but, in this case, the cause, in and of itself, makes the hypothesis essential.

The more difficult it is to gain an overview of a case, the greater is the temptation to begin impromptu treatment. The danger of starting complex treatment without – as a minimum – a skeleton treatment plan in place is that the client and the therapist gradually become enmeshed in a complex transference and countertransference relationship, which increases the risk that the treatment will end unsatisfactorily. This frustrates the client as well as the therapist, because both have invested in the improvement of the client's mental state. A hypothesis regarding the aetiology and maintenance of the client's complex problems can prevent this and keep the therapist from slipping into a pattern of treating impromptu symptoms. It is therefore useful to start treatment by paying explicit attention to gaining an overview of the case and using that to formulate a treatment plan. The theoretical background of such a plan is less important: as long as there is a plan agreed with the client, the treatment will have a solid footing.

Case conceptualization is the formulation of a hypothesis about the symptoms in relation to maintenance and possible causal factors; it also describes the relationship between symptoms, coping strategies, and core cognitions. It is often useful to determine biological factors that may affect the client's treatment, such as level of intelligence and ability to learn.

Whatever the unpredictable effects biological factors may have on the therapeutic process, at the very least it should be documented in the case conceptualization. Different models can be used to develop a case conceptualization, such as holistic theory (Orlemans et al., 1995), function analysis and consequence analysis, cognitive case conceptualization (Tarrier, 2006), and schema-focused therapy (Young et al., 2003). The choice of which model is used is partially determined by the therapist's training and preferences.

A case conceptualization can only be developed in collaboration with the client and will need to be adapted constantly during the course of treatment, given that new information constantly comes to light. It is appropriate to be flexible with the hypotheses and to adapt them as more information is gradually revealed, especially when dealing with clients who have particularly complex problems.

It should be noted that, although case conceptualization at the start of treatment is the ideal, in reality, this ideal is impossible to achieve when dealing with complex trauma, given that the trauma symptoms that disrupt the client's daily life are so dysregulating that it is difficult for the therapist to obtain a complete overview of the case. In many cases the first phase of the treatment merely clarifies the hypothesis about the aetiology and maintenance of the trauma problems. Review and adaptation of a previously developed case conceptualization – to whatever extent it was possible to formulate – also takes place during the initial phase.

Important aspects of case conceptualization:

- Early cognitive schemas that usually determine the basis of the personality structure
- Coping styles that help a client endure, based on cognitive schemas
- Traumatic experiences
- Current trauma symptomology
- Constructive facets that help clients endure
- Turning point in life when the quality of life decreased
- Style used to make contact with people around them
- Current problems and symptoms
- Presence or absence of a supportive social network
- Resilience
- Presenting problem.

Analysing the problem together with the client is very enlightening; indeed, it is often helpful to write out the problem analysis. While writing out the factors (being incidents, feelings, thoughts, and messages) that contribute to an understanding of the interplay between symptoms and personal history, detailed memories pop up and often an overview as well as insight is being obtained. The client receives the assignment to write the text out on a regular sheet of paper and to return a copy to the therapist, who saves the analysis in the client's file. In this way the client has the opportunity to explore problems more deeply and to play an active role in their treatment.

4.3. Treatment indication

The indication of the type and intensity of treatment is determined by a number of client-related factors, such as the presenting problem, distress, resilience, and stability. It is also determined by the severity of the trauma, when the trauma took place, and the client's ability to deal with a disproportionate amount of tension. Treatment of complex trauma is individualized, which makes it impossible to draw up anything other than general guidelines, for which the three-phase model described in Chapter 2 can be used.

The treatment of complex trauma starts with phase 1, when therapist and client get acquainted, medical history is taken, and rapport necessary for a therapeutic relationship is developed. This is followed by a period of psychoeducation and stabilization, and once stability is achieved, the therapeutic processing in phase 2 can begin, followed by phase 3, which is called the integration phase. The time required depends on the client-related factors (presenting problem, distress, resilience, and stability) mentioned above and will always be adapted to the client's individual needs. Two issues in particular have a major impact on the treatment options: when the trauma took place (generally delineated as happening either before or after adolescence) and the degree of social integration and stability of the client. These are both discussed below in terms of treatment options.

4.3.1. Treatment options

Figure 4.1 shows a diagram that can be used to quickly scan for a client's treatment options. The two axes indicate when traumatization occurred and the degree of social integration, with each quadrant illustrating the degree of stability. The horizontal line represents the timeframe of the trauma (early/late), with the midpoint marking the end of adolescence, when basic psychological development is more or less complete (Carr, 2006; Verhofstadt-Deneve et al., 2003). The vertical line represents a client's degree of integration in society (isolation/integration). Good integration in society is reflected by a satisfying job or volunteer work, a stable social life and decent housing, and few problems in the domains of social contacts, relationships, work, legal issues, housing, and finances. Poor integration indicates problems in the above-mentioned domains, for instance, addiction problems, but also the problems associated with seeking asylum. A high degree of isolation is often an indicator of the existence, or possible risk of, structural problems or personality problems. The four quadrants (described in more detail below) describe psychological and psychiatric symptomatology which can be used as indications for treatment. The phases referred to are those corresponding to the model described in Chapter 2.

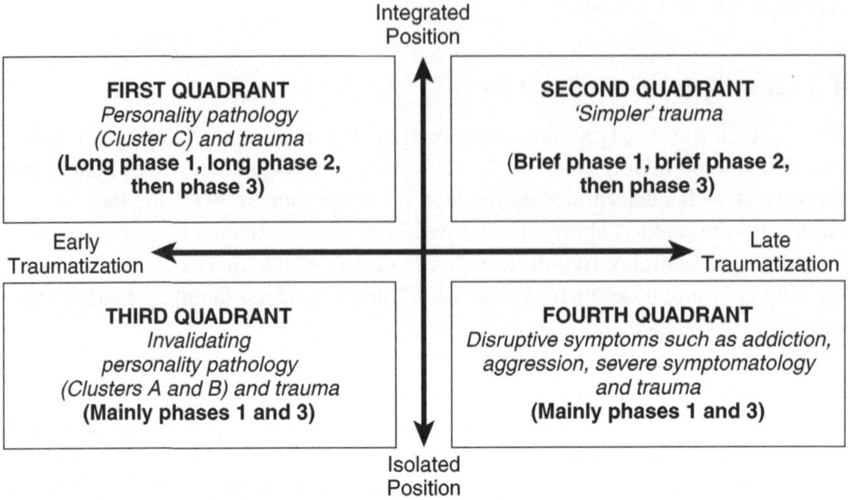

Figure 4.1 Symptomology and treatment options of complex trauma

First quadrant: early traumatization–integrated position

This first quadrant represents people who are reasonably well integrated in society, but who have experienced a relatively early traumatic event whose symptoms persist. Examples are people who experienced traumatic war-related events at a young age (called child survivors), refugees who were traumatized at an early age, second-generation survivors, and people who were exposed to early childhood traumas. These individuals, however, have found an integrated position in life, which is beneficial from the perspective of treatment. Generally speaking, a possible treatment option would be a somewhat longer phase 1 (because the early traumatization resulted in intense dysregulation in the here-and-now), followed by a longer phase 2 (because the early traumatization was distressing and restrictive for psychological development), and rounding off with a standard phase 3.

Second quadrant: late traumatization–integrated position

The second quadrant refers to individuals with a mature personality structure who were traumatized after psychological development was completed; in other words, their structural psychological development was scarcely, if at all, disrupted. These individuals have, nonetheless, an integrated position in society. Examples are war veterans, people exposed to occupation-related trauma, and refugees exposed to trauma after adolescence. The combination of being integrated with traumatization at a later age is beneficial for the treatment options, as the people in this quadrant have the best perspective for successful treatment of their symptoms. Even if the trauma is multiple, the manifestations of traumatic symptoms are very similar to those for simple trauma, so clients belonging in this quadrant are likely to have relatively simple PTSD syndromes. Generally speaking, the treatment for clients with their profile in this quadrant would be the following (referring to the phase model described earlier in this book): a brief phase 1 and a brief phase 2, rounded off by a standard phase 3.

Third quadrant: early traumatization–isolated position

Clients in the third quadrant have the most complex problems, and consequently, the possibilities of successful therapy are also the least favourable. This is due to the combination between exposure to trauma early on in life and poor integration in society. Examples of this type of client are asylum seekers, whose legal status means that they are not integrated in the society of their host country; individuals exposed to traumatic events at a young age, such as child soldiers who have experienced traumatic war-related events at a young age, child survivors, refugees traumatized at an early age, and second-generation survivors; and war veterans with premorbid (sometimes latent) personality disorders who become traumatized during deployment or for whom deployment has a destabilizing effect on a latent personality disorder that caused problems on their return home. These clients are not well integrated in society, so they have various problems with the here-and-now that unfavourably affect the treatment options. This group is also at a greater risk for Cluster A or Cluster B personality problems along with the other symptoms of their trauma. This means that interventions to stabilize the client are an important focus of phase 1. In fact, phase 1 interventions are, in many cases, the only option, as it is difficult to achieve sufficient stability to continue into phase 2. Nonetheless, treatment can proceed directly to phase 3 if sufficient stability is achieved. In phase 3 sessions usually need to be less frequent and extended over a prolonged period in order to prevent relapse.

Fourth quadrant: late traumatization–isolated position

The fourth quadrant refers to individuals who were traumatized after adolescence and whose position in society is one of isolation. Examples are asylum seekers living the uncertainty of their immigration status, refugees who were traumatized as adults, war veterans, and people with occupation-related traumas. The isolated position of these individuals in society is unfavourable regarding treatment options. Poor integration may result in all sorts of symptoms and behaviours related to the client's trauma, including aggression, addiction, or other severe symptomatology.

4.4. Treatment plan

According to legislation concerning medical treatment, a treatment plan must be agreed with the client, as it ensures transparency regarding the goals of the therapy and the intentions of the therapist. This transparency goes some way to neutralizing the mistrust inherent to traumatized clients.

A treatment plan should be dynamic, that is, based on the impressions of a client after a few sessions at the start of treatment, but modified, as necessary, over the course of the treatment. The treatment plan comprises a summary of the treatment goals – formulated as explicitly and verifiably as possible – and describes how goals are phased (for instance, using a model like our three-phase model). More goals may be added at a later date and can also be deleted once they have been achieved or become irrelevant. The plan also should indicate the treatment setting, and which of the therapists involved does what when particular treatment components are to be carried out by different people (e.g., an Eye Movement Desensitization and Reprocessing (EMDR) treatment, social skills training, etc.).

Examples of treatment plans are described below.

Complex trauma treatment plan:

- Determine specific treatment goals derived from the client's presenting problems.
- Categorize the goals in phases.
- Structure the treatment in accordance with the three-phase model.
- Determine specific treatment techniques.
- Designate the therapists.
- Determine the setting.

The following are two examples of a treatment plan.

Treatment plan 1

The treatment plan for a man from Turkish Kurdistan who was imprisoned for years and tortured because of suspicion of being a member of the Kurdistan Workers' Party.

Goals

- Less distress from reexperiences and nightmares
- Less depression, from an average of 7 (on a scale from 1 to 10) to at least 3
- Start making plans for the future again: education and work
- More social contacts
- Get finances in order, eliminate debt

Phasing

- Introductions
- Explanation of the treatment
- Explanation and psychoeducation about his trauma symptoms
- Get finances in order, proper arrangement of benefits

- Sharing traumatic experiences in a non-specific, general way
- Detailed therapeutic trauma processing using EMDR
- How to live after therapeutic processing; planning for education and work

Setting and therapist

- Individual treatment with therapist X

Treatment plan 2

Jewish woman grew up in a family with two parents who were traumatized by the war. She was emotionally neglected, which led to her not learning how to make room in her life for herself and was repeatedly abused by men.

Goals

- Learn to assert herself better
- Function in a relationship in a mutually equal way
- Gain clarity about how the way she was raised caused her negative self-image
- Think more positively about herself, gain more self-trust
- Therapeutically processing disturbing experiences from her youth, with compassion for the difficult circumstances her parents underwent with the war
- Therapeutically processing negative experiences from relationships
- Plan for the immediate future
- Phasing (including setting and therapists)
- Introductions
- Explanation about the treatment
- Prioritizing the practical problems present
- Participation in assertiveness training sessions with therapist N
- Inventorying the underlying negative core cognitions
- Group therapy with people who have the same problems, direct and indirect manner of changing these core cognitions with therapist U
- After group therapy, use EMDR to deal with these core cognitions with therapist U
- How to continue living with this history but also with more awareness of permitting herself to be who she is

4.5. Treatment context

The treatment of clients with complex trauma often requires a special approach. This section addresses the collaboration between the different disciplines involved in the therapeutic process, the selection of the treatment setting, and the impact on the client's relationships and social network.

4.5.1. Different disciplines

The treatment of the multiple, and often layered, problems of clients with complex trauma frequently requires expertise from different disciplines, for instance, a psychiatrist to prescribe medication, a psychologist to carry out the relationship sessions with clients and their partners, another psychologist to conduct the individual trauma-focused sessions, a community psychiatric nurse to provide supportive counselling, and a social worker to help with the clients' practical and financial affairs.

Multidisciplinary treatment usually involves formal or informal conferencing between the different therapists so that activities are coordinated and harmonized with each other. It is strongly recommended to designate a primary therapist to carry out the largest portion of the treatment so as to ensure that the provision of services to the client is coordinated. The appointment of a coordinating therapist is especially necessary when therapists from external sources are involved in the care of the client, for instance, staff members from the council for asylum seekers, social workers, occupational physicians and therapists from addiction services.

4.5.2. Treatment setting

The treatment for complex trauma can be designed in many ways. With regard to the treatment setting a choice needs to be made between outpatient clinic, day clinic, and clinical treatment, and whether it will be group treatment or individual treatment.

Clinical treatment, outpatient clinic, or day clinic

Clinical treatment is indicated when there is severe, dysregulated symptomatology or when very intensive psychotherapeutic treatment is needed. Outpatient clinical treatment or a day clinic (part-time) treatment is indicated when the symptomology is less dysregulated. The choice depends on the severity of the client's symptomatology, the client's presenting problems, or the presenting problems of the social network as well as the available treatment programme.

Group treatment or individual treatment

It is strongly recommended that group treatment for severely traumatized people be provided by agencies in the treatment of complex trauma. The clients should have enough resilience and social skills at their disposal to be able to benefit from group interactions. Clients receive acknowledgement and validation more readily when they are in contact with others who have had similar experiences. Furthermore, a group helps break through the social isolation that is a usual outcome of traumatic experiences. A group experience also exposes clients to how other people deal with their problems. Often new group members feel encouraged from seeing that other people have made progress in dealing with their problems.

When choosing group treatment as an option, the composition of the group must be taken into consideration; the choice is between a homogeneous group of clients with the same traumatic background (veterans, refugees, second-generation survivors), or a heterogeneous group of clients with different backgrounds. Although a homogeneous group is more likely to generate feelings of safety and trust, it has the drawback that an individual may hide behind the collectivity of the group and never manage to work on their own personal development.

Individual treatment is indicated when the client has poor social skills, a great sense of mistrust, too little resilience, an overly high level of anxiety, or just because the client has no time because of a job or daily activities. Another situation for which group treatment may not be suitable is when the client has a great need to testify about a trauma. The explicit therapeutic trauma processing carried out in phase 2 requires too much time for someone to adjust to a group, so should be done in individual sessions, accompanied, if necessary, by group sessions.

4.5.3. Social network

The problems associated with complex trauma inevitably have consequences for the clients' partners and their social networks. In the first place, the fact that the individual has been traumatized by something other people did to them damages their capacity to trust other people, and this affects all the people in their social surroundings. The client's partner and children, in particular, will notice this damage the most and will also have the most difficulty with it. In the second place, family members are also likely to have second-hand experience of all sorts of symptoms that will eventually test their endurance: reexperiencing, nightmares, irritability, depression, distrust, and all types of social conflicts.

Relationships with partners are usually strained under such stressful circumstances. In fact, relationship problems are often the motivation for the client's decision to seek help; the partner is unable to continue sharing the burden and threatens to end the relationship, or takes on board the care for the traumatized person to the extent that they lose their autonomy. It is also common for partners (especially if female) to identify so much with the clients that they become not only the clients' nurses but also their advocates. Their involvement in treatment alleviates their duties, keeps them informed, and involves them as supportive co-therapists. In later treatment phases it may be worthwhile to involve the partner in specific forms of treatment such as exposure or EMDR, as they can help the clients cope if they become destabilized.

In general, however, treatment during phase 2 is better conducted without the partner's direct presence. This is because clients do not always want to tell their partners what happened to them or they are ashamed of their deeds, reactions to the trauma, or the emotions that may arise during the therapeutic process. Sometimes, however, a client feels stronger with the partner close by and the partner may transmit a sense of security during the therapeutic process which encourages the client even more. That is why – as with the entire course of treatment – the decision as to whether to involve the partner in the treatment is always based on the client's needs.

A woman who, as a child, was raped by her father repeatedly over many years actually felt safer with her partner present during the EMDR sessions. A positive added effect was that the partner was also aware of what was happening during the treatment sessions, and so could support his wife more effectively.

The therapist has to explain to the partner that very minor situations can serve as triggers for memories of traumatic events, and that the clients' reactions are disproportionate in regard to the triggers. This puts the partners at ease and they feel validated in what they have been experiencing. It becomes clear to them that the clients' intense reactions have not been or are not now directed at them per se. It relieves them from the misconception that they have done something wrong. This helps develop a sense of ease within their relationship.

Part III

Treatments

Chapter 5

Phase 1 – the stabilization phase

The first phase of the three-phase model has two main goals (Van der Hart & Nijenhuis, 2007): (1) to establish a safe therapeutic relationship and (2) to stabilize the patient or alleviate symptoms. The overall aim is to make the client's life more liveable and less disrupted by the trauma symptoms and their consequences.

Given the large number of phase 1 techniques available, for the sake of readability their descriptions have been distributed through Chapters 5 to 9. We provide a general introduction to the components of phase 1 in the next few sections of this chapter; then we discuss the therapeutic relationship, touch on the topic of medication, and conclude with an overview of the different techniques that can be used to promote stabilization in the client's life and a discussion of when the transition to phase 2 can take place. Chapter 6 describes how psychoeducation can be implemented during phase 1; Chapter 7 discusses a few general life-control techniques appropriate for dealing with complex trauma; Chapter 8 covers different relaxation techniques for the client to learn; and Chapter 9 discusses specific techniques to improve dealing with trauma symptoms.

5.1. Phase 1 goals

The first goal – of developing a relationship of trust and collaboration – is usually much more complicated and takes more time for clients with complex trauma than for clients with other problems. A safe therapeutic relationship is needed in order to actually start processing the trauma in a concrete therapeutic way in phase 2. This chapter describes a few problems and solutions to creating a safe therapeutic relationship.

The second goal – stabilization or symptom reduction – involves establishing safety and control over the current living situation. A variety of techniques can be implemented to help to accomplish this (some described briefly in Chapters 7 to 9). Some are evidence-based, while others are more practice-based (Duncan et al., 2004) or rely on clinical wisdom (Van der Kolk et al., 1996a). Many of the techniques rely on the therapist's creativity, and even though they are founded on scientific knowledge, they have not yet been researched scientifically.

The intention here is to provide an overview of the different types of techniques that are available, although note that this overview is in no way comprehensive. That said, a therapist is at liberty to use this overview to stimulate them to create their own original techniques derived from personal experience to adapt treatment to their client's needs.

5.2. The three-phase model and the layered complex trauma model

The essence of the three-phase model (Figure 5.1) is embedded in the layered model of complex trauma referred to in Chapters 1 and 3. The three-phase model depicts the outer layer as the easiest to influence and so the best place to start phase 1 treatment, consisting of stabilizing the client's 'malaise', which encompasses relationship problems, depression, and the heightened arousal that accompanies posttraumatic stress disorder (PTSD). Therapy can next shift to phase 2 which deals with the distress caused by the actual traumatic experiences, such as the distress arising during reexperiences and nightmares. When the treatment shifts to phase 3, the emphasis is shifted to the client's external world.

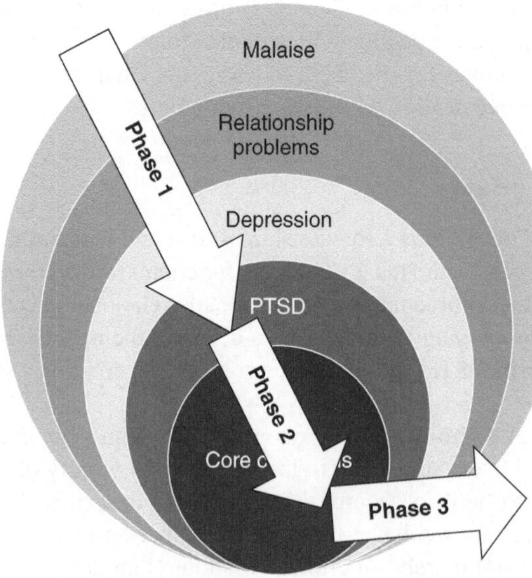

Figure 5.1 Three-phase model and complex trauma components

5.3. Window of tolerance

The goals of phase 1 are to establish a safe therapeutic relationship with the client while achieving stabilization and symptom reduction, thereby enabling the client to therapeutically process the trauma in phase 2 and make life liveable again. To achieve some form of stabilization, the window of tolerance model (Ogden & Minton, 2000) is used to set lower and upper regulatory boundaries of arousal. Figure 5.2 depicts the range and fluctuations between the minimum and maximum boundaries. Although trauma therapy requires some amount of arousal that reflects the issues the client is dealing with, it also has a ceiling. Clients should not be inundated with an excess of reexperiences and emotions during their therapeutic processing of traumatic events, as this will only overwhelm them and diminish any sense of safety and control they may have over the therapeutic process. An excessive degree of arousal is actually a contraindication for processing trauma because the emotional dysregulation is only reinforced, making it counterproductive. However, some degree of arousal is necessary for therapy to work. Treatment is still possible, however, even in the absence of arousal. This occurs with clients who constantly numb themselves with alcohol or drugs, or who are in some form of a dissociative state.

5.4. Comorbid problems

Many clients with complex trauma also present with Diagnostic and Statistical Manual of Mental Disorders (DSM) Axis I conditions such as anxiety disorders (generalized anxiety, specific phobias, and obsessive-compulsive disorders), depression, addiction, eating disorders, and psychoses. If comorbid problems are functionally isolated and interfere with treatment of the trauma, it is advisable to treat these first. The case conceptualization should reflect whether treating

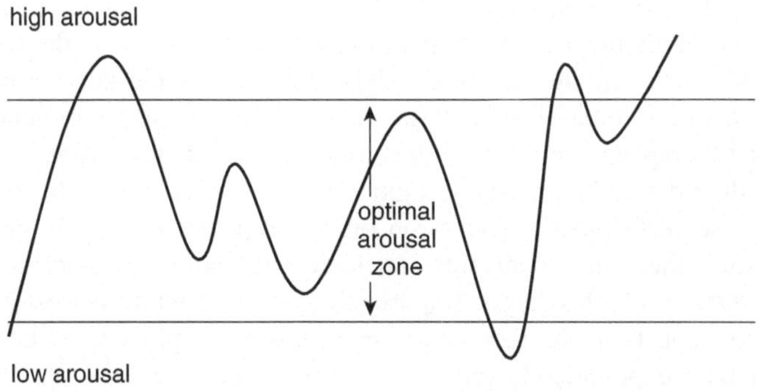

Figure 5.2 Window of tolerance
Source: Ogden & Minton (2000)

these disorders first is indeed helpful. In other cases, it may be better to treat the trauma first and then deal with the comorbid problem. For example, an obsessive-compulsive disorder may actually have the function of managing trauma-related restlessness. In general, any reduction of stress levels promotes effective treatment of traumatic events.

5.5. Therapeutic relationship

When a trauma is caused by people – as opposed to natural events – trust in fellow human beings is breached in a profound way. This makes building a trusting relationship with a therapist a very difficult process. A safe therapeutic relationship is essential to therapy in general, but crucial when treating what are most likely the most difficult experiences someone has ever endured. Building a safe therapeutic relationship in phase 1 is crucial for therapy.

This process of developing a relationship can be met with awkward resistance. A sign of an inability to surrender to the treatment is when a client verbally or non-verbally competes with the therapist for control of the therapeutic situation. This may indicate mistrust based on the traumatic experiences, but can also originate from personality disorders. This section deals with mistrust based on traumatic experiences. Clients often demonstrate behaviours that indicate difficulties with relinquishing autonomy or in presenting with vulnerabilities. This can be expressed in a variety of behaviours: not making or keeping appointments, disagreeing on the treatment plan, questioning the therapist's expertise, having explicit doubts about the purpose of therapy, or expressing a desire to progress slowly. The client may also test the therapist by, for example, asking if the therapist remembers the historic context of the events the client has undergone. Clients may also give the appearance of cooperating during treatment, but may be holding back their worst traumatic experiences until they feel that the therapeutic relationship is safe and trusting. Clinical practice and research have shown that a good therapeutic relationship is an essential prerequisite for successful treatment (Bachelor & Horvath, 1999).

Developing a therapeutic relationship requires time and it is the therapist's responsibility to facilitate the process. The therapist should keep in mind that the client with a trauma disorder has difficulty trusting people in general, and not just the therapist. The therapist has to allow the client to express this mistrust and should simultaneously recognize that it has a function for the client. It can also serve to open a discussion on the topic of mistrust in general. A caring attitude that gently confronts the client with reality is also known as limited *reparenting*, which is a good approach to dealing with mistrust and other problematic aspects of the therapeutic relationship. Applicable details on this topic have been expounded in various publications on schema therapy (Arntz & Bögels, 2000). The following paragraphs describe other aspects of the therapeutic relationship.

5.5.1. Reliability and clarity

The context of the treatment must be clear to the clients in order for them to develop trust in the therapist and in the treatment. They need to know what the treatment will entail, the frequency of the sessions, and how long the sessions will be. This also means that appointments need to be kept and to start on time. A therapist must be careful to avoid cancelling an appointment and must do what has been promised (for example, create a treatment plan, call a referrer, or send a letter to the occupational health and safety service). This gives the client a sense of security and of being in control.

5.5.2. Availability of the therapist between sessions

Predetermined agreements on how and when a client can contact a therapist between sessions clarify matters even further. Many clients find a sense of security in the idea that they can reach their therapist between sessions, yet experience has shown that clients hardly use this option. Using e-mail is a convenient way for the client to reach the therapist directly, leaving the therapist free to reply whenever it is convenient. If a client oversteps boundaries by making inappropriate contact, then the therapist must clarify an agreed frequency of contacts and inform the client of the potential responses to be expected.

5.5.3. Realistic goals

Clarity as to what a client may expect also means that the therapist must demonstrate exemplary realistic goals reflected in their own behaviour. Every therapist wants to avoid a client being disillusioned yet again in life.

5.5.4. Stop sign

It is advisable to agree, at the start of the treatment, on a specific stop sign in case things get too difficult for the client. Experience has shown, however, that clients almost never use the stop sign. The knowledge that they can control when to stop seems to be enough.

5.5.5. Professional conduct

Professional conduct with an empathetic and respectful approach is important for all clients, but especially for clients with complex trauma. The most effective therapeutic approach is to ensure procedural and structural clarity while simultaneously leaving enough room for spontaneous needs. The balance will depend on the personalities and needs of the client and the therapist. A therapeutic relationship is always individualized so that the therapist can adapt to the client's potential and limitations.

A refugee from the former Socialist Federal Republic of Yugoslavia initially agreed to all the proposals made by the therapist. The therapist designed a treatment plan: a session was dedicated to explaining PTSD and complex trauma, and another session was spent explaining testimony therapy. Then the therapy began. The first session using testimony therapy went very well, but then became awkward. The client began expressing dissatisfaction about the therapist's behaviour. The therapist was very understanding and tried to preserve the therapeutic relationship, to no avail. The client continued showing up to the sessions, but mentioned more grievances and disappointments about the therapist and treatment each time. Ultimately the client stopped coming to therapy and did not respond to the therapist's attempts to make contact. The therapist had no choice but to close the file.

It is not clear what the client understood about or expected from the treatment. It was assumed that the client had too little trust to speak about his traumas and he either could not or would not voice this. The therapist was working on the wrong assumption, and this led to treatment that progressed too rapidly. This then probably led to the client feeling increasingly less understood and being left with no other option but to discontinue the treatment.

Occasionally this dynamic is unavoidable when treating trauma. Clients do indeed want to have their symptoms alleviated, but they have not yet developed enough trust in other people to enter into a therapeutic relationship, or perhaps they are unable to voice the overwhelming traumatic events. The therapist has to be sensitive to the client's trust issues, and if possible, the therapist should raise the topic for discussion. If a problem with trust is present, but the client does not give any indication that it is a problem, or if the therapist does not detect the problem, the therapy will inevitably stagnate or stop abruptly.

A woman who was imprisoned as a young girl in a Japanese-run internment camp started an ostensibly good therapeutic relationship. She agreed to tell about her experiences in the camp, and talked about a new traumatic event in each of the first three sessions. The experiences intensified in severity and impact each time, and only in the third session did she describe the experience that troubled her most. The treatment then focused more on this event, which led to a successful therapeutic processing and integration of her experience.

In this case the client initially had too little trust to immediately start explaining her worst traumatic experience. The client had tested herself and the therapist, so to speak, by revealing the traumatic experiences in gradual doses of intensity. This ultimately led to successful treatment. The therapist, nonetheless, does not have many options with regard to steering the client in a particular direction. If mistrust is not discussed explicitly – which is common – the therapist cannot know for sure that the client has trouble trusting people and disclosing information. The only thing the therapist can do is to be sensitive and to try to raise the issue of trust and confidentiality for discussion.

5.6. Overview of stabilization techniques

Different techniques and skills can be used during the stabilization phase. In the interest of providing a general overview of these techniques, similar variants of the different techniques are categorized as follows. They will be discussed further in the following chapters.

5.6.1. Stabilization techniques

Psychoeducation

General control techniques:

- Control over living circumstances
- Control to say in the present moment: grounding exercises

Relaxation techniques

- Promote relaxation
- Medication

Regulating trauma symptoms

- Control over sense of safety
- Regulating arousal and aggression
- Control over unpleasant thoughts and reexperiences
- Natural processes: promoting health
- Therapeutically processing cognitions

5.7. Where to begin

A consistent and definitive sequence to implement stabilization techniques does not exist. The choice of techniques and the sequence in which they are applied depends predominantly on the presenting problem and the therapist's preferences. The relationship between the client's symptoms and the context of the client's current life play a role in determining the sequence used (Hummelen, 2008). Whatever the therapist decides regarding the selection and order of techniques for a particular client, one thing is certain: psychoeducation should be the starting point of any treatment.

5.8. Combinations of stabilization techniques

Integrated programmes for trauma treatment have been developed that basically comprise a combination of the stabilization techniques from phase 1; a few also include one or more integration techniques. Examples of these programmes include the PTSD Stabilization Course (Dorrepaal et al., 2008), Skills Training in Affective and Interpersonal Regulation (STAIR) (Cloitre et al., 2006), the Psychotrauma Course (Arnoldus & Markhorst, 2000), VERS training (Heesterman et al., 2004), and the STEPPS programme (Blum et al., 2002). Although the STEPPS programme – very similar to the other trauma programmes mentioned – was developed to reduce the acting-out behaviour of people with borderline personality disorders, it is also effective for traumatized clients. Another stabilization technique is Stress Inoculation Training (SIT) (Foa et al., 1991), a combination of psychoeducation, relaxation training techniques, breathing exercises, role playing, imagery exercises, cognitive techniques, and thought stopping. The Dutch Multidisciplinary Guideline for Anxiety Disorders (Van Balkom et al., 2013) mentions that the SIT can be a fairly effective treatment for PTSD resulting from one-time occurrence of sexual trauma. The PTSD Stabilization Course, STAIR, the Psychotrauma Course, VERS training, and SIT all integrate different stabilization techniques. Rather than address each combined programme, this book discusses separate elements derived from these techniques.

5.9. Medication

Medication can be a helpful resource for treating severe symptoms that develop after overwhelming violent experiences. In contrast with other techniques, medication has the advantage of usually working quickly. From a psychotherapeutic perspective, psychopharmaceuticals also have disadvantages. They may suppress symptoms that interfere with treatment, but may not produce any actual change. Still, they can create parameters that make it possible for therapeutic change to take shape. Alleviation of the symptoms does, however, run the risk of reducing the client's motivation for psychotherapeutic change. Another disadvantage is that some psychopharmaceuticals are addictive. The use of psychopharmaceuticals requires discipline to ensure a regular regime – which is difficult for severely dysregulated clients. However, the quality of life increases immensely for clients for whom medication reduces heightened arousal and agitation.

Psychiatrists and other doctors, such as general practitioners, prescribe medication. The drug prescribed has to conform to the needs of the psychotherapy, which requires proper consultation and coordination between the psychotherapist and the prescribing doctor. This coordination and education regarding medication provides an added dimension of clarity for the client.

In actual practice, many clients with posttraumatic stress take medication even though the clinical effectiveness of psychopharmaceuticals for PTSD is very limited (Jongedijk, 2006). The Dutch Multidisciplinary Guideline for Anxiety

Disorders (Van Balkom et al., 2013) advises against psychopharmaceuticals for trauma symptoms that can be treated effectively without them. Medication is, however, recommended if there are comorbid disorders with complex trauma such as severe depression, heightened irritability, and sleeping disorders.

Paroxetine or mirtazapine are the preferred drugs for mental healthcare in the Netherlands. When clients respond well to the prescribed drug, they are advised to continue taking it for twelve months and gradually taper it off (National Institute for Health and Care Excellence, 2005).

Complex trauma lies somewhere at the juncture between trauma and personality disorders. Research into the effects of pharmacotherapy on personality disorders is, further, still in its infancy. Opler et al. (2009) provide further documentation regarding recommendations for personality problems and the administration of psychopharmaceuticals.

5.10. From stabilization to therapeutic processing

The most important criterion for starting phase 2 is that the client has achieved the necessary emotional and psychiatric stability so that they can handle the emotional dysregulation and concomitant stress the therapeutic process entails. Additional stress-provoking problems reduce the client's ability to handle the added stress that accompanies aspects of their treatment. Therefore it is important to resolve these problems first – or to reduce their emotional burden – and to avoid triggering undue stress.

A few problems have concomitant levels of temporary arousal that make it virtually impossible to treat trauma problems. Perhaps the most obvious example would be psychotic disorders which reduce the client's capacity to deal with arousal. The same can be said for clients who abuse substances because there is a good chance that the extra stress confronting the client will result directly in a counterproductive abuse of substances in an attempt to numb the stress.

Clients who dissociate will use this defence mechanism to deal with the added stress that arises during therapy: the mind will defend against (dissociate) threatening unbearable emotions. This interrupts the associative integration process. Clients whose prominent dissociative coping styles remain unresolved are not yet ready for phase 2.

Therapy is also problematic for clients who are not comfortable with or who are afraid of their own emotions. These clients attempt to avoid or suppress emotions rather than allow them to surface, which is essential for therapy. Examples are clients who have learnt that anger is not acceptable or who think grief is repulsive. This problem needs to be resolved before trauma therapy can be set in motion effectively. Some therapy techniques can still be implemented in the abovementioned situations, although the therapist will need to consider the pros and cons of each technique carefully.

5.10.1. The transition to phase 2

The sensitive decision on when the transition to phase 2 (the confrontational phase) should take place may be complicated even further by a potential misjudgement regarding preparedness. The client may be ready to start therapeutically processing the trauma but the therapist may be too cautious, or the opposite may happen. The client may not yet be ready to start the processing while the therapist may be prepared to take the risk. Experience has shown that therapists tend to over-estimate their client's instability.

Since therapists tend to be more cautious than is necessary, it is important to discuss this dilemma openly with the client without using language that is too technical. When a therapist is in doubt about the client's preparedness, there is the option of implementing a test treatment, for instance, to use a mild, general-exposure technique. The therapist will also need to have a flexible strategy when choosing from the techniques to be administered. The criteria for estimating if a client is ready for the transition to phase 2 are shown below.

The criteria for the transition to phase 2

The client has to have enough psychological stability to be able to confront the increase in tension and distress that arise. This usually means:

- Availability of suitable social support
- No other problems that would be considered unmanageable
- No other dysregulating psychological problems, for example psychotic problems
- Manageable substance use
- Ability to reduce tension using exercises, activities, medication if needed
- Ability to tolerate emotional diversity
- Control over dissociative reactions

5.10.2. Treatment does not always mean resolution

There is a common misconception that successful trauma therapy means the trauma has to be actively resolved in the sense of 'forgive and forget'. Intrusions and avoidance reactions can for the most part disappear after treatment for simple trauma, but the confrontation with traumatic memories is more laborious in phase 2 with complex trauma. Sometimes phase 2 is merely a relatively brief phase at the end of the treatment. Given the severely destabilized situation often inherent to complex trauma, the stabilization phase is of much greater importance and is also more time-consuming. Occasionally concrete resolution of the trauma is not feasible because the client's psychological state never becomes sufficiently stable. This does not mean that trauma therapy cannot succeed. Rather, the focus of the treatment shifts from resolution to successful avoidance. This, incidentally, was the strategy adopted by most people who endured severe trauma during the Second World War (Bramsen, 1995).

5.10.3. Tethering between phase 1 and phase 3

As mentioned above, some cases cannot be treated in phase 2 because too much stress is evoked for the client. Providing support for a successful avoidance strategy then becomes the feasible treatment goal. Some clients in trauma treatment settings have persistently high stress levels that cannot be altered, and the trauma then develops into a chronic condition. The possible explanations are that these clients either have an already existing personality disorder which impairs integration of the trauma, or their traumatic experiences were so severe that it makes integration of the event impossible. The stability of the personality structure also plays a role and another important factor is the healthcare services available immediately after the trauma.

In these cases, treatment should not focus so much on the integration and confrontation of memories, but more on stabilization and learning how to live with the trauma. In terms of the three-phase model, this is a direct transition from phase 1 to phase 3 that skips phase 2 entirely. It also involves occasional regression to phase 1 to implement stabilization techniques as necessary.

Clients with an unstable personality structure have usually seen therapists over a long period at intermittent intervals and have tried many treatment techniques, to no avail. These clients often manage to function independently, yet still maintain a precarious equilibrium in life. Therapists usually want to reduce the frequency of sessions with these clients, whereas the clients generally prefer more frequent contact, so a compromise can provide a solution, for instance, instituting a voucher system with a limited number of appointments per year. These clients often have strong transference towards the therapist and/or the institution. The effective element in their treatment is the positive safe holding environment experienced in the presence of the therapist or when at the institution. E-mail contact – a form of direct access to the therapist – can also serve as an important way of transmitting a sense of safe holding. Another means of low-commitment contact that can be beneficial for these clients is for them to join a support group that meets on an infrequent basis.

In terms of the three-phase model, treatment for this group of clients evolves into a prolonged phase 3. The list below shows when this form of treatment is applicable.

The criteria to focus the treatment on stabilization and integration instead of therapeutic processing:

- The stress level remains high.
- Different stress-reduction techniques have had little or no effect.

- The tension is too high to implement therapeutic processing techniques or therapeutic processing has to be interrupted because of increasingly high and uncontrollable tension.
- The client senses a safe holding with the therapist.
- The termination of the treatment will probably worsen the situation.

A man with affective neglect who developed serious trauma symptoms following his deployment to Lebanon suffered from persistently high levels of stress. Concrete trauma processing techniques led to severe dysregulation and were promptly stopped. Eventually he was declared permanently disabled after a laborious application procedure. As it happens he was offered the opportunity to live in a portable building at the edge of a nature reserve where he did all sorts of odd jobs for the foresters. In return, they tolerated his unusual living arrangements. With the help of three or four visits from his care providers each year, he managed very nicely.

Chapter 6

Phase I – psychoeducation

An important component of treating complex trauma is giving the clients control, or at least a sense of control, over their situation. After all, an essential aspect of trauma problems is the client's lack of control over their situation during the traumatic event(s) (Allen, 2001). One effective way of giving clients control is, at the start of treatment, to provide them with information regarding the symptoms and problems causing them so much distress. It is also important to inform clients about their condition by focusing on the symptoms. Most clients know nothing about posttraumatic stress disorder (PTSD) or its manifestations and usually have never even heard of the concept. Some clients, however, know about PTSD from a previous treatment. It is useful to spend some time explaining the symptoms of complex trauma. This is because people are often put at their ease once they see that their symptoms can be described so succinctly. It provides them with a sense of validation and a feeling of being in control: 'What I have isn't so strange after all', 'That sounds exactly what I went through', and 'I'm not the only one'. This chapter contains a number of examples of how elements of trauma can be explained to the client using psychoeducation.

6.1. Aspects of traumatization

Psychoeducation is a process of explaining a few essential aspects of traumatization – vulnerability, the distinction between then and now, control, and altered cognitions – and will help clients better understand their own symptoms and reactions.

6.1.1. Vulnerability

Psychoeducation provides clients with insight into their dysregulation caused by arousal and distress and insight into which situations evoke that dysregulation. This knowledge, which can help clients actively avoid such situations, is comparable with vulnerability awareness in STEPPS adapted by Heesterman et al. (2004) as VERS training in Dutch (Van Wel et al., 2006). It is also helpful to involve people who are important to the client – in particular partner(s) – in this phase of treatment so that they become fully aware of how vulnerable their traumatized partner actually is.

6.1.2. Then and now

A simplified guideline for clients to sort out and better understand why they react the way they do in certain situations is to introduce a 'then and now' comparison. People with trauma-associated problems often overreact in a situation in the 'now' that is reminiscent of a situation 'then'. This is usually confusing for the client and may be even more so for the people in their environment. Asking clients about the appropriateness of their reactions and whether they are in proportion to the situation now may help them sort out their reactions: if the reaction is overly intense, then aspects from the past (then) are playing a role. It also helps to ask clients to think about whether their reaction is more appropriate of 'then' or 'now'.

6.1.3. Control

Disproportionate reactions by people with complex trauma can be viewed as an awkward attempt at regaining control. The subconscious intention of taking control aims to prevent recurrence of a similar traumatizing situation. That explains the sensitivity and the intense reactions to trauma-associated stimuli, such as excessive aggression or anxiety. Unfortunately, this dynamic is so deeply ingrained in some clients that they react this way even when there are no objective identifiable triggers present. Such clients are no longer able to distinguish between situations that are genuinely threatening and situations that merely are similar to the overwhelming events experienced in the past. It is important to explain to the client that the brain reacts disproportionately to trauma-associated stimuli, even if the stimuli have elements that are only slightly reminiscent of the original trauma (MacLean, 1990). Situations that a client has difficulty grasping or assessing are often appraised as threatening. It is advisable for clients in treatment to avoid these situations until they learn how to identify trauma-associated stimuli in the here-and-now. Some stimuli in the here-and-now have objective identifiable triggers of threat that justify a reaction, whereas others are triggers of perceived threat that originate from the past experience and are not actually threatening in the present moment.

A woman who was abused by soldiers panics when she sees uniforms and military colours in the safe country to which she fled.

A veteran soldier who neglected his personal finances received a growing number of warning notices to the point that his telephone and gas supply were cut off. As his situation became increasingly chaotic, he lost oversight and became increasingly vigilant and tense. This made it difficult for him to solve his current problems and he fell into a vicious circle of losing control. This loss of control jarred loose his trauma memories: his current situation triggering more and more memories of the chaos and disarray of the country where he was deployed as a soldier and where he was exposed to many traumatic experiences.

6.1.4. *Altered cognitions*

Cognitive theories address the close interrelationship between behaviour, emotion, and cognition (Beck & Freeman, 1990). Psychoeducation about the altered cognitions that result from a trauma could be helpful for the client. Altering cognitions is probably not a feasible goal for the start of trauma treatment, because disturbing emotions and behaviours are usually more prominent at that stage. At a later stage of treatment, however, the trauma can be addressed using cognitive interventions. This approach may also be combined with phase 1 or phase 2 techniques (to be addressed in more depth later in this book).

6.2. Metaphors

For clients it is incomprehensible – and also sometimes a source of anxiety – that they may feel just as anxious or sad in a situation 'now' as they did 'then', that is, during the traumatic situation. Metaphors, a convenient tool for explaining psychological mechanisms, can be used to explain how a trauma can affect one's mental state. They provide clarity to clients by placing a safe and palatable distance between their symptoms and the potentially complicated theory regarding the link between these symptoms and the trauma events. This can be very helpful for clients who feel bogged down by their situation. The fact that clients frequently experience their symptoms as egosyntonic makes it difficult for them to realize that certain reactions are inappropriate for the current situation.

> A soldier was traumatized as a result of witnessing numerous aggressive incidents in Bosnia. Although he found it very unpleasant to constantly experience these situations, he had some notion of it being his fate: 'Apparently this is the way I am'. The metaphor of a wedding [see below] proved to be a real eye-opener for him. Only then was he able to realize that his aggressive feelings were not really part of his character but had something to do with his war experience in Bosnia.

Metaphors are recommended because they rely on images and narrative to convey information. Information in this form is usually easier to remember than an explanation that uses just words. Metaphors also provide an anchor to evoke an explanation of the memories associated with particular symptoms. Metaphor can thus be the tool that provides psychoeducation regarding a specific symptom.

6.2.1. *The wedding as a metaphor for trauma processing*

The wedding is a useful metaphor in more ways than one. Weddings transcend different cultural backgrounds, given that certain elements are universal. A wedding is a gathering of family and friends that usually consists of a ceremony, a reception, and a meal, with the main differences between cultures lying in conventions and duration.

The wedding metaphor

A wedding day is always busy and intense. The bride is collected, there are rituals at the city hall and the place of worship and the reception and meal are accompanied by speeches and festivities. At the end of the day the newlyweds depart into the night. That is when fragments of the day replay in their minds, like short films: the intensity of the day made it impossible to therapeutically process all the events that took place, so this processing is postponed until later. The newlyweds will think about the different events in the coming days but eventually, after a week or two, this reliving of events will end. They will have 'processed' the wedding.

Exactly the same occurs with a traumatic event. The great – obvious – difference with trauma is that the short films that play in the mind (reexperiences) are horror films that evoke unpleasant feelings that are preferably avoided. The fact that these short films are prematurely stopped is what hinders natural processing of events. Proper treatment for traumatic events is to play unpleasant films to the end in a safe environment and in a structured way.

6.2.2. A car crash pile-up as a metaphor to explain delayed trauma reactions

Some people have difficulty understanding why trauma is suddenly reexperienced a few weeks, months or even years after the traumatic event took place. The following metaphor can be used to explain how reactions to shocking events occur (note that it is not advisable to use this metaphor with clients who have actually experienced a car accident).

The car crash pile-up metaphor

Imagine driving in your car. The car in front of you unexpectedly brakes and you cannot avoid crashing into it. You also see how the cars behind you crash one into another in a pile-up. At first you are a bit numb from the unexpected event. Then you smell petrol and you become aware of the risk of an explosion. You grab your things from the passenger seat and quickly get out of the car. You run for ten metres, then, from a safe vantage point, you observe the pile-up and it dawns on you what has happened. You then notice how your knees buckle and you begin to feel sick or you become sad. This somewhat delayed reaction seems rather strange; after all, the direct origin of these emotional reactions was the accident. However, there is a mechanism in the human brain that prioritizes physical survival (flight) over and above mental processing. In the pile-up example, emotional reactions were delayed by several minutes. In cases of trauma, the delayed reaction may occur days, many months, or even 30 years later.

Physical survival takes priority over mental processes

The natural mechanism of physical survival taking priority over mental processes means that thinking is postponed to after the severely traumatic situation has taken place. This is the principle of flight, fight, or freeze in action. Faced with a threatening event, an immediate, instinctive mechanism in the human brain sends a message to flee (flight). If that option is not immediately available, the message is to struggle to escape (fight). However, in a situation where a person is overpowered by one or more perpetrators, they become immobile (freeze). When the traumatic event is rape, for instance, this immobility usually leads to subsequent feelings of guilt: 'Why didn't I resist?' Submitting to the situation, however, often offers the best chance of undergoing the least amount of damage and the greatest chance of survival.

An example of this principle is the behaviour displayed by newcomers to a concentration camp. Most people intuitively feel that if they complain about the treatment (fight), they would just be treated worse. In situations such as this, people quickly learn to suppress healthy and assertive reactions of anger and indignation. The longer the threatening situation lasts, the longer reactions are suppressed and avoided. If the person's social environment pays little attention to how the victims perceive their experiences – which is frequently the case in post-war situations – the avoidance behaviour is reinforced. The victim thus finds a 'natural' way to continue avoiding trauma-associated emotions.

People severely traumatized during the Second World War typically chose an avoidance strategy (Bramsen, 1995). This conforms to impressions regarding the first generation of victims – treated at either the Sinai Centrum or Foundation Centrum '45 – who typically did not develop severely disruptive PTSD symptoms for many years. They usually had a very stable life, with flat affect manifesting as the worst of their symptoms. However, many such people began to have problems in their 50s, caused by external precipitating factors, such as their children leaving home, the loss of a job or being sidetracked from their work, tensions with spouses, or physical ailments. Traumatic memories that were successfully avoided for a long time began to manifest themselves in a more pronounced way.

6.3. The retraumatization triangle

At the start of treatment it is advisable to explain that the intensity of emotions does not always have an immediate cause. The 'retraumatization triangle' (Figure 6.1), derived directly from the classical conditioning model in behavioural therapy (Hermans et al., 2007), can be used as an analysis model to provide insights into the aetiology of the symptoms, and as a point of intervention – a guideline to manage symptoms. It also helps clients regain control over their own reactions.

6.3.1. Analytical model of trauma-associated reactions

Many clients with complex trauma have severe PTSD symptoms. A prominent feature is that something relatively minor in the present moment can trigger an excessively anxious or aggressive reaction. This is problematic for the client and certainly for the client's social environment and may result in the person avoiding certain situations, becoming socially undesirable, or even socially isolated. Examples would be individuals becoming very aggressive towards people committing minor traffic violations, panicking in the presence of uniforms, or crouching in anxiety at the sound of a low-flying airplane.

A diagram of the retraumatization triangle can explain how these reactions develop. It starts at the point the client becomes overwhelmed by intense feelings in a certain – neutral – situation. The retraumatization triangle is then drawn using a broken line from 'situation', in the upper left corner ('now' is added later), to 'reaction' ('then' is added later). One of the client's recent experiences should preferably be used for illustration purposes.

A courteous, well-mannered Iranian man was in a supermarket queuing to pay for his groceries. Suddenly a boy cut ahead in the small space between him and the person in front of him. The Iranian man turned white with anger and started swearing in Farsi. He then threw his basket of groceries to the floor and stomped out of the store. Outside his anger quickly subsided and he was ashamed of his behaviour.

The situation (trigger) evoked a reaction (as indicated by the broken line in Figure 6.1). If the reaction to a certain situation is disproportionately intense, then

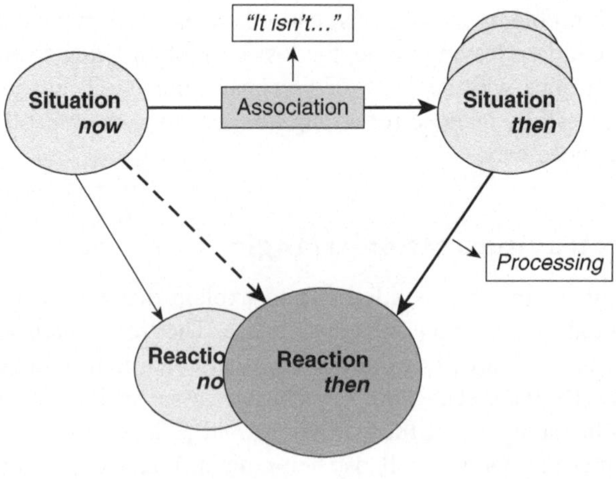

Figure 6.1 The retraumatization triangle

the intensity of the reaction is considered to be determined by another situation; thus, the first of these situations apparently has some element that is associated with the second of these situations. Using the illustration (Figure 6.1), a line is drawn from the upper left 'situation' – reflecting 'now' – to the upper right 'situation' – reflecting 'then'. The 'situation then' – which can also be several situations – causes the intensity of the 'reaction now'. Now the therapist can search for the association between the 'situation now' and the 'situation(s) then'. Note that 'then' can be five minutes ago, but may well be as far back in time as 50 years ago.

Clients sometimes know immediately which situations from 'then' were involved. Asking clients what they think is the worst aspect of the 'situation now' or if they have ever gone through a similar situation can sometimes help pinpoint the association. Alternatively, the therapist may more directly enquire about the first time the client ever experienced such an overwhelming situation. The cognitive theme sought has to do with powerlessness, injustice, or danger. This theme is often directly traceable to one or more deeply overwhelming incidents from the past, namely, the 'situation(s) then' (Figure 6.1).

The Iranian man saw injustice in someone spontaneously taking his place in the queue and this was associated with a traumatic experience in prison in Iran. Afterwards he realized that the uncontainable anger that he expressed was actually focused on the men who had tortured him in the past.

The 'situation now' is usually a somewhat evocative situation in the present (for instance, for the Iranian man, someone cutting ahead in a queue) which also deserves an appropriate 'reaction now'. This can be represented in the retraumatization triangle by drawing a small circle labelled 'reaction now' that appears behind the 'reaction then' circle. The point is that clients need to understand that they may sometimes fail to make an emotional distinction between what is appropriate for now and their overreaction based on an association with their trauma. Different colours can be used in the triangle for the parts that have to do with 'then' and with 'now'.

Clients usually immediately recognize their reactions in this model, whose value is its schematic way of explaining how intense reactions can develop. The model also offers clients an easy way to explain intense behaviours to their partners or other people close to them.

A war-stricken Indian man was in treatment. His wife, who came for one session, mentioned that her husband seemed to be unreasonably aggressive towards adolescents who ran along the walkway in front of their flat. As far as she was concerned they were only playing around but she was worried about her husband's behaviour.

When the therapist explained this situation using the retraumatization triangle, it turned out that there was a clear link with the client's very traumatic experiences during the Bersiap period which unfolded directly after the Japanese surrender to Dutch-occupied Indonesia. In those days the Native Indonesian

boys of the same age as the boys on the walkway walked around armed with spears: they had threatened the client's life and had shot people dead in front of him. This explained his behaviour; his wife understood the implications immediately and was better able to deal with it from then on.

The reader familiar with behavioural therapy will clearly see that this model is nothing more than Pavlov's classical conditioning model further expounded upon by Korrelboom and Ten Broeke (2004) in their consequence analysis model (see also Lazarus, 1971).

6.3.2. Point of intervention

The retraumatization triangle (Figure 6.1) can also be used to treat trauma problems. Once one of the sides of the triangle is broken through, intense reactions will no longer occur.

Connection between the 'situation now' and the 'reaction now'

The connection between the 'situation now' and the 'reaction now' does not need to be broken through as the reaction is entirely healthy and appropriate.

Connection between the 'situation then' and the 'reaction then'

Breaking through the connection between the 'situation then' and the 'reaction then' means that intense reaction in the 'now' no longer occurs when someone thinks back to the traumatic 'situation then'. This is possible when the symptoms associated with the memories of the 'situation then' are processed, as happens in phase 2 of the three-phase model. Although this area of the triangle allows the most thorough and effective intervention, it is not indicated for people with little mental stability. An additional drawback is that this kind of intervention is time-consuming.

Associative connection between the 'situation now' and the 'situation then'

The essence of this connection is a cognitive fusion between the 'situation now' and the 'situation then', resulting in both situations being experienced in the same way. The cognition is so overwhelming that the 'situation now' is just as threatening and anxiety provoking as the 'situation then'. This is actually serving a function, as the mind is guarding against the development of a situation similar to the one in which the original traumatization occurred. The warning system is overly sensitive, however, and alarm is triggered in irrelevant or situations with elements associated to the traumatic situation, as if the current situation has the same severity as the original traumatic situation. Theoretically, this oversensitivity for trauma-associated stimuli, which may have elements that are only slightly similar to the trauma, can be reversed by counteracting the cognitive fusion with more accurate, rational thought that emphasizes the time difference ("it is now, not 1947") or the geographical difference ("we are here, not in Liberia") between the two events. This approach is more effective when the rational alternative thought is personal and appropriate. When clients become aware that they may have an inappropriately intense reaction, theoretically they can stop the 'reaction then' by consciously verbalizing alternative thoughts.

Instantaneous associations

The problem with this cognitive technique is that the strength of the alternative rational thought fails to deal with the strength of the emotion of the 'reaction then'. The neurological connection between the cognitive representation of the 'situation now' and the 'reaction then' is made in milliseconds and this connection is too fast and too strong to break through the association using cognitive alteration. The consequence is that the person in the intense 'reaction then' mode is emotionally hypervigilant and tense as a result of an active amygdala at the psychoneurological level (MacLean, 1990). The basic survival functions of the body drive the hormone-driven alarm to take priority over alternative thought in the neocortex, which is not strong enough to overpower that process.

Using pain stimuli to deflect attention away from the primary trauma reaction

A technique to help bring the altered cognition to the forefront, ahead of the biological reactions, is based on reactivating the trauma systems in the brain and deflecting attention away from the primary trauma reaction. A strong stimulus – like pain – is needed to accomplish this. Administering different kinds of pain stimulation deflects attention away from the trauma (this explains why people self-mutilate). As a therapeutic technique, pain is administered in a controlled and constructive way. The purpose of the pain stimulus is to startle the client out of the reexperiences and evoke the alternative thought agreed upon beforehand: 'It is not . . . but . . .'

The hand is the most convenient and easily accessible place for the safe administration of manageable pain stimuli using a suitable object that is easy to carry around discretely. A rubber band that clients can snap against their wrist is commonly used. The disadvantage is, however, that this also has somewhat of a punishing side effect. Experimentation has shown that a 4-centimetre tee fitting for connecting three water pipes (Figure 6.2) meets pain stimulus requirements the best, as squeezing it inflicts mild pain in the hand. It is easy to carry around and to use discretely in a pocket. Other objects that are easy to carry around and easily

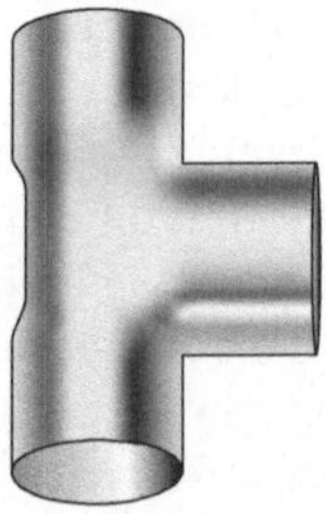

ø	art. nr.	€/3 St.
12 mm	*4121551*	**2.38**
15 mm	*4121557*	**2.25**

Figure 6.2 Tee fitting to administer mild pain stimulation

available may also serve in providing pain stimulation with no risk of abuse through self-mutilation; nonetheless, in our experience, a tee fitting works best. It works immediately with some clients; with others it functions in a more symbolical way, as a positive self-fulfilling prophecy. They know they have the object to control themselves and that thought alone is enough to help them achieve that.

Linking object

The tee fitting, by also functioning as a linking object associated with the therapist and the safe therapeutic situation, can enhance the client's sense of safety in the 'now' and so can delay client associations between the traumatic events and the 'now'.

Using the retraumatization triangle

- Establish which situation is a trigger for intense trauma-associated reactions.
- Enquire about what the worst thing is about the trigger and then ask when the client had experienced that to such an extent in the past. This is to identify the trauma or cluster of traumatic situations that cause the intense reaction.
- Map out this conflation of 'then' and 'now' using the retraumatization triangle following the instructions in Section 6.3.
- Explain how the intense reaction is actually in an inappropriate place and rather belongs with the original trauma or cluster of traumatic situations.
- With the client, think about the association between the trigger and the trauma that seem to have similar meaning in the situation 'now' and then disassociate them. Agree to a brief, mantra-like phrase that has a general meaning such as 'this is now, not then'.
- Explain the tee fitting as an object to be used for mild pain stimulus aimed at awakening the client from the trauma response. After the stimulus, the client should always repeat the previously agreed upon sentence.
- Have the client practise doing this a few times at home before the next session.
- Evaluate the effect the client reports.

Chapter 7

Phase I – control techniques

Clients with complex trauma usually lose oversight of their lives and this leads to a knock-on accumulation of problems. The loss of control over their current life situation in and of itself can be a trigger for trauma-associated reactions and may cause clients to feel despondent and hopeless. When therapy begins, it is important to help clients gain control over their life situation so that daily stressors reduce rather than increase.

7.1. Improving self-care

Depression usually accompanies long-term trauma symptoms. It is a consequence of avoiding the triggers that evoke trauma reactions. To avoid the triggers the person tends to participate in fewer activities and so does not benefit from the enjoyment and self-assurance these activities can provide. The traumatic symptoms are usually also accompanied by depressogenic cognitions such as 'I'm worthless' and 'My life is meaningless'. Lastly, the person's heightened vigilance makes them particularly sensitive to potential triggers and routine issues become less important or receive less attention.

The avoidance of situations, combined with a diminished appreciation of the ordinary things in life, results in fewer pleasant and enjoyable moments in daily living. In addition, these people have many reexperiences and nightmares, which put them at a greater risk for developing depression. Certain life situations after a trauma – refugee camps or asylum centres, for instance – can also be a cause of depression. This frequently results in neglected self-care, which does not help depression.

Simple and effective interventions at the start of treatment that focus on improving self-care may be needed to encourage clients to pay attention to regular and healthy eating habits, good hygiene, clean clothes, and a tidy living space. The deterioration in self-care often leads to personal finances in arrears and neglected paperwork. Intervention might involve organizing various documents and official correspondence, negotiating debt repayments, or dealing with benefits. These practical interventions at the start of complex trauma treatment can quickly and substantially improve the client's mood.

7.1.1. Regular circadian rhythm

An irregular circadian rhythm may indicate depression, but may also be a way to avoid trauma-associated stimuli, as less contact with others means fewer trauma-associated triggers. However, over the long term any shift in the circadian rhythm, which inherently involves avoiding social interactions and losing contact with other people, results in a sense of loss of control.

It is important to obtain a clear impression of the function of the shifted circadian rhythm for the client. The client believes there are benefits of irregular sleep patterns and the therapist needs to approach this discussion by focusing on the options for dealing with those benefits in a more appropriate way.

7.1.2. Structuring current problems

If the client has many current problems, the first priority is to bring some structure to them. A simple and orderly way to do this is to inventory the various problems and problem areas together with the client. Once all the problems have been listed, they can be prioritized based on urgency in a list of specific short-term doable actions. It is helpful to write this action list down and to incorporate it into upcoming sessions. This type of structure will reinforce the clients' sense of control over their current life situation, improve their mood, and reduce the intensity of their trauma symptoms.

7.2. Crisis plan

Uncontrollable spontaneous reexperiences, depression, and anxiety are common in people with complex trauma. A crisis plan can help prevent clients from slipping into a destructive coping style if they become overwhelmed by these experiences and feelings. Many coping styles – excessive drinking, self-mutilation, contentiousness, drug use, reckless driving, etc. – may seem to be effective in the short term but are ultimately destructive. The crisis plan lists circumstances that could lead to a crisis and includes effective measures to be taken in order to manage the accompanying intense emotions.

An essential component of a crisis plan is to include precautionary measures that can avoid a crisis, for example, not watching films with scenes that trigger traumatic memories. Measures that constructively reduce the intensity of emotions can have symmetrical content, which is transcribing the content of the experience precisely. They can also be asymmetrical in content, which means that a conscious effort is made to evoke other – more constructive – emotions to replace the crisis emotions. Examples include some kind of distraction or undertaking physical activities that can release anger and lead to fatigue while also providing a sense of satisfaction or achievement. These activities include sport (cycling on a home trainer or walking, jogging, or cycling outdoors), but they could also include household chores; mopping the floor, for instance, can be a constructive way of scrubbing away emotions. It is useful to include different options for the client to choose from to help them withstand distressing emotions that threaten to overwhelm them (Dorrepaal et al., 2008).

A prescription – or what might even be called a paradoxical prescription – can be a good way to structure the crisis plan. This format contains specific descriptions about the causes of a crisis. Its purpose is to make the client more aware, so that they can recognize risky moments early on and avert a crisis by taking measures in a timely manner. It is useful to include a list of telephone numbers of people who can be contacted in the event of an unforeseen crisis in the crisis plan, which should be stored in an easily accessible location. A crisis plan can also include arrangements with people in clients' social networks to help them through a potential crisis.

Examples of crisis plans

'I've made an agreement with N. to call if I panic and lose my cool. We've agreed that I'll only spend ten minutes raging about everything that's going through my mind and that she doesn't have to do anything except listen. After I hang up, she'll call me back in ten minutes to see how I'm doing. She will come to me or alert someone if I need more specialized care.'

'If I start feeling lousy again, I'll read the newspaper from start to finish. When I'm finished, or sooner if I want to, I'll tear the newspaper up into tiny pieces and then sweep them up into the bin. Then I'll meticulously clean and tidy my bedroom until I've calmed down. If that isn't enough then I'll clean the bathroom and the hallway too. When I start feeling better, I'll do something enjoyable, like have a cup of coffee with a nice snack or watch one of my favourite TV programmes. I could also go to the shop to pick up some of my favourite food to make for dinner'.

7.3. Sleep hygiene

People with complex trauma almost always have sleep problems caused predominantly by worry. In many cases, their lives have gotten out of hand and this leads to many problems and feelings that they no longer have control over their lives. Sleep disturbance also develops because of a disorganized and unstructured way of living that disrupts the circadian rhythm and therefore negatively affects the quality of sleep. The fact that many clients avoid sleep in an attempt to avoid nightmares and reexperiences also has a negative effect on sleep patterns.

Disrupted sleep hygiene reinforces or maintains sleep disturbance. In other words, the causes are acquired habits that do not promote sleep. Examples include:

- Drinking alcoholic beverages to fall asleep faster, which leads to restless and unsound sleep.
- Watching TV as a distraction until falling asleep, which also leads to restless sleep.

- Keeping the bedroom temperature too high.
- Doing activities right before going to bed, such as watching an exciting film, doing physical activities, or tending to personal finances.
- Drinking caffeine-based beverages such as coffee, tea, or cola immediately before going to bed.

The list below shows relatively easy measures to promote good sleep hygiene.

Promoting sleep hygiene:

- Use clean sheets.
- Use a properly supportive bed.
- Make sure the bedroom is well ventilated.
- Make sure the bedroom is not too warm.
- Use nightwear that is appropriate to the temperature.
- Remove stimuli from the sleeping area that increase arousal (e.g., TV or music, except if it actually functions as a relaxant).
- Remove all trauma-associated triggers.
- Have objects associated with a sense of safety on the nightstand for times when awakened by a nightmare (e.g., a bedside lamp for rapid orientation after a nightmare).
- Perform a sleep preparation ritual to make a smooth transition to night-time rest and prepare the body to go to sleep (e.g., gently closing doors, tidying up, turning off lights, shower, oral hygiene).
- Have a set time for going to bed and waking up.
- Do not drink too much alcohol and avoid coffee and other caffeine-based beverages right before going to bed.
- Read something in bed, but nothing that evokes arousal.
- Listen to relaxing music, provided it shuts off automatically.

If these suggestions are not effective, it is not recommended to lie in bed endlessly tossing and worrying, as this can create an aversive association between bed and sleep. Clients should be advised to try to sleep for only 30 minutes and then to get out of bed without becoming too physically active and try to focus their attention on something else, e.g., by watching a relaxing film or going for a brief walk outside. It is advisable that clients who worry very much structure their thoughts (see Section 9.7; also Section 9.6 for information on dealing with nightmares).

It is also important to make sure that clients have enough activities to do during the day to promote the physical need to rest. Naps are not recommended for people with sleep disturbance because that reduces the need to sleep at night. It is better to stay awake, even if with difficulty, until the usual time to go to bed, otherwise unsound sleep at night is reinforced.

7.4. Dealing with substance use

People with complex trauma have many problems with reexperiences, nightmares, and constant vigilance, so it is only natural for them to look for ways to alleviate these troubles. Some use self-medication in the form of alcohol, soft drugs, or hard drugs, seeking their numbing effect. The prevalence of a double diagnosis of posttraumatic stress disorder (PTSD) with some type of substance abuse is very high (Felitti & Anda, 2010; McFarlane, 1998). Such a double diagnosis is a complicated problem because it is accompanied by additional problems related to the substance abuse itself: addiction, social dysfunction, and financial problems. A chronically unstable situation is often present. Abstaining from the substance could improve stability and functioning, but the once-numbed trauma symptoms then typically flare up. Use of these substances destabilizes the situation to the extent that treating the cause of the addiction (the reexperiences, nightmares, and vigilance) becomes impossible.

Many treatment guidelines state that treatment must begin with abstinence (Emmelkamp & Vedel, 2007). However, experience has shown that this is an unrealistic strategy for people with complex trauma, except in cases of very severe addiction problems. It is often possible to start working on two fronts simultaneously: (1) surveying substance use and abuse patterns, and (2) investigating the function of the substance for the client. Attempts can then be made to find alternatives for this function, for instance, medication. In some cases, continuing to use an 'acceptable' substance – soft drugs or alcohol – is the most realistic option. Parallel treatment focused on detoxification in an addiction rehabilitation clinic is a plausible option in cases of pronounced addiction problems (intense hard drug use or severely dysregulated alcohol abuse).

Young people, for instance, young veterans, usually smoke cannabis, in many cases excessively. Older refugees from countries such as Iran or Afghanistan use opium, while refugees from Central Africa sometimes chew on khat (Catha edulis) plant leaves.

7.5. Dissociation and grounding

An important feature of trauma symptoms is alienation from the present moment. Clients may find themselves reexperiencing something that emotionally pulls them out of the present moment. They dissociate and are no longer completely aware of reality in the moment. This usually occurs when they experience something they perceive to be threatening. This type of phasing out is usually not severe and the most important task for the therapist is to show that everything is under control, as this attitude will at least provide the client with a sense of safety. The most important therapeutic measure at times like this is the provision of safe holding.

Dissociation is not a distressing manifestation. It is usually a signal from the brain to indicate that the client has overstepped a boundary. The client is apparently unable to express constructively that things are not going well. Dissociation can manifest itself in all sorts of ways, for instance, the client suddenly no longer reacts, just stares into the distance, faints, or feigns fainting. Hysterical presentations also occur, but it is not recommended that the therapist assume this immediately. Dissociation is usually a defence mechanism of the mind. In cases of severe dissociation it is important to keep the clients' heads cool with water and to monitor their vital functions, as breathing should be even and the pulse should be regular. A doctor should be called if there is any doubt about a client's health. The therapist should analyze precisely what was happening when the client dissociated. What the client was talking about or what the therapist had asked should be examined to gather information about the client's stress tolerance. Incorporating this information into treatment can be potentially fruitful.

Grounding was described by Najavits (2007) as a sensory focus with the aim to distract the client from unpleasant emotions. Grounding techniques, which can keep or bring back a client to the present moment, have generally not been extensively investigated in randomized controlled trials. Below we mainly report our practice-based experiences with different grounding techniques to help clients during and after entering a dissociative state.

7.5.1. Waiting

When clients no longer react to what the therapist says or to stimuli from the immediate environment (e.g., to a moving hand in front of their eyes) or when clients fall away (leaning against a wall, slumping in a chair, or falling to the ground), calmly wait until the client comes around in a return to the present moment. The therapist should describe the situation clearly and audibly, for instance: 'I've lost contact with you so I'm going to my desk to get some work done until you return and make contact with me again'. In group therapy the therapist can inform the other group members and continue with the session. When the client returns, they can be asked if they would prefer to discuss what happened then or later. Clients usually fall away for no longer than ten minutes.

7.5.2. Sitting and watching

This is a very simple technique to encourage clients to return to the present moment. Ask them to sit up straight in their chair and keep their head up so that they can look around. Then ask to make eye contact. Many clients who are in the midst of reexperiencing or dissociating tend to lower their heads and look down, and this also has the unfortunate effect of closing them off even further from stimuli in the present moment. Eye contact causes the client to receive stimulation from the immediate environment in the present moment, making it more difficult to remain in the reexperience or dissociation.

7.5.3. Colours

In addition to making eye contact, the therapist can ask the clients to name objects in the room that have a specific colour: 'Name all the blue things you see'. That forces the clients to focus their attention on the present moment. It also forces them to use and hear their voice in the present moment.

This type of technique uses a counterconditioning procedure (Korrelboom & Ten Broeke, 2004), applicable when the client's attention is focused on a reexperience of the past that results in an unpleasant emotional reaction. The therapist can encourage the client to actively focus on the stimuli in the room in the present moment. The client will then focus less on the stimuli that accompany the reexperience. The therapist can implement variants on this technique by asking the client to do other things, such as list the clothing someone is wearing, or describe a painting in the room.

7.5.4. Stand or sit

A simple technique to help encourage clients to focus on the present moment is to make them become aware of how they are standing or sitting. 'Concentrate on the places on your body that make contact with the chair', 'Concentrate on the places where your feet, through your shoes, make contact with the ground', 'Feel where your body is pressing on the chair the most'.

7.5.5. Sensory perception

Another option for actively keeping a client's attention in the present moment is for them to describe what they perceive through the five senses – sight, hearing, smell, touch, and taste. The five senses are always active, even if a person's thoughts are on something completely different. Focusing attention on sensory perceptions makes a person more aware of the present moment and distracts their concentration and attention away from distressing memories of the past. The instructions are as follows.

- Tell me what you see right now in front of you. Of everything you see, what makes the biggest impression?
- Focus on what you hear right now. Where are the sounds coming from? Which sound grabs your attention the most?
- Focus on the scents you smell right now. Do you recognize those scents? Which scent is the most noticeable?
- Focus on the sense of touch. Where on your body do you feel something different? For example, where does your body touch the chair? You probably feel the air on your face. Which touch sensation do you feel the most right now?

- Your tongue has many taste buds that let you sense the taste of things. What do you taste right now? Is it sweet, salty, bitter? Is it pleasant, unpleasant, or neutral?

The client should notice that their attention and concentration are now more in the present moment. This exercise can also be done by the client on their own, anytime and anywhere.

This exercise is closely associated with techniques from the concept of mindfulness, which is about using meditative techniques to focus on being in the present moment as much as possible (Segal et al., 2002). This is addressed further in Section 7.6.

Dorrepaal's sensory exercises include teaching the client to focus on seeing and listening and on internal sensations (Dorrepaal et al., 2008; derived from Zlotnick et al., 1997), leading to a gradual build-up towards being in the present moment. First the client focuses on five perceptions they are experiencing by naming them, either out loud or to themselves. Five sounds are then made that they listen to, then five physical sensations that they feel (movement, position, temperature). Gradually the number of the things being focused on decrease until there is just one of each. This gradual reduction of the number of sensations that focus on the present moment gradually enhances perception of the last sensation chosen. The client may find it difficult to stay in the present moment initially, but by focusing on increasingly fewer different objects, they will be able to concentrate more and more on the present moment. It is recommended to first demonstrate how the exercise works before implementing it.

A variant of this exercise is to deliberately provide the clients with intense sensations (Zlotnick et al., 1997), for example, holding an ice cube in their hands. This will distract attention from the anxiety-provoking situation. Other examples of stimulating intense sensations are using a stress ball, snapping a rubber band around the wrist, and playing loud music.

7.5.6. Request specific information

Another way of bringing clients' attention back to the present moment is to have them focus on specific and actual information, for example, dates. Ask the client what today's date is and then which day of the week a certain date from next month falls on. The therapist can also ask about someone's birthday and how many days there are until then. Variants of this include questions that involve counting down (subtracting three from one thousand) or about what the client ate yesterday. This technique encourages brain activity by using questions that require attention and concentration, therefore making the brain unavailable for reexperiences or thoughts about trauma-associated issues.

7.5.7. Physical activity

Physical activities performed in and out of the therapy room can also help focus attention in the present moment. An example is throwing a tennis ball to the client to catch it. Another effective exercise is to have the client stand on one leg for as long as possible, forcing them to concentrate on keeping balanced. Activities outside the therapy room include cycling, jogging, or gym workouts. Cleaning is a useful distracting activity that is also very constructive, and gardening works just as well, whether digging, tilling, raking, pruning, sweeping, etc. Another possibility is playing computer games, as they usually require a high level of concentration; they also result in mental fatigue, which helps promote sleep. Another area of activities can be hobbies, especially any requiring a certain amount of concentration, such as jigsaw puzzles, Sudoku, embroidery, or modelling. Holmes et al. (2009) have shown that the computer game Tetris can reduce the number of flashbacks after a relatively mild trauma. The supposition is that it also has a distracting effect because the game involves only focusing on one thing at a time.

7.6. Awareness of the present: mindfulness techniques

Mindfulness, which uses simple meditation techniques from Buddhism, means focusing attention on the present moment. The effectiveness of mindfulness in mental health has been extensively proven in research into prevention of depression (Fjorback et al., 2011; Segal et al., 2002) and the technique is also effective for anxiety disorders (Brantley, 2007). Some practice is necessary for mindfulness techniques to be successful (Germer et al., 2005; Schoorl, 2013).

The essence of this meditation technique is that, by becoming aware of what overcomes them, people learn to resist being driven away by a flush of intense emotion; instead they face the emotion and make a conscious decision to mark distance. In other words, a choice is forced between staying with the emotion or the thought. Mindfulness is radically different from many of the techniques mentioned earlier or the thought-stopping procedures that attempt to actively suppress or avoid memories and reexperiences (see Section 9.2). All thoughts and feelings – including unpleasant ones such as reexperiences and intrusions – are accepted wilfully and non-judgmentally. They are permitted simply because they are there. Clients learn that although they may have these types of feelings and thoughts, they are not at their mercy. The meditation technique teaches clients to experience the emotions and thoughts at a distance, so to speak, so that these thoughts and feelings change or disappear on their own over time. To use a metaphor coined by Schurink (2009), they come, they are, and they go like clouds in the sky.

Mindfulness techniques are also part of training sessions, such as STEPPS training (Heesterman et al., 2004), for dealing with borderline disorders. These basic techniques can be very effective if they are taught properly.

The presence of acute intense emotions stimulates the more primitive parts of the human brain to send out alarm signals, meaning that the executive brain functions in the neocortex are less in control. Techniques that predominantly use executive brain functions, such as mindfulness, will therefore be less effective with acute intense emotions, although they can certainly be effective in the early stages as emotions are building up. A prerequisite for the effectiveness of mindfulness is that the client is able to mark some distance from the emotions or thoughts.

An example of the mindfulness technique in practice

An elderly woman who had experienced heavy bombardments during the Second World War panicked when airplanes that made a certain sound flew low overhead. She knew that the association with the bombardments from long ago was only a memory. She also knew that she had the choice between letting herself be swallowed up by the emotions or letting the association just exist with the awareness that she is in the present moment. This knowledge prevented her from being completely overwhelmed by her thoughts. She was able to keep some distance and fewer emotions arose. To anchor herself in the present moment, she concentrated on her breathing. She did not push the association with the bombardments away but allowed it to remain while focusing on her breathing in the present moment. This technique prevented her from being overwhelmed by distress and reexperiences, and she learnt – much to her own surprise – to tolerate the sound of the airplanes with relative ease. It is important to note that the client first had to learn and practise the technique – using her breathing as an anchor – in order to stay in the present moment.

The fact that emotions are actually in a state of constant change explains why mindfulness techniques are effective. Emotions are often experienced as a never-ending deluge but the reality is that all emotions have a beginning and an end and they come and go like waves (Dorrepaal et al., 2008). It is recommended to explain this to clients so that when they are overwhelmed by their trauma-associated emotions, they can understand that even though the emotion is there now, it will pass in time. The goal is to find distraction so that the emotion can be tolerated and endured.

7.7. Rational rehabilitation for PTSD

Rational rehabilitation uses techniques from behavioural therapy, counterconditioning, and cue-conditioning. It focuses not so much on counteracting symptoms as on improving their management. Thus, instead of focusing on the stimuli that evoke reexperiences, the method focuses on neutralizing the anxiety evoked by the triggers.

Rational rehabilitation:

- Core strategy: a positive experience symbolizing good life experiences.
- Ideal situation: the most suitable positive situation identified by the core strategy.

- Cue-conditioning: in a relaxed situation, the client evokes the ideal situation emotion and internally voices the core strategy. They then take a small object (chosen earlier) and associate the good feeling with it; this acts as the cue. The client practises using the easy-to-carry cue to evoke positive feelings.
- Counterconditioning: the client looks for triggers that usually evoke anxiety and then identifies the cue so that a positive emotion arises that drives away the anxiety.

In their pilot study, performed with a small number of clients, Tomasoa and Appelo (2007) found that rational rehabilitation had a positive effect on the symptoms and well-being of clients with PTSD. After nine 30-minute sessions, clients were less troubled by elevated stress, less avoidant and felt better. Although the traumatic memories did not reduce significantly, the clients were less distressed by them. This procedure is very suitable for clients with complex trauma who require stabilizing techniques because it has no potentially dysregulating confrontation procedures such as with exposure.

A man who had a small successful shop in Bosnia fled because of the war and now lives a depressed existence in the Netherlands. He collected benefits, spoke broken Dutch, and had low self-worth. As much as he would have liked to, he had not been able to find a job. He had trauma symptoms resulting from the war. Rational rehabilitation seemed to be the appropriate technique for him.

- The core strategy was 'I am worth it. I can do something'.
- The ideal situation was the moment right before the war, when his shop was doing well and he had five employees.
- The cue was a coin that he carried with him all the time.
- He applied counterconditioning using the coin when looking for work.

He noticed immediately that his interviews were improving. He realized that it was crucial to improve his Dutch, which up to then he thought he would never do. He took a Dutch language course and ultimately found a satisfying job in the warehouse of a small company. He continues to use the coin, saying that it still has a positive effect.

Chapter 8

Phase I – relaxation techniques

Relaxation exercises are one of the most important ways of counteracting stress, including trauma-related stress. An important prerequisite is that stress levels should not be very high, otherwise relaxation exercises will have little or no effect. Relaxation exercises should also be learnt while in a tranquil location. This may seem self-evident, but while therapists often prescribe relaxation exercises for the client, they do not ensure that the client practises and learns to do them properly.

The best way to teach a client a relaxation exercise is to explain it first and then demonstrate it before assigning it for practice at home. This makes it easier for clients to trust the process and do things they are not accustomed to such as closing their eyes while sitting in certain positions in front of someone. After that, give the instructions for the exercise and then clients can practise it. The clients are then given the assignment to practise at home. Relaxation exercises can effectively reduce trauma-associated symptoms if they are introduced this way, as the secret to success is to have the client acquire positive experiences while practising. Of the wide variety of relaxation exercises available, the most suitable ones will depend on the therapist's experience and skill and on the client's abilities.

8.1. Relaxation exercises

Jacobson's (1938) progressive muscle relaxation technique is the best-known relaxation exercise, as it is very easy and most people benefit from it. It involves alternating between tensing and relaxing different muscle groups, with the idea being for the client to experience clear differences between tension and relaxation. The major disadvantage of the technique is that the full exercise is relatively time-consuming. An element of the progressive muscle relaxation technique is generalizing the effect by cue-conditioning using the word 'relax', so that it can be quickly and easily evoked in everyday situations. McGuigan (1993) described an updated version of this exercise. This and similar relaxation exercises can be downloaded from the Internet. A book that describes relaxation exercises extensively is *The Little Book of Calm* by Wilson (1999). Other relaxation exercises are based more on imagination and hypnotic suggestion. They are usually somewhat more difficult, however, and the therapist has to be suitably trained in order to implement hypnosis-like techniques.

8.2. Breathing exercises

The accelerated breathing that always accompanies stress has a biological explanation. When the human brain senses stress, the body automatically increases respiration in order to take in more oxygen as preparation for the physical exertion of flight. Stressors from an immediate physical threat are not the only conditions that induce this mechanism. Psychological threats – reexperiences or representations of a physical threat – also affect this biological system. Hyperventilation and other symptoms develop when the acceleration in respiration is not followed by physical exertion. Even though the role of hyperventilation is disputed (Hornsveld, 1996), in actual practice it has proven to be effective for clients. Accelerated respiration in the face of psychological threats has been thought of as a possible evolutionary defect. The human brain has difficulties with distinguishing between a real physical threat and an imagined threat. As mentioned above, the body prepares by increasing respiration so that more oxygen enters the blood. The body is preparing to physically exert itself, to quickly flee. Because the client does not actually flee, the preparation is not followed by any physical exertion. Thus, the accelerated respiration leads to hyperventilation, which can be a source of stress. This explains why controlled breathing is an important means of dealing with trauma-associated stress. Breathing techniques are also included as a component of the relaxation exercises described above. Different types of breathing exercises are described below.

Inhaling-exhaling while counting. This is the easiest breathing technique to explain and learn. It relies on the principle that, when exhalation lasts longer than inhalation, breathing becomes slower, deeper, and, hence, calmer. It has the disadvantage that it is somewhat too directive and this may confuse clients about the proper breathing rhythm. The drawback can be alleviated if the therapist first demonstrates how the breathing is done. It is not recommended to practise the exercise simultaneously with clients as this may oblige them to follow the therapist's breathing rhythm rather than their own.

Instructions: Inhaling-exhaling while counting. Breathe calmly in while counting to five using the fingers. Stop for one count, then exhale to the count of seven, slowly and through the mouth with lips pursed. Stop again for one count, then inhale to the count of five again. Repeat three times.

Seven-count exhale. In this exercise the client only has to be aware of exhalation, as the inhalation is allowed to follow naturally. The client simply exhales to the count of seven. Counting with their fingers provides a calm pace for breathing.

Humming. Deliberate humming also focuses on exhalation. The client makes a sound when exhaling and this automatically produces longer and calmer breathing. The lips have to be pursed, just as with the previous exercises.

8.2.1. Sinus line breathing

Another possibility for calm, concentrated breathing is by tracing what is called a sinus line, which is a graph used in mathematics (see Figure 8.1), on paper

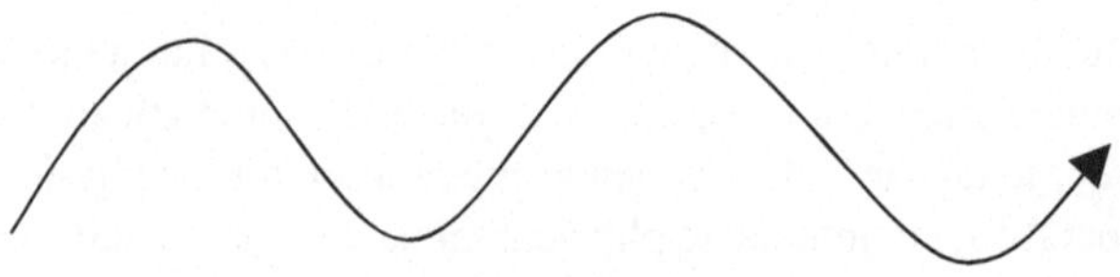

Figure 8.1 The sinus line

synchronously while breathing. Thus, when inhaling the line goes up, and when exhaling the line goes down. Breathing automatically becomes calmer because it adapts to the pace with which the line is traced or drawn. The fact is that the exercise has a similar effect that writing has; it is an activity that requires concentration and relaxation and forces the breathing to follow suit. This exercise can also be performed without pen and paper, for example, when lying in bed and tracing a sinus line in the air or on the sheets.

8.2.2. Abdominal breathing

Another relatively simple way to deepen and slow down breathing to the point of relaxation is to stimulate abdominal breathing, which can also be combined with counting techniques.

Instructions for abdominal breathing: Place a hand on the abdomen and inhale such that the abdomen expands as if breathing into that hand, so to speak. Exhale until the abdomen flattens. Repeat three times.

8.3. Generalizing the relaxation effect

A cue-conditioning technique (Korrelboom & Ten Broeke, 2004) can be used with all the relaxation techniques and breathing exercises described in this chapter. The cue would be a signal that the client incorporates in the exercise so as to evoke the effect later. The high point of the relaxation could be associated with a cue that can easily be attributed to the purpose, for example, saying the word 'relax', gently rubbing the thumb with the index finger or touching the cheek with the index finger. These signals can – even if only temporarily – evoke the associated relaxation at a later stage during a stressful situation. The necessary prerequisite is that the cue has to be practised and repeated often.

8.4. Relaxing activities

Another good way to relax is by doing physical activity. The therapist and the client can inventory which activities the client used to find relaxing in the past and which are still feasible options. The client can also think of new activities that relax, such as different sports, being outdoors in nature, computer games, doing something with a partner or family, listening to favourite music, etc. Another option is 'taking a short vacation from being an adult' (Dorrepaal et al., 2008), that is, consciously and for a limited time creating some sort of accepted regression. Examples are lying in bed in the afternoon for an hour with a beverage or with the blanket over the head, reading or drinking a beverage while having a bath, or withdrawing to a quiet place on the sofa, the balcony, or in the park. In this way clients can create a situation or timeframe that isolates them from the rest of the world and allows them to get back in touch with themselves.

Chapter 9

Phase 1 – regulating trauma symptoms

Clients with complex trauma feel unsafe, are hypervigilant, have difficulty trusting other people, and have a gloomy outlook on life. Constant vigilance and cautiousness, accompanied by unpleasant or unsafe feelings, is exhausting, so clients would benefit greatly from feeling safer. Clients are also often overwhelmed by sudden invasive reexperiences, trauma memories, or nightmares. This chapter discusses a number of techniques that can foster a feeling of safety in the present moment and provide some control over trauma cognitions and reexperiences.

9.1. Inventorying triggers

All types of situations, people, objects, and thoughts can be associated with the specifics of someone's trauma. Examples of objects that evoke these associations are uniforms for people who were arrested and tortured by the police, war scenes in films or in the news for people who experienced war, or love-making scenes for women who were sexually abused. Even seemingly innocent stimuli can be powerful triggers and evoke reexperiences: a wooded area for someone abused in such a place, football games on TV for someone who was tortured in a football stadium, or a barbecue for someone who was burned.

These triggers will evoke anxiety or aggression automatically and unavoidably for as long as the original trauma remains unsuccessfully processed, with these feelings exacerbating the clients' feeling of being unsafe. Therefore, an important component of phase 1 of trauma treatment is for the therapist and the client to inventory potential triggers and their situations in the client's daily life so that a plan to actively avoid those triggers can be rendered with the aim of having the client gain a sense of having a safer life.

Even though it seems logical and obvious, inventorying is uncharted territory for many traumatized clients. Furthermore, clients are often not aware of what exactly the trigger is in a certain situation. They therefore experience the anxiety and/or anger evoked by certain situations as authentic to that situation and as attributable to the present moment.

No additional measures are needed if the client has learnt to successfully avoid the triggers. For situations where occasional confrontations with triggers are unavoidable it is preferable to help the client distinguish between feelings that are attributable to the actual situation and those that are associated with the trauma. It is also advisable to make clear agreements regarding what the client should do in particular situations, for instance, to immediately leave a room when images of war appear on the news.

Examples of triggers

- A man who was tortured by a uniformed policeman in his land of origin became very anxious at the sight of a train conductor.
- A man who was very strictly raised and physically abused by his father became intolerant of traffic infringements and became disproportionately aggressive with cyclists biking in the wrong direction, driving straight into them.
- A Jewish man became extremely anxious in dark spaces and heard unexpected sounds from above. This was because of his memories, as a child, of hiding in an underground hole and hearing the boots of German soldiers stomping on the trapdoor above his head as they were looking for him and his family.
- A man who was traumatized in a Japanese-run internment camp in the Dutch East Indies as a child phoned the therapist when he saw images on the television of the First Gulf War. The therapist helped him by simply recommending him to turn the TV off.

Nonetheless, traumatized people who still seek some degree of acknowledgement and validation obtain a certain amount of satisfaction from their memories of traumatic situations. The original experiences are usually very personal and individual and frequently result in a sense of alienation. There is something of a curative effect when clients see characters in a film experience similar incidents and observe how their response is similar; this can reduce the feeling of alienation because it is often very difficult for clients to explain to people in their social network what the traumatic experience was actually like. Thus, some people deliberately seek out situations that evoke memories of their traumatic situation. This is probably also the reason why war veterans make great efforts to reunite with each other. These reunions are not about discussing the trauma situation, but about the consolation of being with people who have undergone a similar experience.

9.2. Stop mechanism

Reexperiences manifesting themselves frequently can be averted by using a stop mechanism. This technique is an improved form of 'thought stopping', which uses an aversive procedure to stop a thought. However, it can have a rebound effect, as the thought may return more strongly after a period of successful suppression. The stop mechanism is regarded as a variant of counterconditioning (Foa et al., 2000; Foa et al., 2009). The procedure is as follows:

Stop mechanism:

1. Decide which unpleasant thoughts or memories you would like to reduce.
2. Formulate a counter-feeling that is incompatible with the thought or memory.
3. Specify this counter-feeling in terms of situation, physical position, expressions, and associated objects, music or words.
4. Evoke the unpleasant thoughts or memories.
5. Take the physical position that accompanies the counter-feeling; say the phrase associated with that and think about the associated music, object or word so that the counter-feeling is as intensely evoked as possible and push the unpleasant thought or memories away.
6. Practise this several times with a slightly unpleasant memory before using this with unpleasant memories that are more intense.

9.3. Safe objects

Some clients have objects which they always carry with them to reinforce their sense of safety. It is useful to help clients choose 'safe' objects that provide them with a sense of safety. The primary function of the selected object needs to be taken into consideration.

9.3.1. Defence objects

The number of traumatized clients, usually male, who carry some kind of weapon as their safe object is often underestimated. Weapons include firearms, knives, brass knuckles, and clubs. It is advisable to ask traumatized male clients whether they are carrying any weapons and to discuss how the 'safe' object the client carries around should not lead to further problems. The danger lies in using such an object in a situation where it is not necessary. This danger is fairly plausible considering that traumatized people sometimes react to memories and reexperiences of 'then'. It is forbidden to bring any weapons into a treatment setting. Firearms need to be stored in a safe place as quickly as possible. At a minimum, the ammunition and the weapon need to be stored separately at a safe distance. A pocket knife or switchblade can be wrapped tightly with a rubber band to prevent it from being used too quickly, as the delay in removing it will allow time to think things over.

It is furthermore fairly evident that in these cases other 'safe' objects need to be found to replace these dangerous ones.

9.3.2. Objects symbolizing safety

Objects that symbolically represent safety can be very effective. An example is the tee fitting mentioned in the retraumatization triangle (Section 6.3.2). Such an object can have a cognitive meaning – 'It is safe now' – but it can also have an association with the therapist or therapeutic situation perceived as safe. Many objects, memorabilia, can serve the function of safe object, for instance, a small stone or piece of marble, a stuffed animal, a coin, a photo that depicts a place or situation when someone felt strong, a photo of children or other loved ones, among other examples.

9.3.3. Imaginary helpers

Imaginary helpers are devised and conjured up in the client's imagination to prepare for a situation or to ask for help. When a situation becomes difficult, the client can consult their imaginary helper and imagine what advice this helper would give. It is appropriate to practise this in the therapy situation and to have the client engage in an imaginary dialogue with their helper: 'Ask M. what would be the smart thing to do', 'What would M. do?' or 'What do you imagine M. would do if you could get advice for this type of situation?' It is important to encourage the client to actually talk to the helper as an imaginary third person.

9.4. Regulating stress and aggression

Winkel (2007) reports that trauma can be considered an aggression problem because the person is overwhelmed by something unexpected and then became powerless. Regardless of whether or not the feelings of aggression are suppressed, they are always a component of the trauma problems. Disproportionate aggression can be very distressing when it is expressed in situations where it is only partially appropriate.

Aggressive behaviour can be the result of trauma problems, but it can also stem from personality disorders. If the aggression problem is related to the traumatic events then the discharged aggression is mainly attributed to the traumatic event. If a pattern of aggression existed in the veteran's youth before exposure to trauma, it may be an indication of a Cluster B personality problem. This pre-trauma personality problem is not so easy to deal with in people who were traumatized in their youth. A thorough inquiry may be conducted into which stimuli the client reacts to aggressively. If a person reacts mainly to trauma-associated triggers, then they have a trauma problem that may also be partially influenced by a personality problem. If the expression of aggression is less focused, then the problem is probably one of personality.

When the client's aggression problem is caused by traumatic experiences, that is, the aggression problem mainly appears in situations that are somehow trauma-associated, it is important to explain this to the client. It is then a matter of inventorying these situations so that the client can avoid them. Another option is to discuss active distraction strategies so that the client can regulate the aggression. Physical exercise is a particularly effective way to regulate aggression. The aggressive tendency is then converted into a tendency to physical action with a constructive aim and this diminishes the aggression. Some examples of physical activities are sport, floor-scrubbing, tearing up newspapers, tidying up a shed, dancing, gardening.

9.5. Controlling reexperiences

An important component of treatment for traumatized clients is equipping them with skills to deal with the overwhelmingly unpleasant feelings that arise during reexperiences. These skills will also be useful to help the client deal with any temporary increase in arousal that arises as a side effect during the therapeutic processing phase of the treatment. One technique that is easy for clients to use is the imaginary technique that incorporates the principle of imaginary counter-conditioning (Korrelboom & Ten Broeke, 2004). Clients imagine themselves in a situation that evokes unpleasant emotions, but then consciously evoke positive emotions that are incompatible with those unpleasant emotions. To be effective these techniques have to be practised and performed repeatedly, given the severity and intensity of the unpleasant emotions and thoughts. Many of these techniques also have the important component of providing hope, as clients learn to take control of their unpleasant thoughts and reexperiences.

The sections below discuss a few techniques clients can learn in order to control distressing traumatic images. These techniques should be practised with clients first to see which ones work best.

9.5.1. A safe place

The therapist and the client inventory the situations in which the client feels good (those which have already occurred and those foreseen for the future). Clients imagine one of these situations until the desired good feeling develops. The therapist and the client agree on a convenient cue for the client to evoke this situation in their imagination along with the accompanying feeling. Cues can be a word or phrase, a photograph or memorabilia, for instance, a stone or a photograph taken at a beach where the client had a pleasant holiday and felt strong.

9.5.2. The chest

The chest exercise is simple and effective. Have the client imagine a large sturdy wooden chest with a lid and sturdy latches and locks. Instruct them to write down unpleasant thoughts, memories, and feelings on a large piece of paper, fold that paper up, and place it in the chest. The client can also figuratively place in the chest people who played a role in their reexperiences and any trauma-associated factors that cause them distress. The chest is closed, then locked securely. The client can also imagine themselves sitting on top of the chest, especially if they feel that the unpleasant thoughts and feelings are so intense that they could force the lid open. If they imagine that happening, the client can open the lid, place the thoughts and feelings back into the chest, and lock it up again.

This exercise works in either of two ways: first, because the traumatic thoughts and feelings are made to disappear into the background, and second, because the client is so busy visualizing the chest containing their thoughts and feelings that they are less occupied with actually having those thoughts and feelings.

The chest may best work as a coffin for some clients. Alternative images may also be used, for instance, a barrel with a cover that is closed with a hammer. Another image is of a small, comfortable bedroom with a large wooden box; the client imagines lying on the bed and placing any unpleasant thought or feeling that arises in the box.

9.5.3. *The hand as a projection screen*

Have the client open their hand approximately 40 centimetres in front of them. Instruct them to mentally project the distressing image onto the open palm, imagining this to be a projection screen. The client then gradually imagines the projected image moving away from them and finally tosses their hand to one side as if throwing the image away. Shaking the hand to symbolically get rid of the image can be helpful. A variant is for the therapist to ask the client to project the image onto the therapist's hand and for the therapist to gradually move the projected image away from the client.

9.5.4. *Trauma as film*

Ask the client to close their eyes. Have the client imagine being the only person entering the cinema or perhaps accompanied by someone they trust. To make the image as real as possible, ask them to identify and name different parts inside the cinema. A film begins to play that is about the traumatic events that distress the client. Investigate with the client the desired way of dealing with the images; examples include turning the film off in the projection room, advancing the film to more pleasant images, screaming at the film, throwing objects at the screen or tearing the screen to shreds with a knife, leaving the auditorium and taking occasional peeks through the window in the door while the film continues, or leaving the cinema altogether and doing something else. At the end of the exercise, allow the client time to return to the present moment.

This metaphor can be adapted to the individual needs of any client. The aim is to mark a distance from and so control the overwhelming images. The distance also offers the possibility for clients to manipulate the images and redefine the association.

9.5.5. *Trauma as TV film*

Clients can also imagine the film of their traumatic experiences being shown on TV and using the remote control to manipulate the film to reduce the intrusiveness of the images and make them more bearable, for instance, turning off the sound, fast-forwarding through some parts, switching channels, or imagining poor reception.

9.6. Nightmares

Nightmares are common in people with complex trauma (Schreuder, 1999). In dreams, we process the things that are on our minds. If a traumatic event has not been therapeutically processed, there is a good chance it will appear in dreams. Nightmares are dreams containing so much emotion – usually anxiety or aggression – that people wake up screaming. They usually have a strong impact on well-being in that people sleep poorly, wake up early, or wake up frequently during the night. The resulting fatigue causes all sorts of other symptoms such as agitation and irritation. Recurring nightmares cause someone to shy away from sleeping, avoid going to bed or postponing bedtime, and this also negatively affects mental condition. Problems from nightmares can be reduced in three ways.

The first way is to ensure good sleep hygiene (see Section 7.3), which can be combined with practical measures, such as having an object that evokes a feeling of safety nearby, leaving a nightlight on to quickly orientate on awakening from a nightmare, or leaving a household object such as a wet-mop next to the bed to evoke the sensation of being in the present moment on getting out of bed.

The second way is to substantively organize the nightmares by writing them down immediately on being awakened, and later examining this account to see what can be done about the themes. Phase 2 therapeutic processing techniques can be used for the events that appear in these recurring nightmares; for instance, a recurring nightmare can be rewritten (see below).

The third way to deal with nightmares is to do another activity at the time most nightmares occur, usually at the end of the night. For instance, a man who had traumatic experiences as a little boy in a Japanese-run internment camp in the Dutch East Indies took on an early morning newspaper route to deal with his nightmares. The alarm can be set for early in the morning so that the client can undertake an activity such as reading a book or newspaper, doing puzzles, playing computer games, working on a hobby, listening to the radio or gardening, before going back to sleep for a further couple of hours.

9.6.1. Nightmare rescripting

Victor Spoormaker (2005) developed a treatment method to change the meaning of recurring nightmares (also see Krakow et al., 1995), with the client rewriting the usual course of their nightmare so that the ending no longer evokes anxiety, for example, Superman comes and saves the day or the client has some weapon to protect themselves. The results of this method are mixed.

1. Write down how the nightmare usually goes from beginning to end.
2. Change the anxiety-provoking course so that it becomes constructive and positive.
3. Rehearse the new script by reading it for a number of days right before going to bed.
4. Keep a record of how you sleep every day.

We typically use this method in phase 1 because its primary goal is to reduce the symptoms and not to therapeutically process the trauma. If the nightmare content reflects the core of the trauma, nightmare rescripting can also lead to trauma processing.

9.7. A worry place

All trauma problems imply considerable distress, which typically has several causes. The primary distress, caused purely by the trauma symptomology, has a knock-on effect that causes all sorts of practical problems that affect work, relationships, parenting, and financial matters. All of these problems in turn have an effect on the quality of sleep. The absence of the peace and quiet necessary to fall asleep often leads to worrying, which, in turn, leads to restlessness, because there is much to do or because there are so many problems. Sometimes the fact that clients do not want to forget what they are thinking about at night increases the tension and hinders sleep.

Worry is generally not effective, as the person becomes trapped in a vicious thinking cycle. Worry takes the form of constantly posing questions but not bothering to provide an answer. The 'worry place' technique is a simple way of dealing with worry in a more constructive way. The client is first validated by being informed that whatever it is that they are worried about is important, otherwise they would not worry about it. The client also needs to understand that worrying disrupts their ability to sleep and that it would be better to think about problems at a more appropriate time. The technique is based on clients systematically writing down their worries and also possible solutions. Writing down solutions, even if these turn out to be ineffective, brings peace of mind and enables the topic to be put on hold.

A worry place:

- Place a notepad and pen next to the bed.
- If you cannot sleep or awaken because you are worried, write down your problems and thoughts.
- Consider what you can do to solve this problem.
- If you think of a possible solution, write it down.
- If you don't have a solution, write down that you will think about it further and will define the problem more clearly the next morning.
- The next morning, do what you wrote down the night before.

9.8. Natural processes: promoting health

Many techniques aim to change obstructive thoughts, feelings, or behaviours because they are so prominent and simply require urgent attention. Once these obstructive thoughts, feelings and behaviours are more manageable, it might be useful to use techniques based on natural processes. Natural processes are explicitly not about initiating process-focused activities, but about using any emotions, thoughts, and behaviours present in a constructive way – in other words, accepting what is there rather than changing it. The process is initiated using the healthy aspects that are present in the client, and enhancing or reinforcing them.

9.8.1. Thought box

The essence of trauma is that someone has problems with invasive thoughts or images that are not easy to stop. Many of the techniques described above use distraction and displacement of these traumatic thoughts or images. A rather more natural way of dealing with trauma, however, is to give these thoughts and images a suitable place in the client's life. This does not mean evoking more traumatic images which might cause even more distress, but structuring and organizing images and memories. The thought box is one of the ways to accomplish that.

Clients are instructed to set up a designated place in their homes or living environment where they can symbolically collect their images and memories. Clients can also place objects associated with the trauma in this area. It should be a marked off area, so that the client only confronts it when they want. An example is an empty shoe box, a drawer in a wardrobe, or a shelf in the attic. Clients can store objects associated with the trauma in this designated area. It is important that clients do not actively conjure up thoughts and memories to place in the thought box, as this would simply evoke more distress. The idea is to use the thought box only to store thoughts and memories that arise on their own. Clients can express themselves in different ways. For instance, they can write their thoughts on a piece of paper, use a pen to scribble out their anger about what happened, and crumple the paper up in anger. They can put all such papers in the box, along with other items related to the trauma, such as a rock from the place where the trauma took place, photographs, letters, or medals.

Elements from the thought box can be used with exposure techniques implemented in the active therapeutic process of phase 2. Phase 1 does not deal with active therapeutic processing at all, but is more about gaining some type of overview of trauma memories and giving them a designated place. Knowing there is a place where the trauma memories can be stored – or already are stored – reassures clients that they will not be bothered by them in the present moment. The technique also provides a foundation for processing.

9.8.2. Resource Development and Installation

Resource Development and Installation (RDI) is a technique adapted from Eye Movement Desensitization and Reprocessing (EMDR) (Korn & Leeds, 2002; Ten Broeke et al., 2008). Clients imagine difficult situations in the future and use one of their resources or capacities to enable them to confront it more effectively. This is essentially a form of counterconditioning. RDI, which can also be used without the bilateral stimulation typical of EMDR techniques, is similar to the stop mechanism described in Section 9.2 and the anchor exercise described in the next section (Korn & Leeds, 2002).

9.8.3. *Anchor exercise*

This exercise, based on the principle of counterconditioning (Korrelboom & Ten Broeke, 2004), has many variants (see Dorrepaal et al., 2008), for instance, RDI and rational rehabilitation (see Section 7.7). The essence of an anchor exercise is that a certain activity that is quick and easy to carry out – the anchor – is given a positive meaning. A simple gesture such as touching the index finger to the thumb can be associated with a positive feeling during a difficult situation, enabling the client to deal with the difficult situation better. Clients choose their own gesture as their anchor.

Anchor installation:

- Imagine which feeling you would need to cope with a certain situation.
- Think about when in your life you were in touch with that feeling.
- Go sit in a very quiet place in your home. Close your eyes and relax as much as possible. As vividly as possible imagine a situation in which you had that positive feeling. Think about what clothes you wore in that situation and what you were doing when you had that feeling. Use a short phrase to summarize how you feel about yourself, for instance, 'I'm strong' or 'I feel powerful'.
- While imagining yourself in that situation and uttering to yourself the feeling or thought that you want to anchor, gradually bring your index finger to your thumb until they touch. Associate the feeling with this gesture. Repeat three times.
- Open your eyes and look around. Place your index finger on your thumb again and notice how the feeling you anchored returns.
- Practise a number of times for situations that are not too difficult. Then go on to use the anchor gesture for increasingly difficult situations. Compare how you feel in the situation with and without the anchor gesture and notice what a difference it makes.

9.9. Therapeutically processing cognitions

Traumatic images, especially when exposure is repetitive or long term, also lead to cognitive alterations (Kleber, 2007b). Another important goal in treating complex trauma is altering destructive trauma-associated cognitions. This will usually be the indirect outcome of the therapeutic processing techniques used in phase 2, but cognitions can also be immediately targeted in two ways.

The first, more comprehensive, way is to therapeutically process the underlying base cognitions or cognitive schemas using the EMDR 'working right' model.

This intervention, which takes place at a fundamental level of processing, is actually a part of phase 2 therapeutic processing (discussed in Chapters 10 to 12).

The second way is to alter superficial and instrumental cognitions, a less fundamental alteration that belongs squarely in phase 1. An example is the therapist and the client investigating whether the thought that 'all people are dangerous' is true using Socratic dialogue (Ten Broeke et al., 2008). The outcome will probably be the conclusion that this is not a substantive statement, but that people are indeed dangerous in some situations. So, a more suitable, alternative thought would be, 'People in this situation are not dangerous'. To formulate it even more positively, 'This situation is safe.' These thoughts also have to be specifically defined because they are often not specific for the client. This means that the therapist has to attempt to gain and convey a clear impression of the cognitions of a client in a specific situation. This is relatively easy done using further Socratic enquiry.

> A man who survived a Japanese-run internment camp in the Dutch East Indies was often disproportionately angry when people obstructed his way, for whatever reason. This had frequently almost led to scuffles at traffic lights. The therapist asked him, 'What do you think the other person's intention was?' The client quickly responded with, 'He had it in for me'. The therapist then asked, 'Why did he have it in for you?' 'Because he thought I was a threat.' 'Why would he find you threatening?' At this point the client began to have his doubts.

As a result of the therapist's systematic inquiry using Socratic dialogue, the client realized that the other person probably was not thinking about him at all and did not 'have it in for him'. It was the sloppiness and awkwardness of other drivers that was on the other person's mind. That may indeed be irritating, but is no reason for taking action against the client specifically. The client could thus formulate alternative thoughts, 'Other drivers are sometimes so preoccupied they make mistakes or else they drive in a more relaxed way than I do.' The client writes this down on paper and reads it a few times before driving his car. This helps him stay calm when other drivers bother him.

Chapter 10

Phase 2 – general aspects of therapeutic processing

The second phase of the three-phase model focuses on therapeutic processing of the clients' traumatic memories. This chapter discusses a few general aspects of that processing. A decision tree, presented later in this chapter, can help determine whether to start with general trauma processing techniques or specific processing techniques. Both types of techniques are discussed in the following chapters.

Therapeutic processing comprises the gradual alteration or recovery of cognitive schemas. The erratic and overwhelming information that lies deep within when someone has gone through traumatic experiences that cause intense feelings of powerlessness and disrupt someone's life have to be integrated into the person's whole experience (Kleber, 2007b).

According to the Dutch Multidisciplinary Guidelines for Anxiety Disorders (Van Balkom et al., 2013), the 'indicated treatment' for posttraumatic stress disorder (PTSD) is cognitive behavioural therapy in combination with pharmacotherapy if necessary. Most of the evidence for effective treatment is with exposure and Eye Movement Desensitization and Reprocessing (EMDR). The Dutch Multidisciplinary Guidelines for Personality Disorders (2008) also recommend cognitive behavioural therapy and EMDR to treat PTSD. There is a prerequisite, however: 'The exclusive focus on PTSD is advised against in the case of severe personality disorders, particularly with Cluster A or Cluster B personality disorders. In those cases, an integrated approach is recommended, with focus on both PTSD and personality disorder' (National Workinggroup/Trimbos Institute, 2008).

The Dutch Multidisciplinary Guidelines for Anxiety Disorders (2003) are based on the results from many studies, which usually have been performed on uniform study groups; few of the subjects had complex problems and the majority had simple PTSD. Research on the effectiveness of treatment for complex trauma has hardly been conducted. Few studies that incorporated emotion-regulation skills revealed improvement in participants with complex symptoms (e.g., Cloitre et al., 2010; Schoorl, 2013). A few treatment case studies have been conducted (for instance Stöfsel, 2005). This is why treatment interventions to therapeutically process complex trauma symptoms use the evidence available for the treatment of simple trauma. The effectiveness of these methods for the treatment of complex problems has not yet been sufficiently established.

The phase 2 processing of traumatic events involves some form of exposure to traumatic memories. Additionally, the interpretations of the traumatic events are activated even more so than they already may be. These experiences are usually already activated and the emotional reactions resulting from the focused attention they receive during treatment make them broader, more intense, and, hence, more distressing. Even the parts of the traumatic interpretations of the experiences that have been avoided are triggered, which can lead to increased distress. Assessing whether the client can handle the additional stress is the most important criterion in determining whether someone can handle a therapeutic technique.

The therapeutic processing of trauma is processing the associations. Cognitive associative techniques are used to integrate all sorts of images and interpretations of the trauma into memory to alleviate the disproportional emotional load that still manifests itself in the current moment. This therapeutic process can be described in different ways. Kleber (2007b) states the following:

- The 'then' of the trauma should not have control over the 'now', but should be integrated with the 'then'.
- The 'detail' of the trauma should be a part of the person's 'life story'.
- The deep-lying erratic and overwhelming information in the cognitive schemas should be gradually altered.

The treatment plan can be differentiated into general and specific categories. The essence of the general strategy lies in integrating traumatic event into the client's life story, whereas the specific strategy addresses the details of the events more deeply. The higher degree of detail inherent in the specific strategy is more distressing for the client.

Complex trauma is a consequence of multiple traumatic events that may also have taken place over a prolonged period. It is, therefore, usually helpful to start with a general and less distressing trauma processing technique that also brings the different traumatic events into perspective. Clients will have, by then, mentioned and, to some extent, discussed the events, which facilitates the introduction of a more specific technique. Sometimes a general technique is all that is needed to reduce the symptoms.

10.1. Freedom to stop

Some amount of dysregulation and increased distress typically accompany trauma processing techniques. After all, these techniques expose clients to their worst memories. Additionally, a traumatic event is, by definition, a situation in which someone has had absolutely no control or influence over what is happening. Clients will naturally tend to demonstrate avoidance behaviour when dealing with their trauma. The therapist has to encourage clients to be persistent, giving them control over the details they reveal to the therapist. An important means of control for the clients is the explicit freedom to stop whenever they wish. This has a paradoxical effect because it gives clients control over the situation – the kind of control that they did not have 'then'. An additional advantage of the freedom to stop is that clients dare to further confront their most difficult traumatic experiences knowing they can stop whenever they need to. Clients would otherwise probably stop retrieving memories sooner in the process in order to avoid confrontations with the worst parts of their traumas.

In our experience, clients seldom exercise their freedom to stop, even though they value that freedom very much. When a client does want to stop, it is always a good idea to confirm this by asking them if they are sure they want to stop right then. If yes, then the procedure should stop immediately to avoid betraying the client's trust. An explicit question to confirm the wish to stop is necessary because clients sometimes say they want to stop in the throes of their emotions, when in reality they do not want to. It may well be more of a reaction to the severity of the emotions than an expression of their actual wish.

Preventing a trauma treatment from stopping prematurely also reduces the risk of a retraumatization, which would reinforce the traumatic emotional burden without any alleviation. The risk of retraumatization arises when the therapeutic processing technique is stopped at the precise moment the client has a very vivid image of the situation, yet has not added any new – associative – information to the situation.

10.2. When to start therapeutic processing: the risks

It is always difficult to assess when it is appropriate to start with specific or general processing techniques. As discussed in earlier chapters, the most important criterion is that the client is able to deal with the dysregulation that accompanies any processing technique. However, that is never assessed with certitude and there is always the risk that a trauma technique is started too soon. The client may not be stable enough and may be unable to deal with it. There is also the risk of starting too late; the client has been sufficiently stable for some time and could have been relieved of the distressing reexperiences at a much earlier stage.

10.2.1. Transition dilemma

Two things need to be taken into consideration when assessing whether to start with confrontation. The first is that many therapists – understandably – have the tendency to be too cautious. They want to protect their clients from additional yet unmanageable distress. By doing this, however, they can also cause clients to suffer prolonged distress from the trauma symptoms. A client who has trauma problems usually has nightmares and reexperiences daily. Therapeutic processing can generally start earlier than initially seems practicable.

The second point is that, when in doubt, it is possible to start with a mild trauma processing technique – possibly unbeknownst to the client – that can be regarded as a test. If it evokes too much distress, it can be stopped and the therapist can return to techniques that are more stabilizing. Examples of mild trauma processing techniques are testimony therapy or a mild confrontation method. Mild technique here means a technique intended to evoke less stress for the client during and after the treatment. These techniques are discussed in the following chapters.

10.2.2. Encapsulated traumatic experiences

Some clients have encapsulated traumatic experiences such that they scarcely allow them access to, let alone integration with, their memory. These people present for treatment when an intense degree of reexperiences suddenly overwhelms them, for instance, in reaction to a stimulus in their immediate environment. It may well be the case that those memories become encapsulated again, once the foundation is stable enough to therapeutically process the specific traumatic experiences. This is evidenced by the client's significant resistance when inventorying specific trauma experiences. The therapist is confronted with a dilemma and must decide whether it is better to respect the encapsulated memories of the traumatic experiences, or whether the client would benefit more from being confronted. The answer to this question depends on the client's preference and also the presenting problem, the symptoms, and the level of distress. The client will be able to decide once all this dynamic of encapsulated experiences is clearly explained. Many people choose to leave their traumatic memories undisturbed, but can always return for treatment should traumatic reexperiences recur unforeseeably. This in itself reinforces the client's coping mechanisms, enables preparation for potential future reexperiences, and the client agrees that they can still be treated later for this if needed.

Respect for and support of that defence mechanism is the only treatment option for such strongly encapsulated experiences. In the past, such encapsulated memories were broken through with hallucinogenic drugs such as LSD or other narcoleptics (experimentally employed by a well-known and controversial Dutch psychiatrist). The method, however, has never been scientifically substantiated and often leads to pseudomemories (Enning, 2009).

10.3. Decision tree for therapeutically processing traumatic events

A decision tree is a way of arranging and considering the elements affecting the choice of a specific or a general trauma processing technique (Figure 10.1).

The first question is if the client is distressed because of the traumatic experiences. If distress is low, the motivation to undergo burdensome trauma treatment is not strong enough. This may be the case when traumatic experiences are clearly encapsulated, as described above. However, it may also apply to people with a

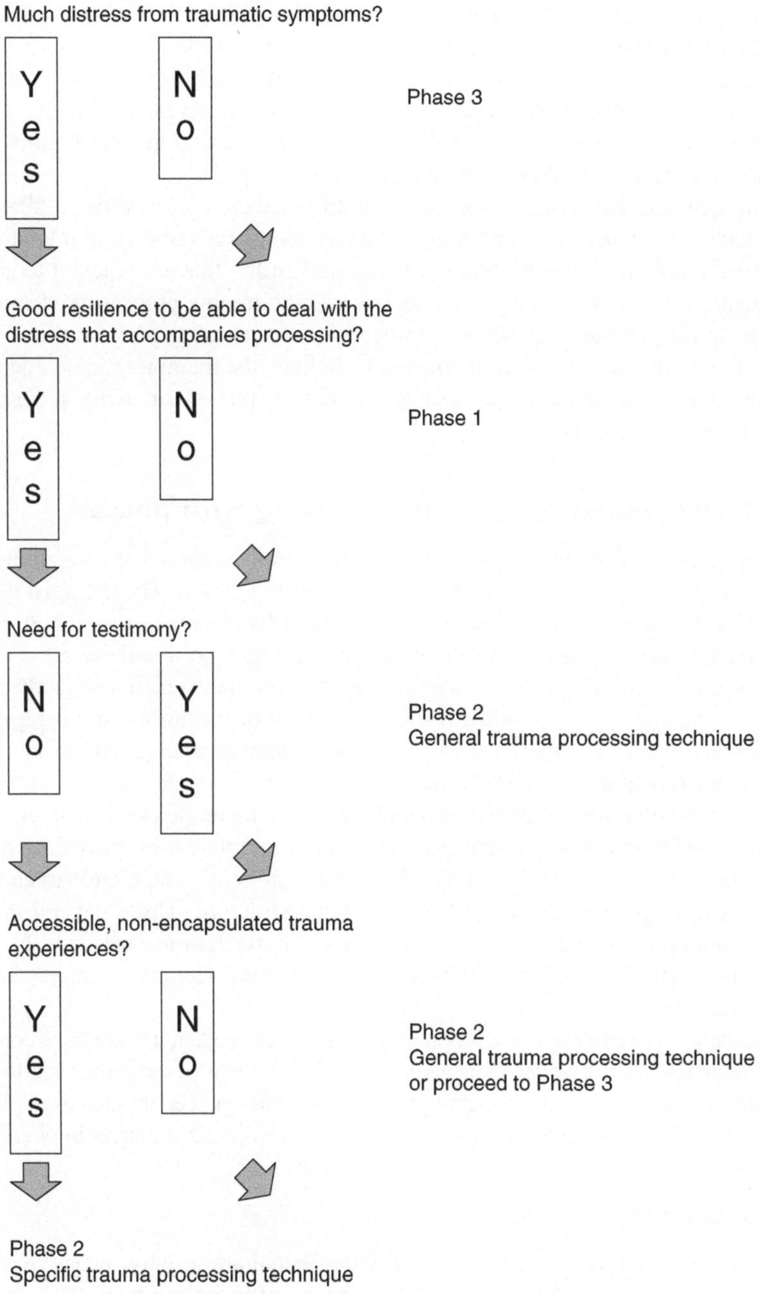

Figure 10.1 Decision tree for therapeutically processing traumatic events

successful avoidance strategy and to people with external motivation to come to treatment, for instance, at the request of a partner or other third parties.

When there is enough distress and adequate resilience, it is important to establish whether clients are ready to zoom in on a specific traumatic experience or need to give testimony and relate their story. In that case, a general trauma processing technique would be a suitable treatment option.

The question still remains, however, as to whether it is feasible to treat the traumatic experience. It is necessary to assess the client's ability to tolerate the different emotions – anger, sadness, shame, and guilt – that are inherent to going through a trauma processing technique. A specific trauma processing technique can be implemented if the client can tolerate a normal range of emotions. When it is not possible to use a specific trauma technique, the therapist should consider using a more general trauma processing technique in phase 2 or, perhaps, consider moving on to phase 3.

10.4. Dysregulation in phase 2: linking with phase 1

While phase 1 of the treatment concentrates on how to establish relaxation and stability, phase 2 techniques inherently cause dysregulation. The therapist needs to know which exercises or techniques the client has learnt in phase 1 in order to gain a sense of control and to re-establish relaxation so that these same techniques can be used again in phase 2. Intense emotional reactions (marked by crying, screaming, and physical restlessness) may occur during the therapeutic processing phase. The therapist has to evaluate whether such reactions integrate into the therapeutic process and remain constructive. Guaranteeing safety is paramount in the treatment of damaged people. This is why therapists have to provide structure by demonstrating their presence, defining boundaries, providing feedback, providing perspective to what the client is going through, and structuring time. A dysregulated client needs this external structure. These general therapeutic requirements equip the client with greater freedom to deal with therapy constructively. They are especially crucial in treating victims of interpersonal violence.

Therapists have to intervene when they sense that clients no longer have control over their reactions or over their panic level. Clients can be brought back to the present moment by using the techniques learnt in phase 1. Techniques from phase 1 are often drawn upon during the therapeutic processing that occurs in phase 2.

10.5. Closure

Successful closure of a traumatic processing technique usually means that the memories of an overwhelming event have been sufficiently processed. In some situations it may be useful to perform a closing ritual; examples are writing a letter to the perpetrator or to God. In such letters it is important to discuss what will happen with the letter afterwards. The client may want to store it in a secret place, burn it, tear it up, bury it in the ground, or shred it and throw it into the air. The chosen action could perhaps be performed in a visit to the place where the trauma took place. Suitable closure could consist of throwing out or burning the client's clothing from the time the overwhelming events took place. The client may also choose to destroy photographs or any other relevant items.

Saying farewell to the treatment and therapist are also part of this phase. Chapter 13 discussed this more extensively.

Chapter 11

Phase 2 – general trauma processing techniques

Occasionally a therapist decides to use a method that focuses on specific traumatic experiences, whereas the client would actually prefer to relate the whole story, because they feel a need to testify everything about their experiences. This need of the client may conflict with the focus required by a detailed procedure such as exposure or Eye Movement Desensitization and Reprocessing (EMDR). This is why it is better in some cases to start with a general trauma processing technique before attempting a more specific one. Sometimes it may be that a general technique is all that is needed. If this is not the case, a specific treatment technique such as EMDR or exposure can still be used.

11.1. Testimony therapy

Testimony therapy was developed in South America when psychologists discovered that writing testimonies for lawyers had a 'cleansing effect' on the health of clients (Cienfuegos & Monelli, 1983; Mooren & Van Dijk, 2004). It is used in the Netherlands in the form of a protocol of twelve sessions in which clients relate their complete chronological life story in a structured way (see Section 2.1.8). The testimony therapy protocol (see below) provides a foundation for the therapist as well as the client, with the client ultimately creating their own document. The method is first explained to the client, who provides their consent to continue. During the therapy, clients write their life story, including the disruptive episode(s). A general chronology results and – if possible – the destination options for the document are discussed. It may be used in legal procedures or just for therapeutic purposes, so it is important to consider who may read the document and where it will be stored. The therapy is closed with a ritual which usually includes something being done with the document.

Testimony therapy protocol

Sessions 1 and 2: Introduction and familiarization with the method

- Explanation and procedure
- Connection between the shocking events and the trauma symptoms

- Purpose of the document
- General structuring for the document

Sessions 3 and 4: Period prior to the traumatic events

- Youth and important life events then

Sessions 5 and 6: The shocking events

- Report of the traumatic events

Sessions 7 and 8: Period after the traumatic events

- Support available
- Experience of returning back to normal life
- Course of life up until now

Session 9: Current life

- Experience of life now

Session 10: Planning for the future

- Expectations for the future
- Potential obstacles

Sessions 11 and 12: Reviewing and signing the document

- Reviewing and revision for possible improvements
- Discussion regarding final destination of the document
- Signature
- Closure

Source: Mooren & Van Dijk (2004)

A man who was emotionally neglected in his youth joined the Foreign Legion seeking adventure. However, he was also exposed to many traumatic events during military interventions against the local populace. After six years, he left the Foreign Legion and embarked on a relatively peaceful existence with his wife and children in the Netherlands. Things went reasonably well until he started having an increasing amount of problems with reexperiences. In one particular case he had recurring nightmares about villagers locked up in a church that was then set alight. He could still hear the screams from the dying people. It was decided to start with testimony therapy because the client had hardly ever spoken about his experiences and also because he had many traumatic experiences during his time in the Foreign Legion and also as a youth. The expectation was that EMDR would be needed for a number of specific traumatic experiences. The testimony procedure was successful and the client was very satisfied with it. The next step would have been to inventory the experiences for which EMDR would be used. The client thought this was no longer necessary because he no longer had problems with traumatic stress symptoms and was no longer bothered by the worst experience (described above). The trauma reactions seemed to have subsided by the three-month follow-up session.

11.1.1. Testimony therapy is not applicable to all trauma problems

Testimony therapy was specifically developed for people who went through traumatic experiences as adults and who had good experiences prior to – and sometimes after – the traumatic experiences.

People who belong to the post-war generation, for instance, have frequently had a problematic and sometimes even traumatic upbringing and actually did not have a 'good period' prior to the traumatic experiences. Huijbregts and colleagues (2008) investigated the effect of testimony therapy on a number of second-generation clients who were burdened in their youth by one or both their parents' war experiences. The conclusion, based on a small study population, was that testimony therapy had neither a positive nor negative effect on symptoms. Most of the participants did mention, however, that they thought the treatment method was valuable (Huijbregts et al., 2008).

11.1.2. Literal transcription

An essential component of testimony therapy is the almost literal description of the client's story. The most reliable way of accomplishing this is to record sessions and to work out precisely the timeframe that the therapist and client determined beforehand. It takes time but it can be done in different ways: simply invest the time needed; delegate it to a secretary; delegate it to therapists in training; have the client type out the recording (although this has the drawback that it may be very confrontational for the client to do this at home and it may be useful to create a crisis plan the client can fall back on); reduce to keywords to convey the general scope; or get the client to create a report using images (e.g., in creative therapy; see Section 12.5).

> Testimony therapy was used for a client who was intellectually challenged and had undergone intense traumatic experiences. This client could not read, so images were used to implement the technique. In one session the client spoke about his traumatic experiences and in the next session he cut out images from magazines that represented his story symbolically. The client and the therapist glued the images on a sheet of paper which then became his own document. This pleased the client immensely.

11.2. Other narrative techniques

Testimony therapy is a narrative technique. The essence of narrative techniques is that the traumatic episode is embedded in the client's life as their story (or narrative). With narrative techniques, clients – with or without the structure or help offered by a therapist – relate their story and embark on very extensive writing projects in the form of memoirs and autobiographies. The usefulness of these narrative techniques may derive from the fact that 'stories structure emotions' (Weine, 2006). Much experience has been gained with this technique in the elderly care sector (Huizing & Tromp, 2007). A specific form is the writing method that is similar to exposure in which the client has to describe a traumatic event very specifically and in detail (Lange et al., 2001). Internet applications have been developed for this method.

A specific form is the writing method that is similar to exposure in which the client has to describe a traumatic event very specifically and in detail (Lange et al., 2001).

11.3. Narrative Exposure Therapy

Narrative Exposure Therapy (NET) is a brief form of treatment that was developed by Schauer and colleagues (Schauer et al., 2005) as a combination of narrative therapy, testimony therapy and exposure. The treatment was developed for refugees and can also be used in settings outside the therapy room, such as refugee camps. It was originally developed during trauma fieldwork in Uganda and has since been applied throughout the world with great success (Schaal et al., 2009; see http://www.vivo.org/resources/net/).

The client's life is extensively inventoried during NET. A cord is laid on the floor to symbolize their life. Stones are placed along the cord to represent the traumatic experiences (larger stones for very overwhelming events and smaller stones for smaller overwhelming events), and (artificial) flowers represent the more pleasant times in the client's life (see Figure 11.1). During the treatment – generally four to twelve sessions – all of the client's important life events are systematically recorded. Much attention is given to the circumstances of the traumatic events, which is when exposure techniques are used.

Figure 11.1 Narrative exposure therapy

Chapter 12

Phase 2 – specific trauma processing techniques

Specific trauma processing techniques target the client's most traumatic event. All such techniques contain a certain degree of exposure. One of the modes of action of exposure can be explained by the bio-informational theory of Lang (1984), which describes three levels of emotional imagery: stimulus information (perceptual codes); meaning information (semantic codes); and response information (response codes). Processing problems exist when too much emphasis is placed on the response information during the emotional representation. By exposing the client as much as possible to all representations of the emotion, an associative process is set into motion whereby the different representations of the emotion affect each other. This cyclical associative process leads to an alteration of the emotional representation (Figure 12.1 illustrates this process using anxiety as the emotion). The response information activates the suppressed stimulus information or meaning information, or both. This is how new information is introduced into the emotional representation, which in turn can alter the emotional representation and cause less anxiety. A time factor usually plays a role in the process. At the stimulus level initially, there is no distinction between 'now' and 'then', but this distinction becomes more apparent as the information is being therapeutically processed.

The adaptive information processing model uses a theoretical model similar to Eye Movement Desensitization and Reprocessing (EMDR) (Shapiro, 2002). Associative processing is induced by techniques similar to exposure (discussed later in this chapter), whose ultimate goal is to reintegrate traumatic experiences that have split apart from someone's life story.

12.1. Exposure

Exposure is a widely used and thoroughly researched behavioural therapy treatment technique. Different variants of exposure have been described (Foa & Rothbaum, 1998; Van Minnen, 2002), such as imaginary exposure, prolonged exposure, intensive exposure, in vitro exposure, and in vivo exposure. Exposure takes place in a safe and structured environment. The client is invited to slowly relate the traumatic events in as much detail as possible while monitoring their gradually increasing arousal level. The client tells about the events in such a way that the images, cognitions, and feelings associated with the traumatic event are

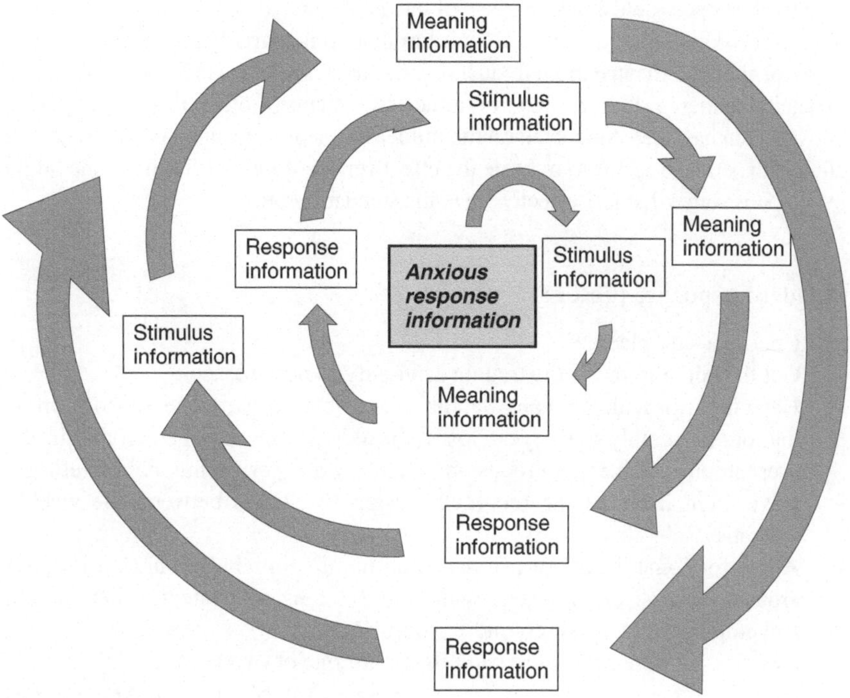

Figure 12.1 Associative processing circle for anxiety

evoked as vividly as possible. The effectiveness of the technique lies in the knowledge that the evoked anxiety can persist for a certain time but will be reduced when the associative processing mentioned in the previous section is implemented.

The validated and most researched version of this treatment lasts ten sessions for each event or cluster of events. In between sessions, the client listens to a recording of the previous session at least four times. This is considered to be a very confrontational form of treatment for the client (Van Minnen & Arntz, 2005), and milder forms are also used with success (Van den Hout & Merkelbach, 1993). The Dutch Multidisciplinary Guidelines for Anxiety Disorders (Van Balkom et al., 2013) recommends cognitive behavioural therapy as an effective treatment for posttraumatic stress disorder, and also states that imaginary exposure is the most researched method with the best methodological research protocols.

Exposure has been studied extensively with very good results. It is, however, a time-consuming treatment to implement. The client has to practise the exposure technique practically every day, either in the sessions or at home while listening to the recordings. The therapist has to invest a great deal of time in implementing exposure, as each traumatic event or cluster thereof requires ten sessions. It is also very intense, as the therapist has to keep the client focused on their most traumatic moments for lengthy periods. These disadvantages mean that exposure is implemented less frequently than one would expect in view of the demonstrated effectiveness of the technique. Accordingly, mild forms of exposure that do not strictly follow the standard protocol are implemented more frequently: the client is asked to talk about the trauma in detail, but there is no recording for home assignments (Stöfsel, 1996). No systematic research has been conducted on the milder forms of exposure, and, although the clinical experience seems to indicate the effectiveness of this approach, as one might expect, it is somewhat less effective than the standard protocol.

Standard exposure protocol:

- Choose a safe place.
- Get the client to recall the trauma as vividly as possible.
- Have them provide as many details as possible, in particular sensory information, preferably with eyes closed, speaking in the first person and in the present tense. Have them focus on imaginary reexperiencing, not on telling.
- Have them listen to the recorded session five times between the weekly sessions.
- Allow for some degree of avoidance during the initial sessions, but because arousal successively increases with more sessions, motivate the client to add and emphasize increasingly more painful details.
- Evaluate how the procedure went in the last one or two sessions.

Source: Van Minnen and Arntz (2005)

A Jewish man, as a child, had hidden underground in constant fear of being discovered by the Germans as they conducted house-to-house searches. As an adult, recovering from a serious illness he began to feel vulnerable and developed severe PTSD symptoms. Unexpected noises greatly frightened him. He received treatment focused on the most traumatic moment in the form of a standard exposure protocol in vitro over ten sessions, followed by listening to session recordings three times between sessions. The trauma symptoms associated with this event disappeared after ten sessions. A few other events were also examined closely using cognitive techniques.

12.1.1. Exposure and complex trauma

Exposure is implemented more easily if several traumatic moments had occurred during one episode. The client relates the entire episode and then the most traumatic events are zoomed in on. There is, however, a limit to the number of traumatic events that can be treated in one procedure. This makes treatment of people with various traumatic events in various episodes somewhat more difficult, which is usually the case with complex trauma. The standard exposure protocol in a series of approximately ten sessions would have to be implemented for each episode. The treatment can therefore be very extensive and long if the client has had many traumatic experiences, and this intensity of treatment can be exhausting for the client as well as the therapist.

12.1.2. Complications

A few potential problems have been reported with using exposure (Van Minnen, 2002). The fact that it can release an enormous amount of anger in the client could have destructive consequences. Clients who listen to their session recordings three to five times a week at home, without the therapist present, may not be able to control their anger. Feelings may also be blocked, rendering further treatment impossible, and anxiety can also be excessively intense and overwhelming, making listening to the recordings at home without the therapist a problem. The therapist will therefore need to properly assess the client's capability. Most important, clients should not exceed their limits, and even though they occasionally have to be encouraged to listen to the unpleasant recordings, they should be able to maintain control. The therapist has to respect and reinforce the client's limitations of how much control they have.

Other potential complications with exposure are comparable to the complications with EMDR, discussed further in Section 12.2.5.

12.1.3. Structured writing

A less rigid type of imaginary exposure is structured writing about traumatic experiences in the form of letters (Lange, 2007). It is less rigid because the client can determine the degree of intensity with which they express their emotions. There is less structure and less support, however, because writing takes place at home without the presence of the therapist. Clear instructions from the therapist are paramount. Schoutrop (2000) reported good results with the letter-writing technique, which includes the writing of uncensored letters that are never sent. Structured writing has three phases (see below).

Structured writing:

- First writing phase: self-control and uncensored letter.
- Second writing phase: cognitive restructuring.
- Third writing phase: the dignified letter as further reorientation, marking a departure from the past.

Source: Lange (2007).

12.2. Eye Movement Desensitization and Reprocessing

EMDR is an extensively researched treatment technique for traumatic events (Shapiro, 2001, 2012), also used to treat other symptoms (Shapiro & Silk Forrest,

1997). Central to this technique is the client visualizing images of the most severe moment of the traumatic event as vividly as possible. The client then receives an alternative stimulus. Originally, this stimulus was the therapist's fingers waved left to right in front of the client's eyes, but now it is more common to use headphones that send alternating audible clicks.

Studies have shown that EMDR is just as effective as exposure (Chemtob et al., 2000), while requiring less time and being less taxing for the client. EMDR has proven to be particularly effective in treating simple PTSD. In the Dutch Multidisciplinary Guidelines for Anxiety Disorders (2003), EMDR is recommended as follows: '[It is] one of the most suitable psychological interventions for PTSD. The method is effective and it is relatively less emotionally taxing for many clients and therapists'.

EMDR, a very well thought-out procedure that uses elements from all sorts of therapeutic schools, has a very rigid procedure. This rigidity is undoubtedly one of the elements that make it effective, as evidenced by the stability it provides the client. It is essential that the procedure be thoroughly explained to the client to reduce their anxiety and give them a sense of control. An important prerequisite for a good outcome is administering the procedure in a structured manner in accordance with the protocol. That is not as easy as it sounds, as this seemingly easy procedure requires proper training and experience. Fortunately there is a growing number of properly trained EMDR therapists available.

The standard EMDR protocol is explained below solely for illustrative purposes; it should not be taken as a guideline for administrating the technique.

Standard EMDR protocol:

- Introduction
- Focusing
- Target selection
- Negative cognition (NC)
- Desired positive cognition (PC)
- Emotion
- Degree of arousal in subjective units of disturbance (SUDs) (0–10)
- Desensitization: concentration on traumatic image and the offer of a distracting stimulus
- Closure at SUD 0
- Installation of the PC
- Body scan
- Reinforcement of the positive experience
- Relaxation exercise (if necessary)

Source: De Jongh & Ten Broeke (2003).

12.2.1. Indication

EMDR is indicated if the client is troubled by obtrusive reexperiences or intrusions. Since it requires the client to focus on the most unpleasant image of a traumatic event it cannot be implemented if there is anxiety without a clear association with a traumatic image. If there is no clear association of the anxious feeling with a memory of a specific event, then more preparatory work needs to be done to find specific and concrete memories that evoke the anxious feeling.

An important prerequisite for EMDR – as with every other therapeutic processing technique – is that the client be able to deal with the dysregulation that accompanies trauma processing. In our opinion this is, in fact, the most important criterion. What this implies is that uncontrolled alcohol or drug use can be a contraindication, because the client might seek refuge in these numbing drugs as a consequence of the increasing arousal that occurs after EMDR treatment. The client must be reasonably stabilized and their life must be somewhat in order.

Our clinical experience has shown that EMDR works very well with refugees and asylum seekers (Stöfsel, 2005). Even though performing therapy through an interpreter causes something of a delay, this is not a major obstacle for refugees and asylum seekers. A greater obstacle for this group is their life of relative isolation and the absence of a support system for sharing their stories with others after the EMDR sessions, as the treatment can exacerbate the sense of social isolation of people unable to share their stories, and this could potentially spiral into withdrawal from treatment.

It can be further inferred that another important criterion is for the client to have a personality structure that can deal with the increase in process-related emotional dysregulation, which people with unstable personality structures are not always capable of doing.

It may be that the traumatic experiences are so chaotic that a clear imagery does not coalesce, which in turn makes EMDR impossible to implement. The client, however, may very well have destabilizing problems caused by their traumatic symptoms, while specifically seeking treatment only for the trauma. This requires tact from the therapist to explain in a respectful way that trauma treatment is not indicated just yet.

12.2.2. EMDR and complex trauma

EMDR is one of the most researched and efficient techniques for simple trauma, but its effectiveness for more complicated conditions has not yet been formally established (Korn & Leeds, 2002) and neither has it been anecdotally reported (Stöfsel, 2005). Nonetheless, EMDR is very suitable for complex trauma. There are two possibilities for obtaining case conceptualizations and administering EMDR for complex trauma, called 'working left' and 'working right' (both Dutch innovations by Ten Broeke et al., 2008). Working left (Ten Broeke et al., 2008) –

the traditional EMDR treatment – involves systematically treating each of the client's traumatic experiences, whereas working right is based on treating the traumatic experiences that are the basis of the invalidating core cognitions (see Section 12.6).

12.2.3. Trauma lists

The client's traumatic experiences have to be categorized in some way in order to be able to work through them systematically. The easiest categorization (addressed below) is according to the severity of the experiences; for a more nuanced way of categorizing traumas, see Ten Broeke and colleagues (2008).

During one or more sessions prior to the implementation of EMDR, an inventory is made of the client's various troublesome traumatic experiences in the here-and-now. The traumatic experiences are then prioritized in a hierarchy from the most to the least traumatic. This results in a list usually consisting of around three to ten traumatic experiences. During this phase of the treatment the events are not discussed substantively; it is enough to just label them so the client knows which experience is which, and so that the traumatic experience can be referred to using few words, a code, a neutral name, or a number. This 'redacted' way of making the list may be necessary for reasons of confidentiality, a language barrier, the intense emotion evoked, or other reasons.

The listed experiences are systematically treated in the EMDR sessions. Therapy usually does not begin with the most difficult experience, as this might be too intrusive or disruptive for the client. It is better to start with an experience that is halfway down the list; for clients who are very anxious or who have trepidations about the technique, an experience from near the end of the list can be chosen. The technique has a better chance of succeeding if a milder experience is chosen, as it increases the client's trust in the treatment. In addition, the successful treatment of a milder experience may ease the intensity of the more severe situations, which, in turn, is likely to make their treatment more successful. It is recommended to discuss the sequence with the client so that the experiences can be treated systematically.

Frequently there is a halo effect which results in the milder experiences on the trauma list no longer needing to be treated with EMDR. This is because the traumatic load has been alleviated by the successful treatment of the more severe traumatic events.

An alternative listing is for the traumas to be arranged in chronological order. The moment the first traumatic experience took place is first identified, as this is regarded as the most conditioned experience. There is then an analysis of what the most representative experience was and what the most recent traumatic experience was (Shapiro, 2001, 2012). Processing the first, most conditioned experience will result in a reprioritization of the severity of the symptoms. Sometimes, however, other experiences have to be therapeutically processed before the client is capable of confronting this first experience.

Although EMDR is generally more effective than other forms of treatment, it is a time-consuming technique when administered for complex trauma. Our clinical experience has shown that complex trauma frequently involves five to ten traumatic experiences and that an average of three to four EMDR sessions are needed for each of those experiences. The treatment of five traumatic experiences would therefore require 15 to 20 sessions, excluding the preparatory sessions.

12.2.4. The EMDR module

Treatments for complex trauma are time-consuming; in particular, stabilization in phase 1 takes a long time. A treatment facility usually has more therapists who are qualified to perform phase 1 techniques than trained to administer EMDR. This problem can be remedied by offering EMDR as a module, meaning that the EMDR sessions are performed by a different therapist as a separate component of the client's treatment. A disadvantage of this is that a client who is finally ready to get more substantively involved in the treatment of the most traumatic experiences in their life often has to do this with a different therapist with whom no therapeutic or trusting relationship has been established. An effective solution to this problem – tested in practice (Stöfsel, 2005) – is to have the phase 1 therapist present during the EMDR module, or at least at its start, as once enough trust has developed between the client and the EMDR therapist the phase 1 therapist may no longer need to be present. This dual approach to therapy requires an information session with the client and both the EMDR and phase 1 therapists. The EMDR therapist explains the EMDR treatment technique and method. If the client agrees to undergo this treatment, appointments are made that enable the phase 1 therapist to be present. The first EMDR session is dedicated to a discussion of the sequence and severity of the various traumatic experiences. After completing the EMDR module, the EMDR therapist withdraws from the therapeutic process and the phase 1 therapist continues with the rest of the treatment.

12.2.5. Complications

It is a big step for a client to submit to EMDR treatment, as emotionally explosive issues are therapeutically processed when EMDR is administered to traumatized people and can result in intense anxiety, sadness, or aggression in clients. In our experience the first sets of clicks or eye movements are frequently the tensest because this is when it becomes evident whether or not the client is able to undergo the EMDR procedure. This is when all sorts of complications may arise, a few of which are discussed below.

Forfeiting control

Since the client has to submit to the structure of the procedure, they have to forfeit control and expose themselves to all sorts of emotions and thoughts that can be evoked by the associative EMDR method. With some clients the anxiety is such that they are unable to submit to the procedure, so the anxiety level has to be reduced and EMDR explained more clearly. Anxiety may also be an indication that a verbal technique such as exposure might be preferable, as better control can be exercised over what a client wants to reveal.

Avoidance of essential emotions

An important prerequisite is for clients to submit to the associative feelings that arise during the desensitization component of the EMDR procedure. Clients are frequently surprised by these feelings and often try to avoid certain emotions, causing the associative EMDR therapeutic process to stagnate. The client, for instance, may be unwilling to express anger. This complicates the therapeutic process because anger keeps them in the state of victimhood typical of traumatized people. Unburdening guilt can also be very difficult for the client, who will need some kind of release from excessive guilt. If the client is unwilling or unable to express emotions, the entire therapeutic process comes to a halt and the EMDR treatment stagnates. In such cases the reasons why someone cannot or does not want to deal with emotions needs to be examined.

Testimony

For clients who scarcely speak about their traumatic experiences, it has been our experience that it helps to dedicate the first (or more if needed) sessions to relating and discussing traumatic experiences in a general way or to use testimony therapy. Sometimes clients who get to the point of visualizing the trauma suddenly have a great need to testify extensively about it. That hinders EMDR treatment, as the technique involves associative internal processing, not verbalization of the traumatic experience.

Overburdening

Because EMDR treatment for complex trauma is time-consuming, it is important to bear in mind the client's capacity for endurance, required for the weekly intensive and extended EMDR sessions. It may be useful to introduce a 'plateau phase', in other words, to cancel EMDR sessions for a certain period and spend the time examining how things are going in the 'here-and-now'. If necessary, time can be spent integrating the results achieved up to that point. Once the client is again ready, the EMDR sessions can recommence and be used to further climb the 'trauma mountain'.

Fluctuating distress

The Subjective Unit of Distress Scale (SUDS) declines even down to 0 (zero), while the client's body language clearly expresses some amount of tension. It is a good idea to do a body scan to see what is the most severe detail in the image. A certain theme in the trauma treatment may appear to be successfully completed, with the client reporting a SUDS of 0, but other arousal-laden trauma channels may still need to be therapeutically processed, and this arousal will be evident in the client's body language.

Dissociation

Dissociation is a defence mechanism of the mind, often used by people with trauma problems. When arousal and anxiety are overwhelming, awareness is temporarily switched off, usually to return on its own in time. Therapeutic processing techniques are inherently about the client experiencing and living through feelings and thoughts related to the trauma. This initiates the associative processing, which also comprises living through and feeling the experiences. The accompanying anxiety and arousal can result in dissociation, which acts as a defence mechanism. However, this defence mechanism stagnates the therapeutic process, making EMDR no longer possible. EMDR for severe dissociative disorders has recently been developed. See Oppenheim and colleagues (2008) for more information.

12.2.6. Realistic expectations

Treating clients with complex trauma and diverse traumatic experiences takes time. Bear in mind that an average of three to four sessions is needed for each traumatic experience, assuming the therapeutic process runs smoothly, which means about 21 to 28 sessions if a client has gone through seven traumatic experiences. Patience is therefore required from the therapist as well as the client, and it is advisable to clearly explain that to the client beforehand.

With complex problems it is usually evident that the therapeutic process is progressing, albeit slowly. It is important that the therapist remains patient and satisfied with gradual progress, for instance, a drop of only one SUDS point, or even no change, especially when body language indicates visible signs of relaxation or therapeutic processing in the client. An important principle for the therapist to bear in mind is that the therapeutic process is about shifting and movement.

Each therapist has their own secret expectations for how the therapy might progress in a client. It is important to realize that expectations are completely irrelevant. The beauty of the EMDR procedure is that it is only about the client's experience. If, for example, the client reports a reduction in SUDS, but the therapist thinks this is illogical, the client's opinion prevails over the therapist's. The EMDR procedure has a number of control mechanisms, such as measuring the credibility of a positive cognition (which has to increase at least a few points if arousal was zero), and the body scan. Body language can also show that the client is relaxed. The decisive factors are these subjective control mechanisms, not the therapist's opinion and expectations.

A woman with a history of abuse went to Asia as a refugee camp doctor working for Doctors Without Borders. She underwent a number of traumatic experiences: robbery with a weapon held to her head, a serious car accident, and being taken hostage with violent threats by soldiers. All this – along with former traumas that were triggered – severely dysregulated the client. Intensive and prolonged psychiatric hospitalization was needed to stabilize her, and after this she was able to therapeutically process the traumatic experiences. With her phase I therapist she made a trauma list containing seven events. Treatment began with event 5, then event 3, both of which were treated successfully by the EMDR therapist. The phase I therapist eventually withdrew from these sessions because enough trust had developed between the client and the EMDR therapist. Event 2 was treated in two sessions and four sessions were devoted to event 1, the most severe event. Events 4, 6, and 7 did not need to be treated as they proved to no longer evoke traumatic reactions. The phase I therapist took over the therapy at this point to carry out the remaining phases. The client was very relieved and liberated from the traumatic experiences from which she had suffered for years, and completed therapy after a short period. A follow-up session six months later proved the results achieved had been sustained.

12.3. Brief Eclectic Psychotherapy for Psychotrauma

Brief Eclectic Psychotherapy for Psychotrauma (BEPP) has proven effective for simple psychotrauma (Gersons et al., 2004; Gersons et al., 2000; Lindauer et al., 2005; Nijdam et al., 2012). In its original form, this brief treatment method with a rigid protocol is not suitable for the treatment of complex trauma. We mention this treatment here because it has a few interesting aspects that can be incorporated into a treatment programme for someone with complex trauma.

The BEPP model has various phases (see below). Memorabilia is used to reinforce exposure – a practice which originated in grief therapy (Ramsay, 1979) – and can also be adapted for the treatment of complex trauma. Giving a positive meaning to the traumatic experiences in sessions 7 and 8 is also important, as people can always get something positive out of going through very unpleasant events (we return to this issue in Chapter 13). Finally, it is also important to finalize the trauma by using a closure ritual (also discussed further in Chapter 13).

BEPP protocol:

- Session 1: psychoeducation
- Session 2: imaginary exposure
- Sessions 3–6: continued imaginary exposure and memorabilia
- Sessions 7–8: writing assignments, meaningfulness and integration
- Session 9: partner or other significant person
- Sessions 10–12: relevant themes not yet discussed
- Sessions 13–16: parting ritual

Source: Gersons & Olff (2005).

12.4. Imaginary confrontation: rescripting

Imaginary confrontation – also known as 'rescripting' (Smucker et al., 1995) – is a variant of exposure in which the client attempts to alter the traumatic situation in their imagination so that the emotional load is reduced to an acceptable level. That is made possible by the client performing the actions they think they should have performed at the time of the traumatic event, for instance, overpowering the offender who robbed them, or saying goodbye to someone who died. Arntz and Weertman (1999) have extensively described techniques for imaginary confrontation and rescripting to therapeutically process memories from childhood.

These interventions, which are often adapted to therapeutically process traumatic situations from childhood, can be very powerful. They are less suitable for situations with unknown perpetrators; this is because the client has to be able to place themselves in the perpetrator's situation and thus has to know them.

The method also requires the therapist to be the director of an imaginary play. Apart from requiring a certain amount of courage, the therapist will need some experience in guiding clients through agreed scenes in a directive way.

Standard imaginary confrontation and rescripting model:

1. Decide on a safe place.
2. Establish which situation will be therapeutically processed.
3. Determine what the client would like to do or say in the situation (things that at that time they did not know, were incapable of doing, or did not dare to do). If the assessment is that the client is unable to imagine any different behaviour, they can imagine coming to their own aid as their adult alter ego (or another person, even the therapist can be brought into the imaginary situation to stand up for them).
4. Instruct the client to imagine themselves in the situation. Ask them to describe it, preferably with eyes closed, speaking in the first person and in the present tense.
5. Instruct the client to say or do what they want, as determined in step 3. If the client reports any obstacles, the therapist can help deal with this by offering cues to using their imagination, for instance, 'Use other people around him that will force him to listen to you'.
6. If the client says or does what they wanted, get them to pay attention to how the other person reacts, and then ask if the client wants to react to that. Try to encourage the development of an imaginary interaction. Continue until the client says they are ready. If this seems to be taking too long, the therapist can direct things towards a symbolic closure: 'Now say what you want to say so that you can leave this situation'.
7. Closure: the client closes the situation by placing it in the past.
8. Have the client return to the safe place.
9. Once there, they return to the here-and-now.
10. Evaluate.

A man with an intense inferiority complex was raised by his mother, who, as a young woman in a Japanese-run internment camp, was sadistically punished physically. The mother created a climate in the home in which she used all sorts of punishments used in the camp on her children (including making them stand absolutely still in the room, locking them up, and rationing food). As a child, the man behaved very obediently and kept all the blame inside without expression. In treatment, the man processed many of these traumatic experiences through exposure. It was decided to close the trauma treatment with an imaginary rescripting of the situation at his mother's deathbed. In the rescripting situation, he told his mother exactly what it meant for him to be raised with all the punishment he went through, and asked her why she did that and if she knew how that would affect his life. The situation he imagined went very well. The client was able to ask his mother extensively why she raised him as she did. To the client's surprise he was also able to imagine how his mother would have reacted, and her calm and open way of responding. It became very clear to him how difficult life was for her in and after the camp. It then dawned on him that his mother had not intended to act that way because she had something against him; rather, her behaviour was determined by her intense feelings of powerlessness. Ultimately he was able to bid farewell to his mother in a heartfelt way. The client returned to the here-and-now exhausted, but also enormously relieved, as a great burden had been lifted from his shoulders. Shortly after that he was able to continue with the closure phase of the treatment.

12.5. Expressive therapies

Words are not always enough to therapeutically process traumatic experiences. Diverse modes of expression related to creativity, movement, drama, and music are frequently very helpful to gain insight into and give meaning to events. Expressive therapies allow the traumatic experiences to continue being therapeutically processed in another way. With creative therapy, the traumatic experiences can be drawn, sculpted, or made into a storyboard. With drama therapy the traumatic situation can be played out.

According to a Dutch handbook on creative therapy (Smeijsters, 2000), there are no specific expressive therapy methods reported for the treatment of complex trauma. Creative therapies can, however, have an important and decisively facilitating effect on the treatment of complex trauma. As Wertheim-Cahen (2007) pointed out, these therapies provide important perspectives on counterbalancing feelings of powerlessness in traumatized people, who, by 'doing something' (empowerment), gain the ability to communicate that which cannot be expressed in words. Creative therapeutic methods can be adapted to exposure therapy, for instance, by having the client draw the traumatic situation on paper, or by drawing the different feelings associated with the traumatic experience. Creative therapy can also be adapted to testimony therapy by having the client draw or sculpt each of their traumatic episodes. Furthermore, creative therapy can be adapted to strengthen the client's identity by using all sorts of techniques from art therapy and music therapy. Creative therapy can also be adapted to teach relaxation, especially with drama therapy and music therapy. Finally, creative therapy can be adapted for rescripting traumatic experiences, for instance, by playing out a situation in which someone still has to say something to their dead father about being abused and neglected. Situations can also be played out in which the client has to deal with trauma-associated triggers, and so learn new behaviours. Readers are referred to Smeijsters (2000) – mentioned above – for further elaboration on all these treatment options.

Expressive therapies are usually implemented, along with group therapy, when indicated for a specific component of individual treatment. The aim may be for the client to express and depict anger or sadness, or to therapeutically process trauma using drawings. Expressive therapies are usually a standard part of clinic or day clinic treatment programmes.

12.6. Cognitive interventions

In accordance with the theory of cognitive therapy described by Beck (1976) and Ellis (1985), the intense emotions that accompany a trauma are the result of cognitions about the situation. Various studies have proven that exposure is the most powerful and effective technique for treating the cognitive representations of traumatic events. Exposure techniques mainly emphasize the situation that evokes the most emotions, with the intention of revealing those emotions so that the client can work through them. Therapeutically processing trauma has the effect of altering and calming thoughts about the trauma as well as the accompanying emotions. This desensitization is also a part of the procedure in the standard EMDR protocol. With EMDR it almost always seems that if the arousal of the traumatic situation has decreased to a SUDS score of zero, the credibility of the negative cognition about the traumatic event has drastically decreased, while the credibility of the positive cognition (opposite to the negative cognition) has, in general, drastically increased. This is why it seems logical that focusing the procedure – initially – on altering cognition can also be effective. Experience has shown that this is actually the case, but frequently the cognitions are less receptive to interventions because the dysfunctional emotions are much more prominent. Usually exposure procedures are initially implemented and then augmented with cognitive procedures if necessary (Stöfsel, 1998). Cognitive interventions can also be used on their own, particularly when the emotions are already somewhat less intense.

12.6.1. Cognitive therapy

Complex trauma situations can also be therapeutically processed with cognitive techniques involving dysfunctional cognitions about self-image, other people, and the traumatic experience itself. Cognitive techniques such as Socratic dialogue, cognitive and experiential challenge techniques, and behavioural experiments, are used in an attempt to alter dysfunctional beliefs. As mentioned earlier, a cognitive technique alone is never enough to therapeutically process complex trauma; it must be augmented with other interventions such as exposure or EMDR. Most of the core cognitions that play a role in complex trauma come from four cognitive domains (see below).

Cognitive domains of (complex) trauma:

- Powerlessness: misjudgement and mistrust, among other things
- Inferiority
- Feeling unsafe
- Injustice

12.6.2. Alterations of meaning and purpose

One of the features of complex trauma in comparison with simple trauma is that the cognitive impact is much greater. In complex trauma, unlike simple trauma, the repeated or prolonged traumatic impact means that the traumatic event can no longer be dismissed, making it an exception to the rule of the naïve positive expectations that we all have about life. These expectations cannot be realistically maintained with complex trauma. Frequently the client's general attitude towards people has also been altered profoundly in the negative sense. This is probably because the trauma is usually the result of some man-made disaster carried out by fellow human beings who knowingly did something to them. A negative self-image also develops whereby the core belief about the self is inferior, small, unimportant, or useless. This impact on the cognitive meaning will also have to be processed in the treatment. Different approaches are possible. Frequently the cognitive meaning alters naturally as a result of a successful treatment with one of the above-mentioned trauma therapeutic processing techniques. Sometimes the alteration of the cognition is part of the treatment technique, as happens with EMDR. The cognitions can also be therapeutically processed with cognitive therapy techniques, for instance, using cognition challenge methods such as Socratic dialogue.

12.6.3. EMDR for use in changing core cognitions

EMDR can also be used to deal with the core cognitions that play a role in complex trauma. The dysfunctional core cognitions are first established, then the client's life is explored to find confirmations of the dysfunctional convictions. It is important to find the earliest experience of a conviction because that is the one that is usually conditioned the most intensely. The search continues in order to find experiences that still serve as emotional confirmation that the core cognition is true. The traumatic moments that are found are usually not very traumatic from an objective viewpoint, yet the client may have attributed a very subjective traumatic cognitive meaning to them. The standard EMDR protocol is subsequently used for such clients.

EMDR 'working right' protocol:

- Establish dysfunctional core cognitions.
- Determine which situations emotionally confirm these core cognitions the most.
- Process these situations therapeutically using the standard EMDR protocol.

Source: Ten Broeke and De Jongh (2008)

A woman was raised in an environment very much marked by her father's stories of when he was in the resistance and his need for hero worship. She was also sexually abused by her father from the age of six to thirteen years old. All her life she worked diligently to live up to her father. She had a good education and career and everything in life seemed to be going reasonably well. However, she was full of self-doubt. She also occasionally had reexperiences about her physically and sexually abusive father.

The essential core cognition was established as 'I'm worthless'. The client was able to identify four important situations: the first time she was abused when she was about six years old, being hit for a minor misdeed, and her punishment after she first stood up to her father. All of these situations were therapeutically processed in fifteen EMDR sessions. At the end of the sessions, the positive cognition – the counterweight to 'I'm worthless' – was validated: 'I'm worth something'. The client felt liberated from the enormous burden of her past and the reexperiences disappeared. A follow-up session four months later proved that the results achieved were being sustained.

12.6.4. Survivor guilt

Survivor guilt is prevalent in people who have been able to live a normal life after surviving an unfavourable situation, such as long-term imprisonment or combat alongside others. This phenomenon became renowned after the Second World War, when many people, Jews in particular, returned to their home country, only to find out that they were the sole or one of a handful of survivors in their family. It was difficult for them to return to a normal life because they felt guilty that they had survived whereas others had not. People seek meaning in surviving, but it is often not there because survival in situations such as this is largely a question of chance. Survivor guilt becomes more intense when people feel that particular fellow prisoners or family members had, for one reason or another, more of a right to live. This feeling of survivor guilt can leave a cloud hanging over one's life.

It also happens with refugees, in whom it is a cognitive problem because the survivor has fixated on the cognition 'I don't deserve to live'. Survival is usually the result of chance combined with some skill in dealing with the bad situation. Chance, however, is very difficult to accept for people when it involves essential aspects of life.

Survivor guilt is a stubborn problem that is difficult to treat, partly because it has an element of a self-fulfilling prophecy: life does indeed stop, so to speak, when someone does not really want to continue living. They do nothing with their lives, and so confirm for themselves that they do not deserve to live on. Survivor guilt frequently hinders effective therapeutic processing of traumatic experiences, because to prove that living has stopped, one has to continue to suffer from the memories of the traumatic experiences.

It is important to gain a clear understanding of the leading cognition when dealing with this problem. It is usually something such as the above-mentioned notion of 'I don't deserve to live'. This cognition needs to be confronted with a challenge. A useful approach is to switch perspective. For instance, with someone traumatized by their imprisonment the challenge could be: 'What would your dead roommate think that you should do with your life?' It can also be useful to get a clear impression on where and how this idea of not being the one who deserves to live originated, for example, with the close camaraderie that is a natural by-product of living in a constricting prison cell. It is important to encourage someone to value the small positive things in life and to broaden that out, as this might initiate a self-reinforcing therapeutic processing of small positive experiences. It might also be useful to investigate what the client's ideals and dreams were before the traumatic events took place, and to examine if and how any of them can still be realized.

A Kurdish man, who was imprisoned and frequently tortured over many years, eventually fled to the Netherlands where he built a new life with his wife and three children. He dutifully did his job in a baking company, even though it was well below his level. Due to his nightmares, reexperiences of the traumas, and depression, he started treatment, which commenced with a few stabilization techniques, followed by EMDR. The client was diligent, but the therapeutic process was tedious: he was unable to get to a SUD score of zero. The therapeutic relationship was good, but the therapeutic processing techniques continually ran aground. It then became clear that the client felt very guilty that he was living a good life while his comrades were still in a Turkish prison. Once this feeling was identified, it could be challenged. The client was encouraged to live out the plans he had made when younger, which gradually led to an improved quality of life. An important side effect was that the traumatic experiences began to automatically fade into the background. Only a few more sessions were needed to successfully complete the treatment.

12.6.5. The function of guilt

Feelings of guilt can sometimes be very stubborn and may play a role in the maintenance of the trauma symptoms. It is important to clarify the function of the guilt (Dorrepaal et al., 2008). It might be survivor guilt as described above. It may also be irrational guilt, because blaming the perpetrator is psychologically less favourable than blaming oneself; an example is the way people blame themselves for the sexual abuse they experienced in their youth. Blaming oneself enables a person to falsely maintain the image of a selfless parent who loves them. When someone has to forfeit that image, they are not only a victim of sexual abuse, but they also lose the illusion of having a protective parent. Guilt can also serve as a form of protection from the reality of grieving or from being confronted with feelings associated with abuse. This self-inflicted suffering stagnates the therapy and protects them from further therapeutic processing any pain.

Trauma problems can be regarded as aggression problems (Winkel, 2007). A perpetrator used aggression, but a necessary and healthy aggressive feeling in return is suppressed (for the most part) because it would only evoke more aggression from the perpetrator. Suppression of the aggression persists after the trauma, and is often a significant hurdle to the therapeutic processing of emotions. Admitting feelings of aggression towards the perpetrators often leads to a great feeling of relief and so can accelerate the therapeutic process. However, when aggressive feelings are no longer suppressed, clients have very destructive fantasies that arise regarding what they would like to do to the perpetrators. Clients with a strong conscience are particularly shocked by the aggressive character of these – in essence healthy – revenge fantasies that are incongruent with their norms and values, because these clients would never do to the perpetrators what they did to them. Because they feel guilty for having their own aggressive fantasies, they end up blocking the therapeutic process. This may affect a client processing feelings associated with their sexual abuse, as suddenly they may have violent fantasies about mutilating the perpetrator's genitals. The therapist must normalize this process and provide some form of psychoeducation. It is useful to explain that taking seriously fantasies that contradict one's norms and values does not necessarily lead to them being carried out. On the contrary, it is the suppression of fantasies that leads to greater obsession, which, in turn, greatly increases the chance of acting on the fantasies.

An African woman had been repeatedly raped by rebels. Therapy, however, was blocked during an exposure procedure, and the reason was not very clear until the therapist enquired about her fantasies. The client admitted to having very vivid fantasies about what she would like to do to her rapists, for which she felt deep shame and guilt. The therapist explained about feelings of guilt in this type of situation, the client was able to allow herself to have these fantasies more easily, and the outcome was an acceleration of her therapy.

12.6.6. Pie-chart technique

The pie-chart technique is a good way to bring guilt into alignment with reality (Sprey, 2002). The technique is effective because clients become aware that they have only been focusing on their own guilt, and are confronted with the fact that they have been apportioning too much blame to themselves. This method of inventorying guilt forces the client to examine the guilt of others. Clients then notice that their own share is much smaller than they previously thought. This starts a process of placing excessive feelings of guilt into proper perspective so that the client feels a more realistic sense of guilt. This also forces them to think differently, and this can be therapeutically processed in further sessions.

Pie-chart technique:

- Establish what the client feels guilty about.
- List who was involved in the guilt situation with the client's name at the top.
- Draw a circle to represent a 'pie', symbolizing guilt.
- Start with the person at the bottom of the list.
- Ask the client how large their share of the pie is.
- Draw out the slice of the pie in accordance with the percentage mentioned.
- Work up the list, representing everyone as a piece of the pie.
- By the time the client reaches their own name, usually no more pie is available.

A sergeant on a UN mission was responsible for six soldiers. He received orders to search a house and sent his men in, but the house turned out to be booby-trapped. One soldier died and another was severely wounded in the explosion. Years later the sergeant felt very guilty that he had sent those young men to death and injury. Inventorying everyone who was involved in the situation (his commander who gave him the order, the soldiers themselves who should have been more careful regarding booby-trap wires, the people who laid the booby traps, and himself), and identifying their share, he noticed, much to his surprise, that his share was much smaller than he had thought. Therapeutic processing of this event then proceeded much faster.

Chapter 13

Phase 3 – integration

Phases 1 and 2 of the three-phase treatment model focus on stabilizing the symptoms and on therapeutic processing of the traumatic past, respectively, whereas the final part of the treatment, phase 3, covers interventions focused on continuing with life after the trauma; in other words, phase 3 focuses on how to continue living into the future and on the obstacles that still need to be addressed. In phase 3 clients have to bring closure to the difficult problems or behavioural patterns that were part of living with their trauma. The focus is on bringing out the stronger facets of the client's personality and reinforcing them.

Clients can arrive at phase 3 of the treatment model after successfully completing both phase 1 and phase 2, or directly from phase 1 if phase 2 turns out to be unachievable.

It is remarkable that, although the literature refers to phase 3, it hardly describes any specific interventions or activities for the therapist to carry out in this phase. This probably has to do with how the approach to phase 3 as well as what happens during it usually does not require many interventions from the therapist. However, this dearth of literature on phase 3 interventions leaves the therapist at a loss in terms of knowing what to do and how to evaluate treatment effectiveness. This chapter discusses a number of phase 3 activities.

13.1. Chronological phase completion

Ideally clients proceed through the three-phase model chronologically: first stabilization (phase 1), then therapeutic processing (phase 2), and finally integration (phase 3). In most cases, when this sequence is followed, phase 3 probably proceeds fluidly and naturally and 'may be seen as the culmination of the previous work and as an exciting time of growth' (Courtois et al., 2009). By phase 3, the obstructive symptoms of the trauma will be subsiding gradually. The client's mood lightens and they notice that there is room for other things in their life than the trauma and its consequences which have consumed so much of their life. When all the therapist has to do is motivate the client to resume planning for the future, phase 3 often proceeds smoothly.

A prison guard underwent a number of traumatic experiences: he was held hostage by a prisoner, he had to take down a prisoner who had hung himself, and he had a car accident. He received little support at the workplace, and eventually developed symptoms of anxiety, panic, and depression that turned out to be difficult to treat. He developed serious marital and financial problems. He went to work in a supermarket where he just could not fit in. Years later he was able to link his problems to the traumatic experiences. He sought help and received Eye Movement Desensitization and Reprocessing (EMDR) treatment. All the symptoms cleared up gradually once the experiences had been successfully processed. Over the course of the years he had developed a specific behavioural pattern with regard to his breathing, which was an important focal point in his treatment during phase 3. His relationship with his wife improved. He became increasingly more aware that he did not like his work, so he started looking for another job. He realized that he did not want to return to working as a prison guard. He finally found a job he liked working in a security company. A number of months later the treatment was terminated after a follow-up session.

13.2. Jumping directly from phase 1 to phase 3

As mentioned earlier, it is not always possible to achieve the stabilization necessary for successful processing in phase 2. When this is the case, the client needs to be told that successful trauma treatment is not possible, and that it would be better to focus the treatment on managing their symptoms and on examining options for the client's future. In fact, this strategy was used by many war survivors after World War II (Bramsen, 1995). Skipping phase 2 does not rule out the possibility of therapeutic processing of the trauma at a later date. When therapy goes directly from phase 1 to phase 3, the therapist has to more actively motivate the client to find some meaning in life and adopt a perspective on the future.

An Afghan witnessed how his father was humiliated and then murdered in a horrible way by the mujahedeen. As soon as he could, he fled the country, eventually arriving in the Netherlands with his family because they too were under threat. He spoke poor Dutch, but after a few years he found work at the packaging department of a large factory. Occasionally he would get excessively angry at the smallest things. He sought help for these symptoms and, in phase 1, was taught a few techniques to curb his outbursts, and also learnt how to schedule relaxing activities into his life. He agreed to relate his story in detail, greatly emphasizing the traumatic experiences, which clearly demonstrated the intensity of tension and emotions these evoked in him. He then refused to follow the specific trauma therapeutic processing technique that was offered, as he was afraid that he would become even more unstable. In fact, he felt that the techniques he had recently learnt would be enough for him to manage his symptoms. The treatment therefore focused on his future. It turned out that the client had been preparing to go to university in Kabul, but war made this plan impossible and the plan was shelved. His work at the packaging department was therefore completely inconsistent with his intellectual abilities and interests. The client was encouraged to improve his Dutch, and he then registered for a part-time degree through the university refugee organization.

13.3. Meaningfulness

The life of severely traumatized people is often characterized by a long period of feeling that they have less control over themselves and their circumstances. The self-confidence needed for dealing with adversity and reacting appropriately when stressed can be severely affected by the trauma. When the traumatic events are occurring, surviving circumstances shaped by others is the priority. Then there is a period of continued survival and arrival to somewhere safe, as happens with refugees. If the traumatic symptoms are intrusive, the client's life is dominated by tolerating, suppressing or avoiding those symptoms as best as possible. A severely traumatized person manages to keep going by adjusting to their external circumstances. When the client gets to the point of leading a life which does not revolve around the traumatic experiences or symptoms, they will engage in living, resume control, and choose their own direction. In other words, they give their life a new meaning.

A personally meaningful experience can be defined in terms of three components (Bohlmeijer et al., 2007): a cognitive component, which is the meaning we give to events (specific values); motivation, which refers to having goals that govern our lives; and the affective colour we give to our life, to feelings of satisfaction, to well-being, and to happiness.

These aspects of meaningfulness are usually disrupted in someone with psychotraumatic problems. The client's understanding of the meaning of their life is often coloured and very restricted by the trauma. Their motivation lacks a long-term perspective and is often defined by simply getting through from day to day. This makes their perspective on life somewhat gloomy.

Once trauma is successfully treated, the client is faced with the difficult task of viewing their life purpose differently. This period, when clients have to explicitly make goals for themselves, can sometimes be very confusing. Sometimes it entails re-establishing goals or falling back on skills from years previously. It is important to spend sufficient time on this process, which may develop in a very natural way, in phase 3. Most important is that the goals are in alignment with the client's own norms and values. Techniques from Acceptance and Commitment Therapy (ACT) can be used. An example is the deathbed metaphor (Hayes, et al., 2003): 'Imagine that you are lying on your deathbed. If you think back on your life starting from now, what would have to change in your life now so that you can look back with satisfaction?' Techniques derived from solution-focused talking therapy can also be used, for instance, 'Imagine you are X years in the future. What would you say in X years was your goal if you looked back to now?'

13.4. Scheduling activities

Phase 3 is not only about returning direction and purpose to the client's life as the previous sections have discussed. Purpose and meaning also have to be fleshed out. In other words, clients have to be encouraged to make practical changes in their lives, potentially affecting important life domains.

13.4.1. Education, work, and volunteerism

In the first place, study, work, or volunteerism is very important, so it is extremely relevant for the therapist and the client to explore the latter's desires, needs, and possibilities. Clients often do not know what they want because their spirit has been broken by the consequences of the trauma which has played such a central role in their lives. They may also have become reconciled with the idea that their original desires and wishes are not achievable. Once these become clear, the practical possibilities of fulfilling them need to be explored. It is useful for the client to do as much of this part of the treatment independently in phase 3. The therapist can also look for support from social workers, student counsellors, civic integration agencies, employers, benefits agencies, and volunteer organizations.

Although age or other limiting factors make it impossible for some people to work, it is important that they have meaningful structured activities in their lives. Volunteer work can meet that need. An orientation visit can be helpful in encouraging clients to do volunteer work; they can be asked, for instance, to identify three appealing activities offered at a local volunteer centre.

13.4.2. Social contacts

It is also important to examine the client's social situation. Psychological problems are often accompanied by reduced social contact and the worsening of a relationship or loss of a partner. It is therefore useful for clients to examine their desires and needs with regard to social contacts, and also what they can do to fulfil those wishes. It may be useful to encourage the client to make contact with old friends. Clients may also need to be encouraged to take action regarding relationships, for instance, registering with a dating agency. Bear in mind, however, that some activities should be postponed, as the client should not be overwhelmed with too many integrative activities. The client also has to be kept aware of the newly acquired cognitions, and should not revert back to trauma-associated cognitions such as 'I'm worthless' or 'I'm a victim', which may require some additional work from the therapist (Van der Hart & Nijenhuis, 2007).

Refugees may be encouraged to participate in cultural activities offered by organizations that help people from a variety of cultures integrate. It is worthwhile for the therapist to be aware of societies or institutes that refugees themselves have established.

13.4.3. Interests and hobbies

It is important to consider where the client's interests lie and to encourage them to take up a hobby. Religious beliefs, for instance, are very important for many people and it may also be useful to explore the client's religious background. It may also be useful to find a religious group that matches the client's needs (Rohlof & Scholte, 2005).

13.5. Posttraumatic growth

The term posttraumatic growth or *benefit finding* (Kleber, 2007a) is often used with regard to trauma. There is even a questionnaire to measure it called the Posttraumatic Growth Inventory (Tedeschi & Calhoun, 1996), which addresses the positive consequences of going through a traumatic experience (see below for examples). Positive consequences can only be present if there is enough stability and harmony in the client's life. The concept of posttraumatic growth is inappropriate for someone who is still struggling with their trauma symptoms. However, when someone recovers their direction in life, positive effects often follow. This is not to deny negative effects, such as a period of loss of enjoyment in life, loss of social position, having fewer job perspectives and education options, and acquiring a bitter view of the world.

In the third phase of treatment it is recommended to not only look at the negative consequences of what the client has gone through, but also at the positive ones. The Brief Eclectic Psychotherapy for Psychotrauma (BEPP) (Gersons et al., 2004) pays special attention to meaningfulness in its fourth domain, namely, meaningfulness and integration. In general, it can be said that if the three-phase model is successfully completed, and if the traumatic experiences and their meanings have been therapeutically processed, the client can largely recover quality of life. There is, of course, the time lost in dealing with the consequences of the traumatic experiences. Nonetheless, successful completion of trauma therapy will usually bring about awareness of being sadder but wiser and of having triumphed.

Possible positive effects after trauma:

- Being less naive
- Dealing more responsibly with oneself and others
- Discovering that one has a strong side
- Learning that persistence can turn negativity around
- Discovering who the supportive and valuable people are in one's life
- Prioritizing what one thinks is important
- Living more intensively

Resilience is the word used for the trait that describes a person's ability to be less affected by severely disruptive events. It is strongly correlated with protective factors (Tol et al., 2009), such as family ties, the degree to which family members protect and support each other, and other social contacts in the client's life. Healthcare professionals often have a biased image of the consequences of trauma in that they think anyone who has gone through a trauma has nothing but problems. The potential resilience in the face of trauma is thus underestimated, whereas in fact, the majority of people who have undergone traumatic experiences are not affected by problems due to whatever their source of resilience may be. Recent studies on the effect of military deployment on veterans reveal that the majority of them value their deployment, even despite the confrontation with war and violence (Schok, 2009).

13.6. Posttraumatic relapse

Posttraumatic relapse could be considered the opposite of posttraumatic growth. In cases of complex trauma it can have pervasive restricting consequences, and quality of life can be lower than prior to the traumatic experiences for a prolonged period. A comparison of quality of life before and after traumatization can only be drawn for people who were traumatized during adulthood. When traumatization occurs during childhood, comparison of quality of life is not possible, because full development has not been completed prior to the traumatic experiences.

When phase 2 therapeutic processing is unsuccessful because the client's situation is not stable enough, residual symptoms will remain, such as mistrust, reexperiences, nightmares, disrupted relationships, social problems, and financial problems (discussed elsewhere in this book), all of which lead to a reduced quality of life. The following sections discuss dealing with stabilization problems.

13.7. Chronic problems: shuttling between phase 1 and phase 3

A number of people with complex trauma find it difficult to successfully complete phase 1. They continue to have a great deal of arousal, and stabilization techniques may seem to have some effect, but not enough. The high level of arousal makes phase 2 therapeutic processing unfeasible. Sometimes attempts made to implement phase 2 techniques are discontinued prematurely because of the increasingly high arousal levels.

According to Breslau (1998), approximately one third of those who develop posttraumatic stress disorder develop a chronic variant and never recover completely, and scarcely any recovery takes place around the six years after a traumatic event takes place (Kessler et al., 1995). This makes for a very large group of people. Some of these people with little or no contact with care workers will have somehow found a way to deal with their nightmares about the traumatic events. They might be able to ignore them completely and may even be able to explain them to their family. Some quality of life is forfeited, but a certain balance has developed. They are also sensitive to trauma-associated triggers, and frequently have a vulnerable personality structure; although it may not be clear if that was present prior to the traumatization or is a consequence of the traumatization. Most cases involve premorbid latent vulnerabilities, which makes management and integration of the trauma difficult. This, in turn, reinforces any pre-existing vulnerabilities, and results in a cluster of symptoms that develop into a vulnerable personality structure that resembles 'complex trauma'. Avoidance is a relatively successful coping mechanism, with alcohol, intensive sports and/or keeping very busy, which are used to numb the trauma symptoms. Most people who respond in this way come from countries ravaged by war where society had been disrupted. This was a predominant coping mechanism for people in the Netherlands after the Second World War (Bramsen, 1995).

People having premorbid latent vulnerabilities only seek help for the symptoms when the vulnerabilities manifest themselves, escalating to the point they can no longer be numbed, or when their social network begins to reject them. Trauma treatment can still be completed successfully for some of these people. For others, attempts to stabilize or therapeutically process emotions will prove that the latitude for change is very narrow. The treatment will then shift to learning to live with the trauma symptoms, and trying to reincorporate structure and perspective in life. A number of people will feel the need to maintain some contact with the therapist because the safety, trust, and predictability of any incidental contact with them is an important factor to prevent problems from worsening. The focus of the therapy is then a combination of stabilization and learning to live with the trauma. In terms of the three-phase model, the treatment switches from phase 1 to phase 3, instead of going through phase 2, with occasional regressions to phase 1.

A man fled from Iraq with his four children, after his wife was killed in an attack. Caring for his children provided him with structure. However, as the children grew older, they did not need him as much and were even rebellious, which he found difficult. He sought help for his posttraumatic stress disorder symptoms and parenting problems. He only wanted to be rid of his children's complaints. All sorts of treatment techniques were implemented, but they were only partially successful, and a substantial amount of tension remained in his life. EMDR treatment was prematurely terminated by the client. Medication had a brief temporary effect. The client then received supportive treatment during sessions scheduled once every six weeks, which he found satisfactory. He rarely spoke about the trauma problems, even though he was still bothered by them. Sessions dealt mainly with how the client should deal with his adolescent children.

13.8. Aftercare

As mentioned earlier, treatment of severe traumatic experiences is only possible if there is a constructive therapeutic relationship. This therapeutic relationship is generally more intensive than with treatments of clients with the Axis I problems who do not present with trauma symptoms. If the treatment is successful, the therapeutic relationship has to be carefully phased out. This is possible by gradually thinning out the frequency of contact, in other words, by increasing intervals between the sessions. Many therapists are hesitant to discuss this with their clients because, after a long and intensive period working together, it may seem as if they are rejecting the client (Courtois et al., 2009). That is usually the case when clients insist on maintaining the intensive frequency of sessions to date. It might help to tell the client that reducing the frequency of contact is actually a consequence of successful treatment and an improvement of their circumstances. Continuing with the present frequency of sessions implies to the client that they are still not doing well, and need a greater frequency of contact than is actually necessary.

13.8.1. Voucher system

It is possible that the client may need more sessions than the therapist thinks they need. One way for the therapist to depart from being the centre of the client's recovery is to offer a symbolic voucher system. That way the client can make, for example, ten appointments in the coming year, if needed, but retains complete control over the need for an appointment. The therapist obviously has to be able to meet any request for a meeting, at least in the short term. This system prevents any uncomfortable negotiation; clients can learn for themselves that they do not need as many sessions as they thought they might, and still have the option to have sessions as needed.

13.8.2. Three-month follow-up

When a treatment has been lengthy and intense, it is useful to have another session after treatment ends – after three months is generally appropriate – in order to check if the decision to terminate was appropriate.

13.8.3. Relapse prevention

It is always possible that the client may unforeseeably relapse into old symptoms, or that external factors disrupt the client's new-found stability, causing the symptoms to return. Clients should be informed about procedures for returning to treatment at the healthcare centre or private practice. In our experience informing clients has a paradoxical effect; the more clearly these procedures of potential future availability are explained, the less the client will make use of it.

13.8.4. Long-term aftercare for chronic problems

Lengthy intervals between sessions with the therapist are often the best option for clients with chronic trauma problems whose symptoms are difficult to stabilize to the point of being able to therapeutically process their trauma more fully.

For these clients, any treatment techniques may have already been attempted, to no avail. They usually manage adequately enough to maintain a certain balance in life, and regular, recurring contact with the therapist is important support for them. Therapists often want to reduce the frequency of sessions with these clients, whereas the clients might prefer the opposite. Ultimately, some type of compromise is reached, whereby it is agreed that sessions should take place at a frequency of once every six weeks to once every six months, with the option of increasing the frequency in the event of a crisis. These clients often have strong transference towards the therapist and/or the institution, and it is sometimes a struggle to obtain management permission for such 'never-ending' treatment.

The effective element in this type of treatment is that it provides clients with a positive holding, which serves them well. Since contact with the therapist becomes part of the client's maintenance strategy, attempts to make the client less dependent often lead to immediate relapse. E-mail correspondence is another option that may meet these clients' need for contact because it offers direct access to the therapist. They could also benefit from a support group that meets infrequently. In terms of the three-phase model, these clients remain chronically in phase 3, with occasional regressions to phase 1. The criteria for deciding an appropriate form of treatment are described below.

Criteria for a long-term low-frequency supportive contact

Focus the treatment on stabilization and integration, and forego therapeutic processing if:

- the client's level of stress is persistently high;
- treatment techniques for reducing tension do not work or have limited effect;
- the client's tension appears to be too high to implement therapeutic processing techniques;
- therapeutic processing techniques have to be terminated due to an elevated level of tension;
- the client seems to react well to contact with the therapist;
- termination of the contact will probably lead to a worsening of the situation.

> A Dutch man was deployed to the former Socialist Federal Republic of Yugoslavia. He carried out secret assignments behind enemy lines and was exposed to extremely severe traumatic events that he still felt very guilty about. All sorts of techniques were implemented in an attempt to therapeutically process these experiences and to make them precipitate less guilt and tension, but to no avail. His attachment to the therapist seemed to have a positive effect on his situation. The client was able to carry on with his life and insisted on keeping in contact with the therapist – not so much for the substance of the contact as for knowing the therapist would be available. A frequency of once every two months seemed to be sufficient, with the option of scheduling sessions more often in the event of a crisis as needed.

13.9. Treatment termination

Ultimately there is the inevitable final session when the client and the therapist must part ways. Some clients will think this is the natural course of events. Other clients will need to spend more time on that process, for instance, by carrying out some form of ritual. It is important that the therapist provides some space during the sessions for rituals, which indeed ease transitions in our lives (Van der Hart, 1992). It is also important for the therapist to provide the client with a brief summary of the results achieved. It can be particularly rewarding to look back on the test results from the intake period, or cite the symptoms from the intake report, or look over the treatment plan. This reinforces the success as well as the decision to conclude the treatment.

Part IV

Client and therapist

Chapter 14

Client groups with complex trauma

This chapter discusses typical categories of clients who have complex trauma. The social, societal, and historical context in which severe violence occurs is an important factor in effectively interpreting a client's specific situation and invaluable for the therapeutic process, both for the client and the therapist. This chapter does not aim to provide an exhaustive description of the client groups; it merely offers some information about dynamics that may be useful during treatment.

In the Netherlands in the decades after the Second World War, clients with complex trauma were predominantly survivors of German concentration camps and Japanese-run internment camps in the Dutch East Indies (including many children, referred to as child survivors), people who participated in the resistance against the Germans, Jews who had lived in hiding, people stricken by civil war, and veterans of police actions in the Dutch East Indies. Most of the people in these groups are now elderly or have died. Since the 1980s increasing attention has been paid to clients who have experienced incest and/or other sexual abuse at a young age. The Dutch mental healthcare system currently treats the following broad client groups for complex trauma:

- People affected by the Second World War (a shrinking group)
- Refugees, including asylum seekers
- War veterans (all adult age groups)
- People with occupational-related traumatization
- Traumatized people from the post-war period, the second generation
- People with early childhood traumatization.

Each group of clients is profiled in terms of a brief description, the main presenting problems, factors affecting treatment, typical cognitions that play a role in the presenting problems, the ideal therapist profile for effective treatment, and finally, treatment recommendations. Each client group is configured according to two dimensions: the life stage when the traumatization occurred, and the degree of integration in society (Figure 14.1). Young's schema therapy is used to illustrate the typical cognitions encountered in each group (Young et al., 2003).

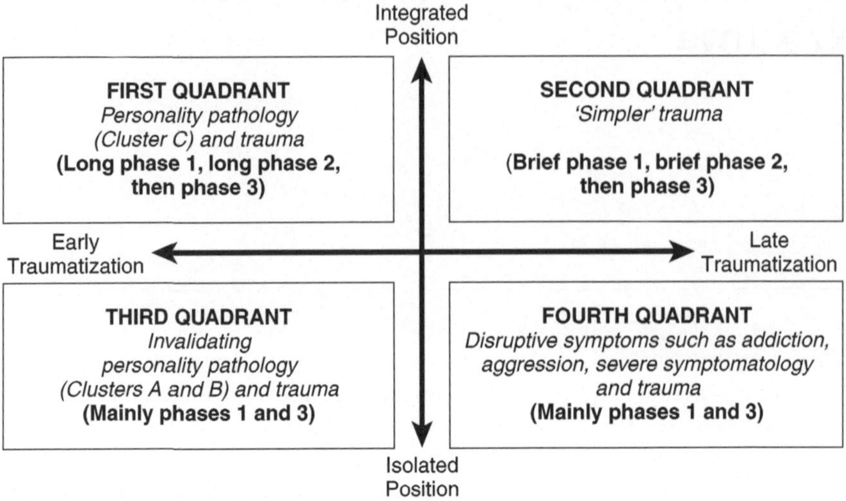

Figure 14.1 Symptomology and treatment options of complex trauma

14.1. People affected by the Second World War

This group includes people who were in German concentration camps, people who were held in Japanese-run internment camps or who suffered some other way during the Japanese occupation in the former Dutch East Indies (for instance, victims of Biersiap, the revolution that took place when the Japanese surrendered), people who experienced civil war, and people who lived in hiding or were persecuted in other ways.

These people, who experienced overwhelming events during the Second World War over 70 years ago, are, by now, mainly elderly and mainly child survivors (traumatized before they became adults), and most are reasonably well integrated in society. They therefore most likely fall into the first quadrant represented in Figure 14.1.

14.1.1. Main presenting problems

Clients traumatized by the Second World War usually present with posttraumatic stress reactions, ageing issues, depression, relationship problems, and family tension.

14.1.2. Factors affecting treatment

Ageing sometimes confronts people with their physical vulnerability more than ever before. People may also feel vulnerable in a psychological sense too, feeling less confident and less competent to protect themselves against overwhelming events. Ageing further undermines a person's natural ability to suppress or avoid thinking about the traumatic experiences, which is how most people coped after the Second World War (Bramsen, 1995). Ageing is also accompanied by fewer routinely structured distractions such as work, and leaving plenty of time to ruminate on the past (Aarts, 2007). This may lead to an increase in the number of nightmares and reexperiences. The limited autonomy that comes with ageing and the growing dependence on others can evoke old feelings of powerlessness in the face of the overwhelming experiences of the past – the opposite of the feelings of control managed in the intervening decades.

14.1.3. Typical cognitions

Clients who were imprisoned for a prolonged period and confronted with severe trauma have cognitions such as 'I cannot trust others', 'I don't deserve to live', 'I cannot be who I want to be', 'You can't do anything to prevent horrible things', 'Life is unsafe and threatening', 'Something bad can happen at any moment', and 'Fate is greater than you are and you can't do anything about it'.

Concentration camp survivors frequently have survivor guilt, a guilty feeling of having survived while others died (Wepster, 2003). This guilt can be a major obstacle for therapeutic processing when people are consumed by thoughts such as 'I don't deserve to live' or 'I get no pleasure from anything' (also see Section 12.6.4).

Young's schema therapy would categorize this client group in the 'Hypervigilance and Inhibition' domain, which addresses 'Negativity/Pessimism', 'Emotional inhibition', 'Unrelenting standards/Hypercriticalness', and 'Punitiveness' (Vreeswijk et al., 2012).

14.1.4. Therapist profile

Therapists will need to have a good command of the history of the Second World War and to be aware of what happened in the Dutch East Indies during and after the Japanese occupation. Familiarity with a bit of the specific terminology associated with these events would be useful too.

The therapist must have the ability to empathize with the client, maintaining sufficient emotional distance while listening to their shocking stories. Providing structure, safety, and trust is crucial because the client usually has all sorts of cognitions regarding mistrust of others. Right from the start of treatment, the therapist should do everything possible to prevent the client from activating these cognitions of mistrust. The therapist must make realistic appointments with the client, be cautious about cancelling appointments, and be punctual. In most cases, the therapist will be much younger than the client, who will possibly test the therapist regarding their 'therapeutic and humane integrity'.

14.1.5. Treatment recommendations

If the client is well integrated in society and their ageing issues do not hinder their abilities, the client can be classified in the first quadrant (Figure 14.1) and therapeutic processing is very possible. If someone is less integrated, the treatment options will more likely come from the third quadrant, meaning that the focus should be stabilization and integration.

Psychoeducation about the trauma processes as well as the ageing issues should be included in the treatment for these clients. Treatment is usually supportive and supervisory, but as mentioned earlier, therapeutic processing techniques may also be implemented. People in this life phase often have a strong need to prepare some type of 'ego document', to document the events that were overwhelming, for themselves to gain a sense of closure, or for their children or grandchildren (Bohlmeijer et al., 2007).

It is usually a good idea to involve the partner or family members in the treatment, especially at the start of treatment in order to inform them about the diagnostic procedure and the treatment plan, and maybe, if necessary, later in the treatment.

14.2. Refugees

This category of clients includes asylum seekers as well as refugees, because the distinction between the two groups is merely a legal technicality: asylum seekers are refugees who have not yet obtained asylum. This diverse group of people can fall into any one of the four quadrants, because being a refugee is not age-dependent and because the degree of social integration is arbitrary. Due to their legal (and often social-societal) status, asylum seekers usually are more isolated and so fall into the third or fourth quadrant. Refugees are often partially integrated in society and so fall into the first or second quadrant; some refugees, however, are not well integrated because of language barriers, among other reasons, so they correspond to the third or fourth quadrant depending on the time in life when they were traumatized.

Refugees in the Dutch mental healthcare system are a heterogeneous group. Many refugees were persecuted in their country of origin for political or religious reasons. They were imprisoned for long periods and in different ways and/or were tortured or abused in some way, often by prison guards. Typical tortures were being beaten with fists, sticks, or whips, being hung by the hands or feet, having their genitals squeezed, electric shocks to the body, mock executions, denailing, water boarding, and standing absolutely still for lengthy periods. In regions where torture is a common practice, the perpetrators are well practised in administering violence without leaving long-term visible damage or scars.

Refugees and asylum seekers from practically all the world's conflictive regions experience torture, although there are regional differences in the type of physical abuse (Van der Veer, 1998). Furthermore, women in prison are usually raped and often refuse to talk about it (Tankink, 2009). Many men imprisoned for long periods have also experienced sexual violence.

The age when the traumatization took place is very important in terms of the consequences, as traumatic experiences during childhood interfere with psychosocial development, which, in turn, can lead to psychological maladjustment. People who were tortured, physically abused, or imprisoned in their youth are referred to as child survivors.

Refugees and asylum seekers usually have been persecuted for political or religious reasons. The fact that someone chose a particular viewpoint and was aware of the risk of torture or imprisonment – in other words, mental preparedness (Moreno et al., 2006) – sometimes has a palliative effect during treatment. The psychological damage is less intense then in refugees who become victims of violence because of arbitrary contingent occurrences. The psychological explanation is that before the persecution, the person has a vague or even a clear idea that they are running a risk of being persecuted and tortured because of their political or religious beliefs. Some political groups even systematically prepare followers to endure imprisonment and torture, as happened with what was called the Dirty War in Argentina.

The refugees' backgrounds vary and their origins depend on where political unrest exists in the world, as well as on political attitudes to asylum provision. A total of 53,000 asylum seekers were recorded in the Netherlands in 1994, and 19,000 in 2002 (Mooren, 2001; Rohlof & Scholte, 2005). Their numbers have decreased significantly in the last decade, due to more strict immigration regulations. The question remains as to how long someone is considered a refugee as opposed to an integrated citizen. Pragmatically, it seems useful to refer to refugee status as long as refugee problems or refugee tasks predominate in the refugee's life, for instance, the language barrier, cultural differences, displacement issues, homesickness, and integration problems. Once someone has achieved a certain degree of integration in a society, their refugee status is still present, but moves into the background.

14.2.1. Main presenting problems

Typical presenting symptoms are anxiety, posttraumatic stress symptoms such as reexperiences, nightmares, being easily startled, vigilance, guilt, shame for surviving, loss of country, grief for the dead, longing for loved ones, difficulty finding a new perspective, insomnia, and flat affect (Van der Veer, 1998).

Refugees usually present with a combination of depression and trauma symptoms. They are often intensely demoralized. They are unable to see a way out, and often no longer know how to carry on with life. The psychological problems are often expressed in all sorts of somatic symptoms such as hyperventilation, abdominal cramps, muscle tension in the neck and shoulders, headache, and insomnia (Hondius et al., 2000). These symptoms partially result from tension, but they can also be attributed to the fact that many cultures only pay attention to physical problems and not psychological problems.

Finally, these people are frequently referred for treatment due to problems in their relationship with their partner and/or children. Asylum seekers, in particular, find themselves in very powerless situations, which can cause much frustration and tension within the family. Because the children of refugees usually learn the host country language faster than their parents, a generation gap develops that reinforces the parents' sense of powerlessness. Parentification is also frequent, a form of role reversal where the children take responsibility for the parents (Figley & Kiser, 2013).

14.2.2. Factors affecting treatment

Asylum seekers

The main problem faced by asylum seekers is that they are not sure if they will be permitted to remain in the country. This is an overwhelming shadow hanging over their heads. The life of an asylum seeker remains, as it were, on hold because their future is uncertain, and they are unable to make plans with regard to work or education. The past usually burdens them, often with horrible memories and experiences of war and violence, and their present is also depressing: it lacks a perspective on the future, the financial situation is tight (below the poverty level), and the living situation is often restless and noisy. There are few opportunities for pleasant social contact in asylum centres. They are, by their very nature, unsettled places due to the presence of many different cultures and many vulnerable, sad, and worried people. In summary, with a traumatic past and an uncertain future, asylum seekers usually do not have an easy time in the present either.

The legal situation regarding asylum and the client's status as an asylum seeker is invariably a topic of discussion during the treatment. Therapists are frequently approached by legal, medical, immigration, and naturalization services to make statements concerning the asylum seekers' psychological condition. This happens, for instance, when a request is made to stay in the country for medical reasons. The therapist therefore has to know what is strategically and legally the most beneficial for the client. In any case, it is pointless to make broad non-nuanced statements about the distressing situation of asylum seekers. The insecurity regarding their asylum status can limit the possibilities of implementing other interventions or therapeutic processing.

Refugees

Once asylum seekers are formally recognized as refugees, they may stay in the host country with reasonable certainty. That offers the perspective of a home and a place to live for the coming years. Other problems may then arise, however, such as learning the language and assimilation into what is usually a radically different culture. In addition, refugees frequently experience downward social mobility: the level of their education or training from their home country is not equivalent to what is possible for them in the host country. Diplomas are frequently not recognized, or compatible, and language problems affect the refugee's possibilities for doing a job commensurate with their education or training. Often they are unsuccessful in finding work and the options for benefits are uncertain. Refugees are often provided with public housing far away from built-up areas, which makes it very difficult for them to integrate into society successfully.

Homesickness

Refugees frequently long to return to the country where they grew up. The tragedy is often that children born or brought up mostly in the host country become so well assimilated that they do not want to leave. For instance, many older refugees from the Balkans who fled to the Netherlands in the mid-1990s in great numbers return home while their children remain in the host country. Refugees continue with their lives in a place to which they fled involuntarily. This usually leads to feelings of displacement and uprootedness and an underlying longing to return to their country of origin. They go through a phase of grief and defiance before integrating within their new society. But the longing to return to the country of origin always remains in the back of their minds (Van Willigen, 2007).

Acculturation is the process of adapting to another culture. It involves learning new skills, maintaining and pursuing social relationships, and adopting or accepting new beliefs (for instance, ways of dealing with parents or children in certain situations) (Mooren, 2001), while maintaining traditions and customs. Acculturation can sometimes cause stress, but migration can also offer new possibilities and challenges. Involuntary migration by refugees from violence or war can make adapting to new surroundings problematic. Of the Bosnian refugees, for instance, the elderly and women generally find it most difficult to root themselves in their new country. Younger and better educated people usually have an easier time resettling. Interaction is necessary for acculturation to take place. It is not only the migrant who affects the acculturation process; the hospitality of the host country and the options it provides also affect integration.

Feelings of demoralization, depression, disappointment, hopelessness, and powerlessness are common in refugees. Among the many causes are their trauma experiences and the fact that they are a refugee. Moreover, the process of assimilation – which usually lasts for years – places people in a lower financial and social category regarding education, work, and housing compared to their country of origin, which, in itself, is demoralizing (Drozdek & Wilson, 2007).

An asylum seeker waited for years to be granted asylum and watched his children grow up in an asylum centre. He found it difficult to tell his family in the home country that he could no longer pay to maintain telephone contact. He felt inferior in his role as father and as a man.

Many refugees and asylum seekers experience an accumulation of disruptive experiences in a short period of time, ranging from the traumatic experiences in the country of origin, the flight itself, and then the uncertainty of asylum-seeking procedure with the proper authorities. This accumulation of events overwhelms many refugees, as they never would have imagined that they would find themselves in such a precarious and dependent situation.

Assimilation

Therapists may have to deal with the refugees' problems with assimilation regulations. Refugees have somewhat of a problem learning the language, as difficulties with concentration and attention span affect most people with traumatic stress symptoms. Although they may be eligible for exemption from compulsory language courses for psychological reasons, refugees should be encouraged to acquire the language, as knowing the language is fundamental for integration in a new society, and, in the long run, reduces the risk of psychological problems.

We culture/me culture

An important cultural difference between Western Europe and other countries or regions is that Western Europe has much more of a 'me culture', whereby life derives its meaning from the idea that the individual – within the spectrum of possibilities – can develop to the fullest. This is fundamentally different from other parts of the world marked by a 'we culture' (Sevinc & Colijn, 2009). Family survival and success is central in a 'we culture', and individuals are considered to be subordinate to the family and its needs. This may play a role in psychological problems, making it important for the therapist to be aware of the client's culture.

Language issues

Language is always an area of concern in the treatment of refugees. Most refugees are not likely to speak the language of the host country on arrival there, so another language or an interpreter will be necessary in order to communicate. The interpreter may be live or via telephone, each with their pros and cons (Bot, 2005), but many therapists have their own specific preferences. The advantage of a live interpreter is that they can also convey the non-verbal aspects of communication, and, if from the same or a similar culture, can also provide the client with a feeling of validation within the otherwise alienating 'foreign' healthcare organization. Note, however, that many refugees and asylum seekers come from countries with major political or religious differences between ethnic groups, so there is the danger that an interpreter can potentially turn out to be a representative from a group which makes the client uncomfortable. The fact that two professionals will be sitting across from the client can also be an obstacle. It may also be possible for the therapist to gain additional cultural information from the interpreter after the session.

Differences in geographical, religious, or political ethnicity play less of a role with telephone interpreters. Even so, regions have a diversity of accents, so a refugee is likely to be able to distinguish which region or ethnic group the interpreter comes from based solely on the first few sentences spoken. A few other disadvantages of a telephone interpreter is that it is somewhat more difficult for the therapist to maintain control of the session and the interpreter cannot convey the client's non-verbal communication; also, hand-free devices need to be obtained or purchased. A paradoxical advantage of the telephone interpreter is in the moments just before and at the end of the session when the interpreter is not present, and both the client and the therapist have an awkward time communicating with each other. This shared experience can be used in the development of the therapeutic relationship.

Family problems

Aggression can escalate in traumatized refugees as a result of the accumulation of problems from the trauma, their flight, their disappointments, and the burden of integration. This may manifest itself in the form of physical abuse within the family that is not discussed because family problems remain concealed (not to wash dirty laundry in public). It is often family problems (including pressuring children to keep silent) that make it difficult to arrive at an effective assessment which is also in agreement with the cultural norms of the country of origin and the host country. It requires some tact to gain useful insight into the problems of refugee families and to remain engaged with them (Cummings et al., 2009; Gewirtz et al., 2008).

Gender issues

Many cultures are patriarchal, so the opinion of the oldest man in the family – the father – is the most important, and, in his absence, the oldest son. All important decisions must therefore be explained to and approved by the eldest man in the family. In Kurdish families, for instance, the oldest son, even if he lives in Western Europe, is consulted by telephone prior to major decision making by family members. Therapists need to deal with this cultural issue with tact and sensitivity, and need to recognize the pressure and responsibility placed on the eldest man in the family. When the psychological circumstances do not allow for the man to fulfil this role, this responsibility is burdensome.

Other cultures also have strict rules regarding contact between men and women, and this needs to be taken into consideration when clients are matched with therapists. This will be especially crucial when dealing with problems encased in shame, such as sexual problems or sexual abuse.

Survivor guilt

Clients who have survived traumatic experiences which comrades, fellow villagers, or family members did not survive, or for which they are still imprisoned, experience intense survivor guilt (Herman, 2013) (also see Section 12.6.4). This guilty feeling often leads to nihilistic thoughts that emerge from their search for the reasons they survived. But usually there is no tangible reason; people usually survive because of a combination of personal coping styles, the coping styles of the guards, and sheer luck. To make the world predictable, people prefer to see some sort of logic to it all. They do not consider themselves exceptional or worth more than those they left behind, and this leaves them asking why they have the right to continue living. The question will need to be therapeutically processed first before the client can make the transition to any further processing or to restarting life constructively.

Drug use

Young male refugees often make excessive use of drugs such as cannabis, khat, and, occasionally, opium. This drug use should not be viewed so much as a problem of addiction, but more as a form of self-medication to numb traumatic symptoms. If drug use or the problems surrounding it, however, are severe, then the addiction needs to be dealt with first.

14.2.3. Typical cognitions

This client group partially falls into Young's schema therapy domain of 'Hypervigilance and Inhibition' with cognitive schemas such as 'Negativity/Pessimism', 'Emotional inhibition', 'Unrelenting standards/Hypercriticalness', and 'Punitiveness'. For people in the third and fourth quadrants (Figure 14.1), who are poorly integrated, the cognitive schemas from the domain 'Disconnection and Rejection' will play a role, namely, 'Abandonment/Instability', 'Mistrust/Abuse', 'Emotional neglect', 'Inferiority/Shame', and 'Social isolation/Alienation' (Young et al., 2003).

The fact that many survivors of torture and long-term imprisonment feel guilty that they have survived or escaped and others did not, can be a major obstacle in therapeutic processing, because they have thoughts such as 'I don't deserve to continue living' and 'I can't be happy as long as my comrades are still in prison'. People who have been tortured and imprisoned have core cognitions such as 'You can't trust anyone', 'I don't deserve to live', 'I can't be who I want to be', 'You can't do anything to prevent horrible things', 'Life is unsafe and threatening', 'Something bad can happen at any moment', and 'Fate is greater than you are and you can't do anything about it'. Typical cognitions for asylum seekers are 'I have to be patient and wait' and 'I hope everything goes well', and for refugees, 'I'm allowed to be here providing I adapt', 'I don't feel welcome', and 'I can't be who I am'.

14.2.4. Therapist profile

Low expectations

When working with refugees, it is important for the therapist to have low expectations. The accumulation of overwhelming problems (trauma, flight, legal uncertainties, acculturation, and assimilation) makes it a challenge for the therapist to deal with the powerlessness and hopelessness of the situation that refugees often find themselves in. Therapy effectiveness with asylum seekers has been found to be minor. Summerfield (1998) reported that therapists sometimes have to be satisfied with being effective by just being 'a decent person'. Many asylum seekers have almost no contact with ordinary people, only with civil servants from immigration services, immigration enforcement officials, and other asylum seekers, so it means a great deal when they can relate their story to someone they regard as a normal person.

Cultural sensitivity

It is important for therapists to be sensitive to cultural differences, and do not let themselves be shocked by them. Cultural differences in actual practice turn out to be much smaller when they are simply respected. With regard to psychological processes, there are fewer differences between cultures, most especially when it comes to very severe problems. The differences are often in the way in which the symptoms are presented. Being culturally sensitive also means being curious, and asking about certain traditions and customs that are important to the client.

Less rigid interpretation of duties

The accumulation of problems in refugees confronts the therapist with all sorts of practical problems that technically fall outside their responsibility. The treatment thus is converted into a pragmatic social work intervention. This is not necessarily a problem, as long as the therapeutic function is maintained (it stabilizes the client or is part of the therapeutic processing of the trauma). It is also helpful to have the therapist occasionally liaise with other agencies dealing with practical problems that may be troubling the client (Van der Veer, 2004).

Several skills, some mentioned earlier, are generally needed for the treatment of psychotrauma:

- Capacity for empathy, but also the ability to keep sufficient emotional distance.
- Ability to endure listening to shocking stories, so the client does not have to worry whether the therapist can cope.

- Ability to provide structure, safety, and trust. Clients often have all sorts of cognitions regarding mistrust of others. It is important, especially in the initial treatment phase, to avoid inadvertently activating cognitions that evoke feelings of mistrust in the client. Make realistic appointments with the client, be cautious about cancelling appointments, and be punctual.
- Knowledge of the course of therapeutically processing traumatic experiences.
- Patience, as due to the frequently long-term and severe traumatization, this type of treatment is lengthy and has fluctuating intensity. There is often a lengthy period of gaining the client's trust, and during the treatment there are periods of intensive processing and periods of support which are less intensive. Sometimes the client terminates treatment prematurely and after a few years returns to complete it.

14.2.5. Treatment recommendations

Treatment options depend on the client's life stage when the trauma took place and degree of integration in their home country. Refugees can fall into any of the four quadrants (Figure 14.1). A large group of refugees and asylum seekers who request help are not well integrated in society and so fall into the fourth quadrant. In this case treatment will mainly comprise support and supervision. Other better integrated refugees fall into the first or second quadrant, meaning that active phase 2 therapeutic processing is possible.

The following aspects are of major importance when treating refugees for trauma.

- Validate their problems. Many traumatized people are under the impression that their trauma was their fate and so experience their problems as unique – which is essentially true. It is usually healing and cleansing, however, when they realize that people with similar war experiences have the same types of problems.
- Explain the interpretation of symptoms. Preventative psychoeducation programmes for refugees have been developed in a number of places in the Netherlands (Mooren & Schoorl, 2009). For an overview of these programmes see Mooren and Schoorl (2006).
- Start with the most problematic symptoms. Tackling these first facilitates the development of a therapeutic relationship (Van der Veer, 1998).
- Provide practical support. This may be limited by the extent to which it falls within the scope of the mental healthcare system in question, for example, medication, easy practical tips, or brief relaxation exercises.
- Offer group therapy. The client will identify with the others in the group and gain a sense of validation. Group composition needs to be taken into consideration, as clients may have difficulty, for instance, sitting in a group of people who used to be or could have been on the side of the enemy. Other clients, nonetheless, may have absolutely no problem with this.

- Promote structure. Structuring the client's life is helpful, whether through work or volunteering, or by encouraging them to participate in social activities, for instance, religious or political organizations, or a special interest group of fellow countrymen. Information on support groups is usually made available to refugees in their host countries. Encourage the client to take up their religion again (if appropriate), take language lessons, and participate in an assimilation programme so as to immediately enhance control over their life (Rohlof & Scholte, 2005).
- Emphasize empowerment. Explore the client's strong facets, sports, or leisure activities they used to do, and any other issues they used to be enthusiastic about.

Although there are limitations to the treatment options for refugees, small, pragmatic changes can make a great difference. The major cause of problems for asylum seekers is that they have little control over their situation, which is a reality that therapists can do little to change. The therapist can help the client view their situation realistically. It is also helpful to explore the aspects that the client can indeed control and where changes – albeit small – are possible. Encourage them to try to cultivate a realistic perspective and to place everything in a timeframe so that, for instance, it becomes clear how long that uncertainty may be expected to last and that they accept that their life will be difficult because of the uncertainty. Place the client's refugee status in proportion within the overall context of their lives. The treatment should also address the other parts of the client's life as well, particularly the events of their life prior to the disruptive events (Van der Veer, 1998).

14.3. War veterans

Veterans in the Netherlands belong to two subgroups: an older group and a younger group. The older veterans are former soldiers deployed by the Dutch government to conflicts during the Second World War, as part of the UN forces in Korea in the 1950s, and to the former Dutch East Indies and in New Guinea (until 1962). This subgroup is shrinking rapidly due to ageing, especially since 2000.

The younger group is composed of Dutch veterans deployed with UN forces in Lebanon (UNIFIL) at the end of the 1980s, in Bosnia, Cambodia, and Iraq, and since 2006 in Afghanistan. Smaller numbers of Dutch soldiers participated in actions as part of UN forces in other parts of the world, for instance, in the Democratic Republic of the Congo in Africa. Some 99,000 Dutch soldiers were deployed to conflictive regions in the period between 1979 and 2007.

Around 4 per cent of this younger subgroup of soldiers is estimated to have posttraumatic stress disorder (PTSD) (Engelhard et al., 2007); this percentage rises to 12 per cent for the Dutch battalion that witnessed the fall of Srebrenica in Bosnia (DUTCHBAT III). A study by the Dutch Ministry of Defence showed that approximately 2 per cent (deployed to Cambodia) to 8 per cent (deployed to the former Socialist Federal Republic of Yugoslavia) of Dutch soldiers deployed as part of UN forces developed PTSD. Incidence was greater for partial PTSD, predominantly heightened vigilance: 11 per cent (deployed to Cambodia) to 20 per cent (deployed to the former Socialist Federal Republic of Yugoslavia) (Schok, 2009). Approximately 25 per cent of veterans suffered guilt and shame for at least some time (Rietveld, 2009). Most soldiers deployed by the Netherlands return home without psychological problems, although, obviously, we can only report on those presenting with problems in the mental health sector.

Veterans usually fall into the second and fourth quadrants of Figure 14.1, generally because they have experienced shocking events in young adulthood; most of the veterans were about 20 years old during their first deployment.

14.3.1. Main presenting problems

Veterans usually present with PTSD symptoms, including concentration difficulties, increased startle reactions (mainly irritation and low frustration tolerance), and a sense of hyperalertness and powerlessness. Further reasons for seeking help are escalated aggression, addiction and/or relationship problems, and sometimes legal problems.

14.3.2. Factors affecting treatment

Soldiers who served in the Dutch army who acquired psychological problems always experience severe traumatic events to some extent, usually in a phase of life right after adolescence, which makes a huge impact on these young men and women. Deployment is also an overwhelming and intensive period in other ways, as camaraderie is exceptional and unfolds in an unknown environment and unfamiliar culture. Deployment can therefore have positive as well as negative aspects.

Upon returning to the home country, the traumatic experiences, the missed camaraderie, and the readjustment to civilian life can take their toll. This combination leads to problems for a small number of veterans. Some people in this group may have some type of latent personality disorder that was probably triggered by the experiences during deployment. Such personality disorders are interwoven with trauma problems, which can be represented on a continuum ranging from traumatic experiences to pathological personality disorders. It can be a complicated task for the therapist to distinguish between the traumatic symptoms and the (latent) pathological personality disorder. Such clients often also strongly and positively identify with being a veteran, sometimes in an effort to hide the pathological personality disorder.

Identity as a veteran

Being a veteran is an important identity for many of these former soldiers as it retrospectively validates their torment. There are also financial compensations for veterans, for instance, they may be eligible for certain benefits and pension. Being a veteran can, however, also be a label for having psychological problems in an honourable way. The difficulty is that, since being a veteran is more beneficial than not being one, the ultimate effect is one of maintaining the suffering, and this, in turn, can then wrongly lead to problems being categorized as 'trauma problems'. Some veterans hide behind their diagnosis – 'I have PTSD' – while secretly concealing their pathological personality difficulties.

Aggression

Trauma problems are essentially suppressed aggression problems (Winkel, 2007), as the person has gone through a situation which made them a victim of external, overwhelming aggression. In veterans the threshold for expressing suppressed aggression is lower than in other trauma groups. Veterans often find themselves in severely violent situations in civilian life, and may even have problems with the law. What complicates the matter further is that the veteran may also find themselves in a vicious circle because these situations have a retraumatizing effect, which maintains, and maybe even worsens, their original problems.

Derailment

A small group of veterans are severely derailed by the combination of trauma symptoms, personality traits, and loss of structure and camaraderie. This often leads to problems with the law, caused by aggression or severe substance use. This group has multiple problems, and therapists have the complicated task of trying to determine which problems to start with.

Tensions in relationships

The sometimes complex cocktail of problems described above frequently causes problems with partners and families. Partners frequently say that the client has become strange and is no longer the same person as before the deployment. That is why it is very important, when necessary, to involve the partner or the family in the treatment.

Addiction problems

The intense trauma symptomology can elicit a great need for substances that numb their effects. The use of alcohol or other numbing substances is the most obvious. Veterans occasionally have severe addiction problems, and, from the treatment perspective, it is important to know if the addiction is primarily for the purpose of numbing the unpleasant PTSD symptoms or if underlying causes existed prior to the trauma. Reducing or abstaining from the substance is only possible if the veteran has an alternative for numbing those symptoms, for instance, medication or a stabilization technique.

Divided loyalties

Armies undertake all sorts of secret missions that the press or parliament hear nothing about. Most veterans who seek psychological help participated in regular missions that, in some cases, also involved military secrets or small-scale top-secret deployments. These are usually carried out by special forces within the military such as marines or commandos, and the soldiers involved are sworn to secrecy. These soldiers are therefore faced with a loyalty problem when they want to discuss experiences that fall under their oath of confidentiality. Therapists must then make their professional ethics code standards clear and will have to help the client decide to either continue suffering from the experiences of the secret mission or to work through them in therapy, even though they are breaching their oath. There is also an immoral component in forcing someone to swear to secrecy when they had no way of knowing what they were promising, so it is important for the client to hear this. It is also sometimes difficult for therapists to believe what soldiers might have gone through in these secret missions. It is important to consult with colleagues who also work with veterans to discuss the credibility of a client's story, given that there are veterans who tell fantasy stories about 'secret missions' because they cannot be verified.

14.3.3. Typical cognitions

Regarding the psychotrauma, typical trauma cognitions are 'I can't be who I want to be', 'You can't trust anyone', 'Danger is everywhere', and 'Life is always unsafe'. Regarding the feeling of alienation, cognitions include 'No one understands me', 'This isn't how it should be', 'I don't know what to do with myself', 'I'm all alone', and 'I have to stand up for myself, no one else will'.

In Young's cognitive schemas (Young et al., 2003) this client group, similar to a group within the refugee group, will mainly fall into the domain 'Hypervigilance and Inhibition' with cognitive schemas such as 'Negativity/Pessimism', 'Emotional inhibition', 'Unrelenting standards/Hypercriticalness', and 'Punitiveness'. But for poorly integrated people in the third and fourth quadrants, the cognitive schemas from the domain 'Disconnection and Rejection' will play a role, with cognitive schemas such as 'Abandonment/Instability', 'Mistrust/Abuse', 'Emotional neglect', 'Inferiority/Shame', and 'Social isolation/Alienation'. Finally, cognitive schemas from the domain 'Impaired limits' also play a role in veterans, for cognitive schemas that include 'Entitlement' and 'Lack of self-control/Self discipline'.

14.3.4. Therapist profile

Knowledge of the military world

For a therapist to work with veterans, it is very useful to have general knowledge of the deployment circumstances, how the military is structured, military ranks and positions, and the atmosphere that prevails in the military. It is also helpful to have general knowledge of the specific benefits available to veterans.

Dealing with the old-boy network

When veterans get together the atmosphere quickly turns into an old-boy network with an unspoken code of solidarity and a feeling of standing united against the external world. Serious matters are often addressed in a humorous way. The therapist has to be able to deal with and partially join in with this type of atmosphere, but also be able to return order if the encounter becomes too unstructured. The therapist must also be ready to be put to the test. Since these clients learnt how to function in a strict military hierarchy, the therapist will be placed in their hierarchy, usually in an authoritarian position, and this can also be exploited.

Professionalism

Many veterans have witnessed horrible things. The therapist has to be able to hear these stories. This topic was discussed extensively in Section 14.2 on refugees.

The therapist should have a number of skills, listed earlier, but repeated here for convenience sake.

- Capacity for empathy, but also the ability to keep sufficient emotional distance.
- Ability to endure listening to shocking stories, so the client does not have to worry whether the therapist can cope.
- Ability to provide structure, safety and trust. Clients often have all sorts of cognitions regarding mistrust of others. It is important, especially in the initial treatment phase, to avoid inadvertently activating cognitions that evoke feelings of mistrust in the client. Make realistic appointments with the client, be cautious about cancelling appointments, and be punctual.
- Knowledge of the course of therapeutic processing of traumatic experiences.

14.3.5. Treatment recommendations

As mentioned, most veterans fall into quadrants two or four (Figure 14.1), depending on the degree of integration, which is determined by the severity of the trauma or possible latent personality disorders. For veterans whose problems are strictly caused by traumatic events, treatment options lie in the second quadrant and are focused on phase 2 therapeutic processing. As for veterans with possible personality disorders, treatment options, mainly comprising stabilization techniques, are drawn from the fourth quadrant.

Identification and validation through group therapy

Veterans, during their military service, functioned in groups, and this assured familiarity. Group therapy would therefore offer room for identification and validation with others. Group therapy would also appeal to the sense of camaraderie that veterans frequently miss after returning home. The risk of group therapy is that the distinctive nature of being a veteran, being special, is overemphasized and some form of counterproductive group narcissism can develop.

Structure

Providing structure is effective when treating this population, as it encourages the client not to continue identifying with the status of veteran – now the 'powerless' veteran – but to focus on the future. Key questions are: What do you want now? What did you want before you went into the army?

Non-Dutch veterans

The Dutch mental healthcare system also attends to veteran soldiers who served with foreign armies, for instance, the Foreign Legion, and to refugee veteran soldiers who served with armies in their country of origin, for instance, Bosnians, Serbians, and Croatians who fought in the Balkan War in the 1990s. The non-Dutch group clearly differs from the Dutch veterans in that, in the continuum of veteran problems, they tend towards the trauma side. Unlike the Dutch veterans, they typically have had severe traumatic experiences over a longer time or repeatedly. Another difference is that, for Dutch veterans, being identified as a veteran can be positive. This is seldom the case for the foreign veterans for whom the traumatic impact predominates over the identification with being a veteran.

It is usually not a good idea to place different groups of veterans in the same therapy group because there are mutual prejudices, and contingencies often arise. Treatment for the non-Dutch veterans, more affected by the impact of trauma, has to focus more on learning how to deal with the traumatic experiences through the three-phase model. The circumstances of their arrival in the Netherlands also play a role in that the usual refugee problems also affect this group (see Section 14.2). If the problems of being a refugee are more prominent than those of being a veteran, the traumatic experiences can perhaps be postponed until the client is more socially integrated in the Netherlands.

Many veterans from Western countries have immigrated to the Netherlands for family reasons. Belgium, compared to the Netherlands, has more young men who were in the Foreign Legion, mainly because there was no language barrier. Under the combined Dutch-Belgian collaborations, a number of Foreign Legion veterans who live in the Netherlands had horrible experiences in war and clearly have very severe trauma problems. Depending on their degree of integration in society, which is restricted by unrestrained behaviour or earlier problems, their treatment will take place as outlined in the second quadrant.

14.4. Occupational-related traumatization

People can become traumatized by practising their profession. Professions particularly affected include police agents, prison personnel, ambulance personnel, security workers, and train personnel. These people are at a high risk for traumatic events associated with their jobs. This occupational-related risk is the reason why a candidate's stability and integration into society is assessed during the recruitment procedure for these positions. In general, the second quadrant (Figure 14.1) would be the appropriate strategy, given the level of integration in society and the fact that the traumatization would occur in adulthood. However, clinical experience has shown that people in this group, like veterans, may have latent problems or even personality disorders. Although the problems do not hinder being selected for the job, they may develop into a more dysregulated set of symptoms when triggered by a trauma, which, in turn, increases the risk of severe problems and of greater isolation in society. These clients would therefore be reflected by the fourth quadrant.

14.4.1. Main presenting problems

Symptoms in people who have been traumatized by events related to their profession are PTSD, depression, anxiety, and panic.

14.4.2. Factors affecting treatment

These clients may be confronted repeatedly by severe violence or may experience very traumatizing circumstances. The feeling of having lost their invulnerability typically causes intense demoralization. In general, clients from this group, who often work in a macho environment, may not have learnt how to express their emotions effectively.

Inability to express feelings

Police, security, and prison-related professions that carry the risk of traumatic experiences have a macho image, and often attract men and women who, figuratively speaking, wear emotional armour and have learnt not to express their emotions. There is also a macho atmosphere on the work floor in such professions. Traumatic experiences are discussed openly, but the assumption is that everyone is capable of dealing with them. A consequence of this situation is that someone who is overrun by all sorts of feelings (for instance, when on the verge of developing PTSD) senses that the work environment is not the place to discuss the issue.

Sensation of failure

There is a great risk that having symptoms after a trauma is experienced as a personal failure, because of the macho atmosphere on the work floor, where it is assumed that everyone is capable of handling any kind of situation that might arise. It is useful to explicitly pay attention to this sensation of failure during treatment, and if possible and appropriate, to contact the client's supervisors to discuss potential solutions for them.

Employer/occupational health and safety pressures

People who have been traumatized on the job are usually still working with the same employer, and the employer or the occupational health and safety service might pressure the client to go back to work during the treatment. In such cases it is advisable to contact the employer or the occupational health and safety service to set up some prerequisites for treatment or to discuss a reintegration scheme.

14.4.3. Typical cognitions

Typical trauma-associated cognitions are 'The world is dangerous', 'I'm vulnerable', and 'Danger is everywhere'. Cognitions about self-worth can also play a major role because the sense of failure frequently conflicts with an atmosphere of invulnerability that comes with these occupations, such as 'I failed' and 'I'm weak'.

Young's schema therapy would categorize this client group in the domain 'Hypervigilance and Inhibition' with cognitive schemas such as 'Negativity/Pessimism', 'Emotional inhibition', 'Unrelenting standards/Hypercriticalness' and 'Punitiveness'. If the client had problems prior to the traumatic event, other schemas may also play a role, for instance, from the domain 'Disconnection and Rejection' or 'Impaired limits'.

14.4.4. Therapist profile

Some knowledge of the specific occupation would be useful as the basis for a good therapeutic relationship. Although this is not so important for phase 2 therapeutic processing, it is very useful to know what the client's job entails in order to be able to constructively discuss reintegration at work during phase 3.

The following skills – some already mentioned in relation to other client groups – are also necessary:

- Capacity for empathy, but also the ability to keep sufficient emotional distance.
- Ability to endure listening to shocking stories, so the client does not have to worry whether the therapist can cope.
- Ability to provide structure, safety, and trust. Clients often have all sorts of cognitions regarding mistrust of others. It is important, especially in the initial treatment phase, to avoid inadvertently activating cognitions that evoke feelings of mistrust in the client. Make realistic appointments with the client, be cautious about cancelling appointments, and be punctual.
- Knowledge of the course of therapeutic processing of traumatic experiences.

14.4.5. Treatment recommendations

Treatment options for these clients, usually drawn from the second quadrant (Figure 14.1), are focused on active trauma processing in phase 2, with the length of the prior phase 1 stabilization period depending on the client's current stability. Because the client's trauma happened in the workplace, it is important to consult the client's employer and/or the occupational health and safety service about work reintegration in a therapeutically appropriate way.

14.5. Traumatized people from the post-war generation

The generation born to people affected by the Second World War is also known as the 'second generation'. Few post-war generation members were exposed to long-term or repeated violence and so do not develop complex trauma symptoms. They were, however, raised by people who had complex trauma or were the offspring of refugees. As children, their development was affected by their parents' problems, developed as a consequence of their exposure to war and violence. The determining factor is probably not whether the parents have gone through traumatic experiences, but whether the parents have developed PTSD or other problems. As far as we know, this distinction has not been drawn in any research into the second generation.

Since these clients had problems at an early stage of life, they fall into the first or third quadrant (Figure 14.1), depending on the degree of integration. Most of this group fall into the first quadrant, but there is also a group with psychological damage that places them in the third quadrant. These clients are similar to children who have parents with psychiatric problems, at a greater risk for psychiatric problems. Special consideration for the second generation has to be taken regarding the historical specifics (when and where) of their parents' experiences of war. The number of second-generation members who seek help is obviously shrinking. In contrast, the number of people from traumatized refugee families is expected to increase in the coming years considering the large influx in Western European countries during previous decades.

Second-generation problems are psychological problems related to growing up in a family in which one or both parents were traumatized by the Second World War. Often the traumatic experiences and the war are not spoken about, yet may be very prominent in the climate in the home. Not all the children that grow up in such a family will necessarily develop problems. The offspring's traumatization depends on the severity of the parents' own traumatization and how this has affected the family; it also depends on the child's capacity to deal with it. Ordinal position in the family also plays a role, with younger children often protected by their older siblings. Various studies (meta-analyzed by Van IJzendoorn et al., 2003) have shown that there is no general tendency for second-generation children to have more psychological problems than peers whose parents have not been traumatized. Clinical experience has shown that intense problems resulting from family or child-rearing problems can develop at the individual level during a child's development. Having traumatized parents also results in a specific pattern of symptoms and problems. This is at times manifested in the form of parentification, leading to a complicated separation and individuation process, which, in turn, generates problems that have to do with autonomy, assertiveness, and basic self-identity (Sleijpen et al., 2009). But other disturbances in the parent-child relationship occur as well that may lead to a variety of developmental difficulties (Scheeringa & Zeanah, 2001; Van Ee et al., 2012; Van Ee et al., 2014).

14.5.1. Main presenting problems

Clients often present with autonomy problems, assertiveness problems, depression, questions about identity, and personality problems such as dependence and evasive personality traits. Compulsive behaviour alleviates depression and tension to some extent. These clients usually seek help because of their difficulty in committing to and maintaining intimate relationships. They have learnt to mask their vulnerability and to keep others at an emotional distance, which is what makes seeking help difficult. Typical problems are over-adapting to and adjusting to others, ignoring one's own interests, not standing up for oneself, sub-assertiveness, not asking for one's own space, inability to identify one's needs properly, impaired relationship attachment, inability to conflict with parents, problematic identification with same-sexed parent, difficulty separating from parents or the home, parentification, poor autonomy development and experience, conflict avoidance, repressed anger, being a giver and not a taker, avoiding being bothersome and being vulnerable, and internalizing high expectations from the parents.

14.5.2. Factors affecting treatment

Cultural identity

Second-generation problems involve the circumstances of war of which geography (regions) or ethnicity (culture) are inherent. Cultural aspects can certainly affect treatment, such as how some cultures do not discuss difficult matters instead of talking about them directly. For instance, the Indo post-war generation identify strongly with Indonesia, which was formerly a Dutch colony occupied by the Japanese during the Second World War. All people with Dutch heritage, particularly those with white skin, were imprisoned in Japanese-run internment camps, whereas mixed blooded, so-called Indos, were also imprisoned later. Many of them underwent horrifically traumatic experiences and suffered deprivation in these camps. Identification with either Indo or white ('toto') culture was (and still is) associated with a reluctant, modest, and withdrawn attitude towards others and a direct, open, and extravert attitude respectively. Further, the importance of certain rituals and ceremonies may be derived from a client's cultural background.

Parents as traitors

Children whose parents chose to take sides with the Germans during the Second World War often have to deal with discrimination based on their parents' choices. For this group, the war is a taboo subject, so they have tended to remain silent about the war and also about problems that resulted from having parents who were traitors. Even healthcare professionals are sometimes taken aback about openly providing help to these people for fear of gaining a bad reputation.

Impaired relationship with siblings

The combination of children burdened with this taboo, secrets within the family, and loyalty to war-stricken parents can result in the children having relationships of divergent quality with the parents. Sometimes the more burdened child seeks support from a sibling but, due to loyalty to the parents, cannot find any validation for their problems and is sometimes even rejected. This can lead to major tensions between siblings.

Relationship problems

The impaired development of identity, problems with assertiveness, problems setting boundaries, and a poor self-image often cause problems in relationships. The client is usually in a subordinate position; they reveal little of themselves and tend to adjust to others, just as they learnt in their family.

14.5.3. Typical cognitions

This group usually has cognitions involving the absence of individualism, poor self-worth, and adaptation to others: 'I cannot be who I am', 'I can only be accepted conditionally', 'I'm not worth the effort', 'I should serve others', 'I must have respect', and 'I must not be bothersome'.

In Young's cognitive schemas (Young et al., 2003), these clients will mainly fall into the domain 'Impaired autonomy and performance', with cognitive schemas 'Dependence/Incompetence', 'Vulnerability to harm or illness', 'Enmeshment/Undeveloped self', and 'Failure to achieve'. The cognitive schemas from the domain 'Other-directness' will also play a role, including 'Subjugation', 'Self-sacrifice', and 'Approval-seeking'. Schemas from the domain 'Disconnection and rejection' will also play a role, namely, 'Abandonment/Instability', 'Mistrust/Abuse', 'Emotional neglect', 'Inferiority/Shame', and 'Social isolation/Alienation'. Cognitive schemas from the domain 'Impaired limits' may also play a minor role.

14.5.4. Therapist profile

Transference provides the opportunity for the therapist to provide positive attachment to an authority figure. The client will somehow ascribe elements of the parental role to the therapist. From a healthy attachment with the parental figure, the client will be able, to some extent, to recover their impaired attachment. For all sorts of reason, however, this process may advance in a complicated way, with the therapist possibly becoming the target of the aggression that was never directed towards the parents.

Adaptive coping style as healthy social behaviour

These clients often developed all sorts of clever coping styles to acquire warmth and attention from their parents while avoiding abuse or neglect. This behaviour served a function in the unhealthy family situation, but when this continues later in life it hinders clients from making room for their own wishes and needs. Gaining insights into the effect that impaired attachment relationships have had on the client's psychological development helps the therapist understand the issues that arise in the therapeutic relationship.

The therapist should have some general historical knowledge about the culture and/or war experienced by the parents.

14.5.5. Treatment recommendations

As mentioned, this group of clients usually falls into the first or third quadrant (Figure 14.1). People reflected in the third quadrant usually undergo long-term treatment and often have a long history with the healthcare sector. People reflected in the first quadrant have more favourable treatment options, determined by their integration and the extent of their structural personality problems. A complication with these clients, especially if they are not well integrated, is that their problems put them at a greater risk for situations that traumatize them once again.

Group therapy

Elements of a family situation recur in a group setting, in which the therapist(s) is(are) parental figure(s) and the other clients are siblings. Unhealthy attachment relationships become clearly distinguishable in the group dynamics, providing an opportunity to experiment with effective attachment styles. Such groups comprise clients with similar backgrounds who can identify with and validate each other, which all have a general psychological healing effect.

Exploring and challenging loyalty to parents

It is important that clients become aware of how strong their loyalty to their parents was and often still is, and gain insight into how their loyalty has been an obstacle. The parents' responsibility for the psychologically unhealthy facets of the family system should also be explored and identified, as a prelude to taking more emotional distance from the parents.

Departure

The process of departure leads to clients becoming more aware of their disappointment, anger, and sadness regarding the love and devotion they failed to receive in return from their parents. A client can then see that it is better to adopt distance from the expectations they had for their parents, and face the fact that they will never receive the attention and love from them that they missed as a child.

Separation and individuation

By letting go of the adaptive coping style and becoming aware of the attention and love they missed, clients can separate from the loyalty to their parents and so become more aware of their own identity and the accompanying expectations. The clients learn how to be in contact with their own feelings. This provides the opportunity to learn more appropriate social behaviour and to be assertive. They begin to realize that the world will not come to an end if they stand up for themselves.

Traumatic experiences

Over the course of treatment, it may be important to therapeutically process childhood traumatic experiences (see Chapter 7). Eye Movement Desensitization and Reprocessing (EMDR) 'working right', for instance, can be implemented to repair self-image (see Chapter 12).

14.6. People traumatized in early childhood

People traumatized in early childhood are a diverse group because the traumatization can take many different forms. Attachment problems are generally common. Parentification sometimes develops, and problems with individuation later in life and in relationships almost always arise. Similar to second-generation clients, these clients are reflected in the first or third quadrants (Figure 14.1), depending on the current degree of integration. What distinguishes second-generation clients from people with early childhood traumatization is their parents' specific historical war experiences. Most of this group fall into the first quadrant, but there is also a group with psychological damage that places them in the third quadrant.

Chronic early childhood traumatization includes the harmful psychological, biological, and social consequences of traumas that started before the age of eight. Examples are abuse (emotional, physical, sexual), emotional neglect, war, painful medical interventions, traumatic loss of family members, and witnessing violence in childhood. The criterion for traumatization is not the nature or the severity of the event, but rather the subjective response of the individual to being exposed to the event.

14.6.1. Main presenting problems

The typical presenting symptoms of adult clients who were traumatized in early childhood are depression, impaired sense of self, fragmented self-image, low self-worth, all sorts of undefined anxieties, sub-assertive problems or an enormous overcompensation thereof, posttraumatic stress symptoms, hyperalertness, hypervigilance, difficulty trusting, all sorts of relationship and collaboration problems, inability to relax, emotional dysregulation, and personality problems with dependent and avoidant tendencies.

14.6.2. Factors affecting treatment

Impaired attachment

Early childhood physical abuse, sexual abuse, and neglect make healthy parent-child attachment difficult. This affects all relationships later in life, and also affects development of a self-image. Contact with others is that of an adaptive child with adaptive social behaviour. The aetiology of this adaptive behaviour is to avoid evoking any offence in an attempt to prevent any physical or sexual abuse. This adaptive behaviour conceals a submerged world of emotion in which sadness, anxiety, disappointment, aggression, and negligence play major roles, even though they are suppressed as much as possible.

Problematic relationships

Clients often have difficulty forming relationships. Some clients have a pattern of turbulence, unstable relationships, fear of abandonment or of being dominated, difficulty with boundaries, and difficulty developing an integrated identity.

Dissociation

Dissociation is highly prevalent in children who were traumatized at a young age, with children traumatized in the preverbal period at a greater risk for dissociation.

Client's unrealistic treatment expectations

The consequences of early childhood traumatization are often dramatic and treatment may take a long time. A satisfying result for the client is not always possible, so it is useful to neither raise nor dim the client's hopes too much.

Victimhood – oppositional behaviour – sabotage

Adaptive behaviour had the function of avoiding further physical or sexual abuse from parents, but, in the present moment, this coping style maintains the adaptive behaviour and sometimes leads to passive behaviour. The suppressed feelings of anger and frustration can be expressed in a safer environment, and, in the present moment, can lead to oppositional behaviour or sabotage. This fluctuation in coping styles can be difficult to deal with in treatment.

14.6.3. Typical cognitions

In Young's cognitive schemas (Young et al., 2003), these clients will mainly fall into the domain 'Impaired autonomy and performance', with cognitive schemas 'Dependence/Incompetence', 'Vulnerability to harm or illness', 'Enmeshment/Undeveloped self', and 'Failure to achieve'. The cognitive schemas from the domain 'Other-directness' will also play a role, including 'Subjugation', 'Self-sacrifice', and 'Approval-seeking'. Schemas from the domain 'Disconnection and rejection' will also play a role, namely, 'Abandonment/Instability', 'Mistrust/Abuse', 'Emotional neglect', 'Inferiority/Shame', and 'Social isolation/Alienation'. Cognitive schemas from the domain 'Impaired limits' may also play a minor role. They also have cognitions such as 'You can't trust people', 'I'm not worth it', 'You're not worth it', 'First you have to prove you're trustworthy', and many other cognitions and feelings of imperfection, combined with difficulty trusting others and a low self-image.

14.6.4. Therapist profile

When treating people whose trust in other people was damaged during their youth it is important to be cautious regarding intense transference and countertransference dynamics. These clients often consider other people to be threatening and untrustworthy. An effective treatment relationship can be established as follows:

- Provide the opportunity for positive attachment to an authority figure.
- Be knowledgeable about developmental psychology regarding the effect of impaired attachment relationships on psychological development.
- Collaborate with therapists who perform expressive therapies. Some children are exposed to violence before they have acquired an ability to speak. Expressive therapies can be implemented to work in non-verbal ways, for instance, with images, sound, or movement.
- Tolerate their complex ways of making contact which shifts from keeping emotional distance and seeking intimacy, demanding trust but not giving it.

Finally, clients' stories of violent experiences at a young age may evoke disgust or anger in the therapist, who should also identify and recognize their own countertransference (Nicolai, 2008). Furthermore, the treatment of these clients requires a great deal of patience.

14.6.5. Treatment recommendations

As mentioned earlier, this group of clients usually falls into the first or third quadrant (Figure 14.1), so the treatment options are similar to those for second-generation clients. People in the third quadrant usually undergo long-term treatment and often have a long history with the healthcare sector. People in the first quadrant have more favourable treatment options, determined by their integration and structural personality problems. A complication with these clients is that their problems place them at a greater risk of being in situations that traumatize them once again.

The treatment of people with early childhood attachment impairments practically always needs time, so the client has the opportunity to attach to the therapist and so gradually dare to be vulnerable. Being validated for the problems is also very important. Only then can phase 2 be implemented, to process the coping style, the inaccurate self-assessment, and the traumatic memories. This process is often so lengthy in which the tension escalates so high that temporary regression to phase 1 techniques may be necessary. The therapist needs to create a safe and trusting framework by demonstrating exemplary behaviour during sessions and by faithfully keeping to appointments.

The treatment can comprise individual psychotherapy sessions that can take place in combination with other types of treatment such as day care, (brief) hospital admissions, crisis support, group therapy, movement therapy, psychiatric home care, or reintegration supervision. Medication can help to counteract depression, anxiety attacks, or insomnia. Group therapy is also possible, although specific therapeutic processing activities might be better tackled during individual sessions.

Chapter 15

Therapist boundaries

It is emotionally taxing for therapists to work with severely traumatized people. The clients' traumatic experiences can evoke in therapists intense emotional reactions such as horror, anxiety, and disgust. However, they also evoke intense positive engagement with the traumatized clients. A recent study (Smith, 2009) showed that trauma therapists are no more anxious or depressed than other therapists. Nonetheless, the emotional burden can lead to different types of problems that are discussed in this chapter, which also includes a few recommendations for dealing with these problems.

15.1. Transference and countertransference

The essence of complex trauma is the harm people inflict on their fellow human beings. This has an impact on spontaneous, naive trust in other people, and making contact with others is burdensome. Clients therefore have problems developing relationships. Even their relationship with the therapist will be initially affected by this basic mistrust in others. Therapists should be prepared for clients who may direct their mistrust of other people inappropriately towards them. The therapist has to be conscious of the fact that expressions of mistrust and insecurity, and doubts about the therapist's professionalism involve more than just the therapeutic relationship. The therapist must also bear in mind that it was the trauma that caused this fundamental mistrust in other people, not what is happening in the therapy room. The therapist must be cautious in dealing with this and not react impulsively to the client's malcontent (Hafkenscheid, 2005).

An impulsive reaction to the types of allegations that put the therapist's professionalism in question may lead the therapist to react with countertransference. The therapist who reacts with countertransference is not actually reacting to the situation created by the client's expression of mistrust; rather, the reaction is more an expression of a personal issue for the therapist, an example of which is having the conviction not to tolerate any unjustifiable accusations. A therapist reacting from their own emotional issues may fuel the client's mistrust and this may eventually lead to mutual disappointment and humiliation, and to an unproductive working relationship.

A therapist should consult with a colleague if they suspect their reaction is countertransference. A colleague can then help explore the part of the therapist's feelings which were evoked by the client's transference (the situation) and the part of the therapist's feelings that caused the countertransference (the therapist's past). The therapist has to then reconcile this countertransference in order to avoid any further problems in the sessions with their client. Two scenarios are possible. One scenario is that the therapist's ability to deal with clients empathetically and to understand what they went though more deeply increases when they deal with countertransference carefully. The therapist has to explore the significance of their own anxiety and resistance to the client's treatment, as otherwise the second scenario would be that their empathy could be impaired and eventually destroy the therapeutic relationship. Then, there is a third possibility with the therapist acknowledging their feelings of countertransference and accepting that they hinder the client's treatment, which only leaves the option of transferring the client's treatment to a colleague.

A man who was frequently tortured in prison in Iraq sought help for diverse trauma symptoms. He agreed to a treatment plan developed by his therapist. However, the sessions quickly became mere monologues by the client. The therapist felt increasingly less respected and became irritated at the fact that the agreed upon treatment plan was being ignored. It seemed as though the client was ignoring the therapist's interventions, which had become nothing more than the impetus for new monologues. The client also failed to show up for several months, then made new appointments for sessions and he repeated the pattern.

After the client and the therapist had not seen each other for six months, the client reported that things were going very well with him. The therapist took advantage of this opportunity for terminating the relationship with this annoying client, and proposed ending the treatment since things were going so well. The client became explosively angry, claiming to feel rejected and misunderstood, and with so many problems that he had not yet begun to talk about. Out of desperation the therapist agreed to yet another appointment.

15.2. Audience to shocking stories

Working with severely traumatized people confronts therapists with the horrors of what happened to their clients. Therapists are also familiar with the reactions from others at social occasions: 'How can you listen to all those stories?' 'How do therapists do that?' There are three ways to successfully deal with the intensity of the therapist's work: adaptation, professional distance, stability and balanced caseload.

15.2.1. Adaptation

Everyone who works in healthcare is at some time exposed to accounts of the terrible things people do to each other and the resulting long-term consequences.

Exposure is initially through clinical examples in textbooks, then through face-to-face contact with clients in actual practice. A type of natural selection takes place whereby those who are better able to tolerate hearing about severe problems become more proficient in providing clinical mental care.

An ability to adapt is also a necessary skill for therapists. Over the course of time, people working in mental healthcare gradually see a narrower range of clients, which naturally results in seeing fewer variations in their clients' problems and stories; in other words, therapists seldom hear new themes in their new clients' shocking stories. Of course each client's personal story is unique and is, in that sense, new. The therapist does, however, become less shocked by, and more accustomed to, these stories because the variation of themes within each specialism is limited. To use behavioural therapy terms, you could say that some form of exposure takes place over time.

In actual practice therapists seldom take their clients' stories home with them, although some therapists do report that they still think about new severe trauma stories on their way home. It is not a problem if the therapist is still slightly preoccupied with the story up to approximately 24 hours after hearing it. If for longer, however, or if the therapist is more than just slightly preoccupied, then more thorough exploration is necessary concerning what is actually happening and what may need to be done about it. As would be expected, younger or less experienced therapists frequently take longer to adapt because they have more information to adapt to.

It is important to make sure that the process of adapting to the themes does not lead to emotional numbness in the therapist, and that the therapist remains adequately sensitive to the clients' stories. Therapists run the risk of overlooking the details of someone's unique story if they inadvertently dismiss it as simply a repetitive theme that they have heard before. The advantage of successful adaptation over time is that the therapist has more experience and expertise in dealing with the clients' problems more effectively. Emotional numbness is not due to being shocked by the content of a story the therapist is hearing for the first time. It is the result of how clients deal with their horrible experiences; even though two people experience the same event, the uniqueness of their stories is due to the coping processes they each exercise.

The fact that becoming accustomed to listening does not necessarily lead to emotional numbness is evidenced by the presence of well-seasoned trauma therapists who work in forensic psychiatry. Such a therapist is not so easily shocked by stories about death and homicide. Their ability to adapt has been put to the test to the point that they know how to deal with these topics. Most trauma therapists also know how to deal effectively with milder problems in that they do not trivialize them, which is what would be expected from someone who is emotionally numb.

Dr Charles Figley compared therapists being touched by their clients' pain to carpenters having a sore thumb at one time or another: 'Those who walk around worrying about their thumbs should probably look for other work.' The point is therefore not to be bothered by the emotional impact, but to adapt.

15.2.2. Professional distance

It is important that therapists consciously maintain their professional distance when listening to their clients' horror stories. This requires marking a certain degree of emotional distance between the therapist and the client, but also between the therapist and the client's story. Therapists do not need to identify with the client's story. Even more so, they may not identify with it, otherwise they will find themselves in a position comparable to that of the client and are no longer the healthcare provider. This necessary professional separation also helps keep the impact of the client's story at somewhat of a safe distance.

A therapist had a client who was a veteran of the Second World War. The client had been physically abused in POW camps in the Dutch East Indies and had witnessed horrible scenes while working on the Burma railway, also known as the Death Railway. The treatment plan for phase 2 included the client writing out his story (using the testimony therapy format) after each session at home and mailing it to the therapist. The goal was to break his story up into episodes, so to speak. The client read each episode out in the following session for discussion. The therapist noticed that reading the stories sent in the mail was much more depressing than listening to the client relate the story in the therapy room, and realized that this was because of the professional distance maintained in the presence of the client. When reading the story in the first person, he automatically identified much more with the client and felt emotions more intensely. As a therapist he was more of a spectator of the client's emotions. The distance was greater and the therapist was less distracted by the emotional content of the story.

Second-hand emotions

Therapists only have to identify and empathize with clients in a general sense, because the clients are in the same room doing all the necessary emoting right there in front of them. Therapists are usually not affected by the emotions evoked by the stories, but more by the emotions the clients express when talking about their traumas. They are empathizing with the emotions the client is experiencing in the moment. It could be said that the therapist's emotional reactions to the story content are second-hand, whereas the client feels the first-hand emotions themselves in the therapy room.

An exception is when clients relate their traumatic experiences with little or no emotional expression. The therapist may then feel the emotions first-hand. This says something about the client's problems: there may be some dissociation or emotional numbness, or even a Cluster A or Cluster B personality problem.

In summary therapists have to consciously maintain professional distance and not identify with the content of the client's story to protect themselves from the effects of listening to the horrors.

15.2.3. Stability

It is important that therapists leave their work at work. Therapists need to be aware of their own emotions to prevent these from merging with those of the clients. They also have to maintain their own emotional distance and not identify with the problems and emotions of the clients. The completely stable therapist does not exist, but a certain amount of inner stability is required for the therapist to resolve their own problems and traumas and maintain their role as care provider. If the therapist's emotions are going to be too much in sync with those of the client, the therapist will easily find themselves in a position comparable to the client.

Therapists are just people too and are occasionally confronted with unpleasant experiences in life. A common issue is when a therapist has to deal with the death of a parent while a client is also dealing with that issue. The therapist may need to consider transferring that client over to a colleague, as the client's stories could potentially evoke too many of the therapist's emotions. It may also be useful to have a colleague to consult with about maintaining effective emotional distance from the client.

15.2.4. Balanced caseload

Having a balanced caseload helps deal with difficult stories. A caseload with too many of the same kind of problems runs the risk of the therapist becoming emotionally numb, and reduces the ability of retaining a sense of proportion and marking distance from the problems. It is also advisable for therapists not to work exclusively with severe trauma. Admittedly this is difficult in organizations that specialize in trauma therapy, but the therapists could work with a diverse group of clients, for instance, with a mix of refugees, rape victims, and veterans.

15.3. The impact of clients' problems

Working with severely traumatized people affects therapists. Various terms have been used over the years, for instance, secondary traumatization, compassion fatigue (Figley, 1995), or vicarious traumatization (McCann & Pearlman, 1990). These terms seem to indicate that working with traumatized clients may lead to specific symptoms similar to those for posttraumatic stress disorder (PTSD) and may even cause personality changes. There is, however, little scientific evidence to support these claims. Smith and colleagues (Smith et al., 2007a; Smith et al., 2007b) reported that working with severely traumatized people had a great emotional impact on the therapists, but seldom caused psychopathological consequences or other negative long-term changes, as suggested by the terms secondary traumatization and vicarious traumatization. These findings confirm our own clinical experience: our therapists are neither traumatized nor do they acquire trauma symptoms because of clients' stories.

Although the impact is limited by a protective and emotionally distant stance, the traumatic stories of clients do indeed influence therapists. Listening to traumatic stories about someone's wife who was physically abused and murdered by the Taliban, for instance, may result in the therapist being less neutral when watching any news about Afghanistan. Another example would be listening to, and being affected by, clients' stories about violence, hunger, powerlessness, and helplessness. Emotional distance is crucial to reducing the impact of the clients' traumatic stories, but therapists are inevitably affected by such stories.

15.3.1. Realistic treatment goals

The effectiveness of their interventions indicates whether the therapist is being overly affected by a client's story. After all, the goal of treatment is relief of the client's symptoms in their daily life. Achieving that goal will be the therapist's and client's main objective for treatment. The impact of the content of the client's story becomes less important. If the treatment is unsuccessful, there is a greater likelihood that the therapist was affected by the emotions of the client's story.

Success has much to do with the therapist's expectations of their interventions. If therapists expect too much, they may be disappointed about the effect of the treatment, and the client's symptoms and problems will still remain. This increases the chance that the therapist becomes pulled down into the client's emotional world of, for instance, depression or powerlessness. The possibilities of success are greater when therapists set lower goals. A realistic expectation – underscoring the importance of establishing realistic goals at the start of treatment – sets a strong foundation for moving on and the treatment can then focus less on the client's symptoms and problems.

Clients whose problems are difficult to therapeutically process or alter often have a sense of powerlessness and helplessness – which can potentially affect the therapist's feelings. In this case it is even more important to set realistic goals, preferably together with the client. When clients are unable to collaborate with the therapist in setting the goals, then it is important that therapists set realistic expectations for themselves, which in turn prevents disappointment and any merging of emotions between the client and therapist and also reduces the risk of countertransference.

The content of clients' stories can also affect their therapist's behaviour. For instance, working with clients who experienced starvation when they were children may affect how a therapist deals with their own children's eating behaviour. Changing behaviour because of these stories only becomes a problem if a therapist has become too emotionally affected by the clients' stories and is dealing with them pathologically.

15.4. Therapist guilt

Dealing with severely traumatized people on a frequent basis evokes a lot of compassion. Compassion combined with professional distance has a positive effect on the therapeutic relationship. A part of that compassion comprises elements of identification with the client's situation, which make therapists aware of the differences between their own situation and role from that of the clients, whose mental, social, and financial situations are usually a radical contrast with their own (Hafkenscheid, 2005). This can evoke guilt in a therapist for their own well-being and good fortune; this understandable countertransference reaction does not favour the therapeutic relationship, as the client should not be burdened with this guilt (Van Minnen et al., 1998). If the therapist has persistent internal struggles with this feeling of guilt, intervision or supervision with colleagues is needed.

The danger of compassion combined with guilt is that the therapist will be tempted to rescue the client by adopting a paternalistic and protective attitude. This type of countertransference risks a counterproductive underestimation of the client's strength and healthy facets. It is patronizing to think the client needs to be saved. It is quite possible that the therapist's emotions are overly in sync with those of the client through a conspiracy of silence (Danieli, 1984), a coping style that many severely traumatized people rely on as a survival mechanism. In other words, this defence mechanism is being perpetuated rather than processed.

15.5. Sharing feelings

Emotions in therapists which do not promote an effectively functioning therapeutic relationship must be dealt with outside the therapy room with colleagues, perhaps in the form of intervision. Mental health organizations should provide systematic intervision or case consultations, with scheduled time for therapists to discuss their feelings in an atmosphere where it is safe to present vulnerabilities. However, systematic intervision is usually neglected or occurs infrequently in practice. Group dynamics also evoke feelings of insecurity, which prevent therapists from revealing their vulnerabilities in front of colleagues.

It may be more productive to seek support – if needed – from just one person, for instance, a supervisor. Supervisors can effectively and systematically explore the feelings evoked in the therapist by working with particular clients. A supervisory relationship is generally safe, because the supervisor is there for the therapist, and there is no question of losing face before the team. The reality is, however, that the majority of seasoned therapists no longer arrange supervision.

Countertransference usually arises suddenly and is the therapist's problem, although it must be dealt with as soon as possible with someone they trust. Having someone to consult with who works in close proximity and is easily available is perhaps more desirable than a formal, structured supervisory procedure. It is important to invest in a team to create an atmosphere of mutual trust and open communication (Nicolai, 2008). Instituting a buddy system is possibly an option so that everyone has immediate support when things become difficult.

If a team is dealing with clients with problems that evoke a great deal of countertransference in team members, it is important to have systematic intervision, supervision, or vocational training for dealing with severely traumatized clients (Smith, 2009).

15.6. The challenges posed by traumatized clients

Many therapists work in organizations specialized in treating clients who have been severely traumatized at some time in their lives. These institutions, departments, or private practices are forensic or deal with a specific form of severe trauma. Various factors play a role in why therapists work in this type of institutions.

It can be challenging for a therapist to work with people with severely traumatic experiences because it confronts them with issues that test the boundaries of the human spirit: death, the will to survive, arbitrary circumstances, human cruelty, the capacity for torture and to endure torture, human resilience, and the meaning of life. These themes bring the therapist in contact with the very essence of life. This has an enriching component, but there is also an undeniably sensational and irresistible component to listening to descriptions of unpleasant traumatic experiences, which is not necessarily problematic, providing it does not become dysfunctional.

Working with refugees and veterans puts the therapist in contact with people from war-stricken regions in the world. You could say that the therapist is 'on top of the news', albeit one to three years later. The time lag exists because veterans usually do not seek help for their problems at mental health institutions from the outset. Veterans typically first attempt to deal with problems on their own and then seek help from veteran help services. They continue having their problems before ultimately visiting a trauma specialist. This process takes anywhere from one to three years after returning home. Refugees and asylum seekers require about the same amount of time before they seek help. They start with deciding to flee, fleeing, and finding a host country. Then the trauma symptoms develop and finally they acknowledge that they need help. Working with people who participated in tragedies that took place in the world a few years previously has a certain appeal for therapists. They hear directly from the clients how major conflicts played out on specific individuals and they receive insights about these events that are not covered in the media. It is 'inside information' on world problems, so to speak.

War trauma always has a historic context. The clients' stories about their trauma contain personal information about the history of a conflict which is usually only referred to in the media at the macro level. Refugees and asylum seekers bring with them their culture, their stories, their trauma, their clothing, their traditions, and their language. It has been said that working with refugees and asylum seekers is like taking a trip around the world in the therapy room. Therapists come in contact with all sorts of cultures that they otherwise would not get to know so intensely. This makes working with refugees and asylum seekers very interesting.

Complex trauma involves severe problems that have an intense impact on the client's life. As mentioned earlier in this book, it is often impossible to alleviate trauma problems completely, but remarkable improvement in the quality of their life is often possible. The therapist can feel good about having contributed to that improvement. Furthermore, clients with complex trauma usually have an impaired capacity to make contact with others because of their mistrust, suspicion, and their complicated way of conveying information. The therapist's challenge of creating a workable therapeutic relationship and of treating the client within that dynamic requires great effort, but it is very rewarding when it is successful.

Appendix 1[1]

Criteria for Posttraumatic Stress Disorder (DSM-IV-TR)

A The person has been exposed to a traumatic event in which both of the following were present:

(1) The person experienced, witnessed, or was confronted with an event or events that involved actual or threatened death or serious injury, or a threat to the physical integrity of self or others.
(2) The person's response involved intense fear, helplessness, or horror. Note: In children, this may be expressed instead by disorganized or agitated behavior.

B The traumatic event is persistently reexperienced in one (or more) of the following ways:

(3) Recurrent and intrusive distressing recollections of the event, including images, thoughts, or perceptions. Note: In young children, repetitive play may occur in which themes or aspects of the trauma are expressed.
(4) Recurrent distressing dreams of the event. Note: In children, there may be frightening dreams without recognizable content.
(5) Acting or feeling as if the traumatic event were recurring (includes a sense of reliving the experience; illusions, hallucinations, and dissociative flashback episodes, including those that occur on awakening or when intoxicated). Note: In young children, trauma-specific reenactment may occur.
(6) Intense psychological distress at exposure to internal or external cues that symbolize or resemble an aspect of the traumatic event.
(7) Physiological reactivity on exposure to internal or external cues that symbolize or resemble an aspect of the traumatic event.

C Persistent avoidance of stimuli associated with the trauma and numbing of general responsiveness (not present before the trauma), as indicated by three (or more) of the following:

(8) Efforts to avoid thoughts, feelings, or conversations associated with the trauma

(9) Efforts to avoid activities, places, or people that arouse recollections of the trauma
(10) Inability to recall an important aspect of the trauma
(11) Markedly diminished interest or participation in significant activities
(12) Feeling of detachment or estrangement from others
(13) Restricted range of affect (e.g., unable to have loving feelings)
(14) Sense of a foreshortened future (e.g., does not expect to have a career, marriage, children, or a normal lifespan)

D Persistent symptoms of increased arousal (not present before the trauma), as indicated by two (or more) of the following:

(15) Difficulty falling or staying asleep
(16) Irritability or outbursts of anger
(17) Difficulty concentrating
(18) Hypervigilance
(19) Exaggerated startle response

E Duration of the disturbance (symptoms in Criteria B, C, and D) is more than 1 month.
F The disturbance causes clinically significant distress or impairment in social, occupational, or other important areas of functioning.

Specify if:

Acute: if duration of symptoms is less than 3 months
Chronic: if duration of symptoms is 3 months or more

Specify if:

With Delayed Onset: if onset of symptoms is at least 6 months after the stressor.

Note

1. Reprinted with permission from the Diagnostic and Statistical Manual of Mental Disorders, Fourth Edition, (Copyright © 2000). American Psychiatric Association. All rights reserved.

Appendix 2

Criteria for Disorders of Extreme Stress Not Otherwise Specified (DESNOS)

(I) Alteration in Regulation of Affect and Impulses (A and one of B to F required)

A. affect regulation
B. modulation of anger
C. self-destructive behavior
D. suicidal preoccupation
E. difficulty modulating sexual involvement
F. excessive risk-taking

(II) Alterations in Attention or Consciousness (A or B required)

A. amnesia
B. transient dissociative episodes and depersonalization

(III) Alterations in Self-Perception (Two of A to F required)

A. ineffectiveness
B. permanent damage
C. guilt and responsibility
D. shame
E. nobody can understand
F. minimizing

(IV) Alterations in Relations with Others (One of A to C required)

A. inability to trust
B. revictimization
C. victimizing others

(V) Somatization (Two of A to E required)

A. problems with the digestive system
B. chronic pain
C. cardiopulmonary symptoms
D. conversion symptoms
E. sexual symptoms

(VI) Alterations in Systems of Meaning (A or B required)

A. despair and hopelessness
B. loss of previously sustaining beliefs

Source

(Luxenberg, Spinazzola & Van der Kolk, 2001)

Appendix 3

Criteria for Developmental Trauma Disorder (DTD)

A. Exposure

The child or adolescent has experienced or witnessed multiple or prolonged extremely stressful traumatic events over a period of at least one year beginning in childhood or early adolescence, including:

1) Direct experience or witnessing of repeated and severe episodes of interpersonal violence, and
2) Significant disruptions of protective care giving as a result of repeated changes in primary caregiver, repeated separation from the primary caregiver, or exposure to severe and persistent emotional abuse.

B. Affective and physiological dysregulation

The child exhibits impaired normative developmental competencies related to arousal regulation, including at least two of the following:

1) Inability to modulate, tolerate, or recover from extreme affect states (e.g. fear, anger, shame), including prolonged and extreme tantrums, or immobilization,
2) Disturbances in regulation of bodily functions (e.g. persistent disturbances in sleeping, eating, and elimination; over-reactivity or under-reactivity to touch and sounds; disorganization during routine transitions),
3) Diminished awareness/dissociation of sensations, emotions, and bodily states, and/or
4) Impaired capacity to describe emotions or bodily states.

C. Attentional and behavioral dysregulation

The child exhibits impaired normative developmental competencies related to sustained attention, learning, or coping with stress, including at least three of the following:

1) Preoccupation with threat or impaired capacity to perceive threat, including misreading of safety and danger cues,

2) Impaired capacity for self-protection, including extreme risk-taking or thrill-seeking,
3) Maladaptive attempts at self-soothing (e.g. rocking and other rhythmical movements, compulsive masturbation),
4) Habitual (intentional or automatic) or reactive selfharm, and/or
5) Inability to initiate or sustain goal-directed behavior.

D. Self and relational deregulation

The child exhibits impaired normative developmental competencies in his/her sense of personal identity and involvement in relationships, including at least three of the following:

1) Intense preoccupation with safety of the caregiver or other loved ones (including precocious care giving) or difficulty tolerating reunion with them after separation,
2) Persistent negative sense of self, including self-loathing, helplessness, worthlessness, ineffectiveness, or defectiveness,
3) Extreme and persistent distrust, defiance or lack of reciprocal behavior in close relationships with adults or peers,
4) Reactive physical or verbal aggression toward peers, caregivers, or other adults,
5) Inappropriate (excessive or promiscuous) attempts to achieve intimate contact (including but not limited to sexual or physical intimacy), or excessive reliance on peers or adults for safety and reassurance, and/or
6) Impaired capacity to regulate empathic arousal as evidenced by lack of empathy for, or intolerance of, expressions of distress of others, or excessive responsiveness to the distress of others.

E. Post-traumatic spectrum symptoms

The child exhibits at least one symptom in at least two of the three PTSD symptom clusters B, C, and D.

Source

(Schmid et al., 2013; Van der Kolk, 2005)

Appendix 4

Criteria for Enduring personality change after catastrophic experience

Enduring personality change, present for at least two years, following exposure to catastrophic stress. The stress must be so extreme that it is not necessary to consider personal vulnerability in order to explain its profound effect on the personality. The disorder is characterized by a hostile or distrustful attitude toward the world, social withdrawal, feelings of emptiness or hopelessness, a chronic feeling of 'being on edge' as if constantly threatened, and estrangement. Post-traumatic stress disorder (F43.1) may precede this type of personality change.

Personality change after:

A. concentration camp experiences
B. disasters
C. prolonged:

   captivity with an imminent possibility of being killed exposure to life-threatening situations such as being a victim of terrorism

D. torture

Excl.:

post-traumatic stress disorder

Source

(WHO, 2007)

Appendix 5[1]

Posttraumatic stress disorder in the DSM-5

Criterion A: Stressor

The person was exposed to: death, threatened death, actual or threatened serious injury, or actual or threatened sexual violence, as follows: **(1 required)**

E. Direct exposure.
F. Witnessing, in person.
G. Indirectly, by learning that a close relative or close friend was exposed to trauma. If the event involved actual or threatened death, it must have been violent or accidental.
H. Repeated or extreme indirect exposure to aversive details of the event(s), usually in the course of professional duties (e.g., first responders, collecting body parts; professionals repeatedly exposed to details of child abuse). This does not include indirect non-professional exposure through electronic media, television, movies, or pictures.

Criterion B: intrusion symptoms

The traumatic event is persistently re-experienced in the following way(s): **(1 required)**

A. Recurrent, involuntary, and intrusive memories. Note: Children older than 6 may express this symptom in repetitive play.
B. Traumatic nightmares. Note: Children may have frightening dreams without content related to the trauma(s).
C. Dissociative reactions (e.g., flashbacks) which may occur on a continuum from brief episodes to complete loss of consciousness. Note: Children may reenact the event in play.
D. Intense or prolonged distress after exposure to traumatic reminders.
E. Marked physiologic reactivity after exposure to trauma-related stimuli.

Criterion C: avoidance

Persistent effortful avoidance of distressing trauma-related stimuli after the event: **(1 required)**

A. Trauma-related thoughts or feelings.
B. Trauma-related external reminders (e.g., people, places, conversations, activities, objects, or situations).

Criterion D: negative alterations in cognitions and mood

Negative alterations in cognitions and mood that began or worsened after the traumatic event: **(2 required)**

A. Inability to recall key features of the traumatic event (usually dissociative amnesia; not due to head injury, alcohol or drugs).
B. Persistent (and often distorted) negative beliefs and expectations about oneself or the world (e.g., 'I am bad', 'The world is completely dangerous').
C. Persistent distorted blame of self or others for causing the traumatic event or for resulting consequences.
D. Persistent negative trauma-related emotions (e.g., fear, horror, anger, guilt or shame).
E. Markedly diminished interest in (pre-traumatic) significant activities.
F. Feeling alienated from others (e.g., detachment or estrangement).
G. Constricted affect: persistent inability to experience positive emotions.

Criterion E: alterations in arousal and reactivity

Trauma-related alterations in arousal and reactivity that began or worsened after the traumatic event: **(2 required)**

A. Irritable or aggressive behavior.
B. Self-destructive or reckless behavior.
C. Hypervigilance.
D. Exaggerated startle response.
E. Problems in concentration.
F. Sleep disturbance.

Criterion F: duration

Persistence of symptoms (in Criteria B, C, D and E) for more than one month.

Criterion G: functional significance

Significant symptom-related distress or functional impairment (e.g., social, occupational).

Criterion H: exclusion

Disturbance is not due to medication, substance use, or other illness.

Specify if: With dissociative symptoms.

In addition to meeting criteria for diagnosis, an individual experiences high levels of either of the following in reaction to trauma-related stimuli:

D. Depersonalization: experience of being an outside observer of or detached from oneself (e.g., feeling as if 'this is not happening to me' or one were in a dream).
E. Derealization: experience of unreality, distance, or distortion (e.g., 'things are not real').

Specify if: With delayed expression.

Full diagnosis is not met until at least 6 months after the trauma(s), although onset of symptoms may occur immediately.

Note

1. Reprinted with permission from the Diagnostic and Statistical Manual of Mental Disorders, Fifth Edition, (Copyright ©2013). American Psychiatric Association. All Rights Reserved.

References

Aarts, P.G.H. (2007). Veroudering en trauma [Growing older and trauma]. In: P. Aarts & W. Visser (ed.), *Trauma, diagnostiek en behandeling [Trauma, assessment and treatment]* (pp. 448–463). Houten: Bohn Stafleu van Loghum.

Allen, J.G. (2001). *Traumatic relationships and serious mental disorders*. Chichester, UK: John Wiley & Sons.

Allen, J.G. (2013). *Restoring mentalizing in attachment relationships: treating trauma with plain old therapy.* Washington, D.C.: American Psychiatric Publishing.

Allen, J.G., Fonagy, P. & Bateman, A.W. (2008). *Mentalising in clinical practice.* Washington DC: American Psychiatric Publishing.

American Psychiatric Association (2000; 2013). *Diagnostic and statistical manual of mental disorders*, 4th edn text revised. Washington, DC: American Psychiatric Association.

Antonovsky, A., McCubbin, H.I., Thompson, E.A., Thompson, A.I., & Fromer, J.E. (1998). *Stress, coping, and health in families: sense of coherence and resiliency*. Thousand Oaks, CA US: Sage Publications, Inc.

Arnoldus, M.P.E. & Markhorst, C.M. (2000). *Traumacursus, handleiding [Trauma training, manual]*. Groningen: GGZ Groningen.

Arntz, A. & Bögels, S. (2000). *Schemagerichte cognitieve therapie voor persoonlijkheidsstoornissen [Schema-focused cognitive therapy for personality disorders].* Houten: Bohn Stafleu van Loghum.

Arntz, A. & Weertman, A. (1999). Treatment of childhood memories: theory and practice. *Behaviour Research and Therapy, 37*, 715–740.

Arrindell, W.A. & Ettema, J.H.M. (1986). *SCL-90: Handleiding bij een multidimensionele psychopathologie-indicator. [Manual to a multidimensional indicator of psychopathology]*. Lisse: Swets & Zeitlinger.

Arrindell, W.A., Groot, P.M., & Walburg, J.A. (1984). *Handleiding Schaal voor Interpersoonlijk Gedrag, SIG.* [Manual Scale for interpersonal behavior]. Lisse: Swets & Zeitlinger.

Bachelor, A. & Horvath, A. (1999). The therapeutic relationship. In: M. Hubble, B. Duncan & S. Miller (Eds.), *The heart and soul of change* (pp. 133–178). Washington, DC: APA Press.

Balkom, A.L.J.M. van, Vliet, I.M. van, Emmelkamp, P.M.G., Bockting, C.L.H., Spijker, J., Hermens, M.L.M., & Meeuwissen, J.A.C. (2013). *Multidisciplinaire richtlijn Angststoornissen (Derde revisie). [Multidisciplinairy guideline for anxiety disorders, 3rd revision].* Utrecht: Trimbos-instituut.

Barker, P. (1991). *The regeneration trilogy*. London: Penguin Books.

Bastiaans, J. (1974). Het KZ-syndrooom en de menselijke vrijheid. [The KZ-syndrome and human freedom]. *Nederlands Tijdschrift voor Geneeskunde, 118*, 1173–1178.

Bateman, A.W. & Fonagy, P. (2004). Mentalization-based treatment of BPD. *Journal of Personality Disorders, 18*, 1, 36–51.

Beck, A.T. (1976). *Cognitive therapy and the emotional disorders*. New York: International Universities Press.

Beck, A.T. & Freeman, A.M. (1990). *Cognitive therapy of personality disorders*. New York: Guilford Press.

Beck, A.T., Ward, C.H., Mendelson, M., Mock, J., & Erbaugh, J. (1961). An inventory for measuring depression. *Archives of General Psychiatry, 4*, 561–571.

Beck, A.T., Steer, R.A. & Brown, G.K. (1996). *Manual for Beck Depression Inventory-II*. San Antonio, TX: Psychological Corporation.

Beck, A.T., Emery, G., & Greenberg, R.L. (2005). *Anxiety disorders and phobias: a cognitive perspective*. New York: Basic Books.

Beltran, R.O. & Silove, D. (1999). Expert opinions about the ICD-10 category of enduring personality change after catastrophic experience. *Comprehensive Psychiatry, 40*, 396–403.

Bernstein, E.M. & Putnam, F.W. (1986). Development, reliability, and validity of a dissociation scale. *Journal of Nervous and Mental Disease, 174*, 727–735.

Blake, D.D., Weathers, F.W., Nagy, L.M., Kaloupek, D.G., Klauminzer, G., Charney, D.S., & Keane, T.M. (1990). A clinician rating scale for assessing current and liftetime PTSD: the CAPS-1. *Behavioural Therapy, 13*, 187–188.

Blijham, H. (1984). Het specifieke bij het existentieel emotioneel stress syndroom. [The specifics of the existential emotional stress syndrome]. *Tijdschrift voor Psychiatrie, 26*, 564–573.

Blum, N., Pfohl, B., St. John, D., Monahan, P., & Black, D. (2002). STEPPS: A cognitive behavorial systems-based group treatment for outpatients with borderline personality disorder: A preliminary report. *Comprehensive Psychiatry, 43*, 301–310.

Bohlmeijer, E., Mies, L., & Westerhof, G. (ed.) (2007). *De betekenis van levensverhalen, theoretische beschouwingen en toepassingen in onderzoek en praktijk. [The meaning of life stories, theoretical perspectives and implications for research and practice]*. Houten: Bohn Stafleu van Loghum.

Bonanno, G. (2004). Loss, trauma, and human resilience. *American Psychologist, 59*, 20–28.

Boon, S. & Draijer, N. (2007). Diagnostiek van dissociatieve stoornissen met de SCID-D: mogelijkheden en beperkingen. [Assessment of dissociative disorders with the SCID-D: possibilities and restraints]. *Psychopraxis, 9*, 27–32.

Bot, H. (2005). *Dialogue interpreting in mental health*. Amsterdam/New York: Rodopi.

Bramsen, I. (1995). *The long-term psychological adjustment of World War II survivors in the Netherlands*. (Dissertation.) Delft: Eburon Press.

Brantley, J. (2007). *Angst beheersen met aandacht [Controlling fear with attention]*. Amsterdam: Nieuwezijds.

Breslau, N. (1998). Epidemiology of trauma and posttraumatic stress disorder. In: R. Yehuda (Ed.), *Psychological trauma* (pp. 1–30). Washington DC: American Psychiatric Press.

Breslau, N., Chilcoat, H.D., Kessler, R.C., Peterson, E.L., & Lucia, V.C. (1999). Vulnerability to assaultive violence: further specification of the sex difference in post-traumatic stress disorder. *Psychological Medicine, 29*, 813–821.

Brewin, C.R., Dalgleish, T., & Joseph, S. (1996). A dual representation theory of posttraumatic stress disorder. *Psychological Review, 103*, 670–686.

Brom, D. & Kleber, R.J. (1985). De Schok Verwerkings Lijst (SVL) [The Dutch Impact of Event Scale]. *Nederlands Tijdschrift voor de Psychologie, 40*, 164–168.

Calhoun, L.G. & Tedeschi, R.G. (1999). *Facilitating posttraumatic growth. A clinician's guide*. New Jersey: Taylor & Francis.

Carr, A. (2006). *The handbook of child and adolescent clinical psychology. A contextual approach* (2nd edn). London: Routledge.

Chemtob, M.C., Tolin, D.F., Kolk, B.A. van der, & Pitman, R.K. (2000). Eye Movement Desensitization and Reprocessing. In: E.B. Foa, T.M. Keane & M.J. Friedman (Eds.), *Effective treatments for PTSD: practice guidelines from the International Society for Traumatic Stress Studies* (pp. 139–154). London: Guilford Press.

Chu, J.A. (2011). *Rebuilding shattered lives. Treating complex PTSD and dissociative disorders* (2nd edn). Hoboken: John Wiley & Sons.

Cienfuegos, A.J. & Monelli, C. (1983). The testimony of political repression as a therapeutic instrument. *American Journal of Orthopsychiatry, 53*, 43–51.

Classen, C.C., Palesh, O.G., & Aggarwal, R. (2005). Sexual revictimization: a review of the empirical literature. *Trauma, Violence and Abuse, 6*, 103–129.

Cloitre, M. (2009). Effective psychotherapies for posttraumatic stress disorder: a review and critique. *CNS Spectrums, 14*, 1 (Suppl. 1), 32–43.

Cloitre, M., Cohen, L.R., & Koenen, K.C. (2006). *Treating survivors of childhood abuse. Psychotherapy for the interrupted life*. New York: Guilford Press.

Cloitre, M., Stovall-McClough, K.C., Nooner, K., Zorbas, P., Cherry, S., Jackson C.L., Gan, W., & Petkova, E. (2010). Treatment for PTSD related to childhood abuse: a randomized controlled trial. *American Journal of Psychiatry, 167*, 915–924. DOI: 10.1176/appi.ajp.2010.09081247.

Cloitre, M., Garvert, D.W., Brewin, C.R., Bryant, R.A., & Maercker, A. (2013). Evidence for proposed ICD-11 PTSD and complex PTSD: a latent profile analysis. *European Journal of Psychotraumatology, 4*, 20706. http://dx.doi.org/10/3402/ejpt.v4i020706.

Cohen, E.A. (1969). Het post-concentratiekampsyndroom. [The post-concentration camp syndrome]. *Nederlands Tijdschrift voor Geneeskunde, 113*, 2049–2054.

Courtois, C.A. & Ford, J.D. (2013). *Treatment of complex trauma. A sequenced, relationship-based approach.* New York: Guilford Press.

Courtois C.A., Ford, J.D., & Cloitre, M. (2009). Best practice in psychotherapy for adults. In: C.A. Courtois & J.D. Ford (Eds), *Treating complex traumatic stress disorders, an evidence-based guide* (pp. 82–103). New York: Guilford Press.

Cukor, J., Spitalnick, J., Difede, J.A., Rizzo, A., & Rothbaum, B.O. (2009). Emerging treatments for PTSD. *Clinical Psychology Review, 29*, 715–726.

Cummings, E.M., Goeke-Morey, M.C., Schermerhorn, A.C., Merrilees, C.W, & Cairns, Ed. (2009). Children and political violence from a social ecological perspective: implications from research on children and families in Northern Ireland. *Clinical Child and Family Psychology Review, 12*, 16–38.

Danieli, Y. (1984). Psychotherapists' participation in the conspiracy of silence about the Holocaust. *Psychoanalytic Psychology, 1*, 23–42.

Debats, D. (1996). *Meaning in life. Psychometric, clinical and phenomenological aspects* (doctoral dissertation). Groningen: Groningen University.

Derksen, J.J.L., Meij, H.R.A. de, Sloore, H., & Hellenbosch, G. (1996). *MMPI-2. Handleiding bij afname, scoring en interpretatie. [MMPI-2, manual for testing, scoring and interpretation}.* Nijmegen: PEN Test Publisher.

Derogatis L.R., Lipman R.S. & Covi L. (1973). SCL-90, an outpatient psychiatric rating scale-preliminary report. *Psychopharmacology Bulletin, 9*, 13–28.

Dorrepaal, E., Thomaes, K., & Draijer, N. (2008). *Vroeger en verder. Stabilisatiecursus na misbruik of mishandeling [Earlier and beyond. Stabilization training after abuse or maltreatment].* Amsterdam: Harcourt.

Draijer, N. (1988). *Een lege plek in mijn geheugen. Seksueel misbruik van meisjes door verwanten. [An empty spot in my memory. Sexual abuse of girls by relatives].* Den Haag: Ministerie van Sociale Zaken en Werkgelegenheid.

Drozdek, B. & Wilson, J.P. (2007). *Voices of trauma.* New York: Springer.

Duncan, B.L., Miller, S.D. & Sparks, J. (2004). *The Heroic Client*, 2nd ed. San Francisco, CA: Jossey-Bass.

Ebert, A. & Dyck, M.J. (2004). The experience of mental death: the core feature of complex posttraumatic stress disorder. *Clinical Psychology Review, 24*, 617–635.

Ee, E. van, Kleber, R.J., & Mooren, T.M. (2012). War trauma lingers on… Associations between maternal PTSD, parent-child interaction and child development. *Infant Mental Health Journal, 33* (5), 459–468. DOI: 10.1002/imhj.21324.

Ee, E. van, Mooren, T.M., & Kleber, R.J. (2014). Broken mirrors: shattered relationships in refugee families. In R. Pat-Horenczyk, D. Brom, C. Chemtob & J. Vogel (Eds.). *Helping children cope with trauma: individual, family and community perspectives* (pp. 146–162). New York/Oxford: Routledge.

Ehlers, A. & Clark, D.M. (2000). A cognitive model of posttraumatic stress disorder. *Behaviour Research and Therapy, 38*, 319–345.

Ehlers, A., Bisson, J., Clark, D.M., Creamer, M., Pilling, S., Richards, D., Schnurr, P.P., Turner, S. & Yule, W. (2010). Do all psychological treatments really work the same in posttraumatic stress disorder? *Clinical Psychology Review, 30*, 269–276.

Ellis, A. (1985). *Overcoming resistance: rational-emotive therapy with difficult clients.* New York: Springer.

Elzinga, B.M., Spinhoven, P., Berretty, E., Jong, P. de & Roelofs, K. (2010). The role of childhood abuse in HPA-axis reactivity in Social Anxiety Disorder: A pilot study. *Biological Psychology, 83*, 1–6.

Emmelkamp, P. & Vedel, E. (2007). *Alcohol- en drugsverslaving, een gids voor effectief gebleken behandelingen [Alcohol and drug addiction, a guide for effective treatments].* Amsterdam: Uitgeverij Nieuwezijds.

Engelhard, I.M., Hout, M.A. van den, Weerts, J., Arntz, A., Hox, J.J.C.M. & McNally, R.J. (2007). Deployment-related stress and trauma in Dutch soldiers returning from Iraq. *British Journal of Psychiatry, 191*, 140–145.

Engelhard, I.M., Hout, M.A. van den, Janssen, W.C. & Beek, J. van der (2010). Eye movements reduce vividness and emotionality of 'flashforwards'. *Behaviour Research and Therapy, 48*, 442–447.

Enning, B. (2009). *De oorlog van Bastiaans. De LSD-behandeling van het kampsydroom. [The war of Bastiaans. The LSD treatment of the camp syndrome].* Amsterdam: Augustus.

Eurelings-Bontekoe, E.H.M. & Snellen, W.M. (red.) (2003). *Dynamische persoonlijkheidsdiagnostiek [Dynamic assessment of personality].* Lisse: Swets & Zeitlinger.

Fazel, M., Wheeler, J. & Danesh, J. (2005). Prevalence of serious mental disorder in 7000 refugees resettled in western countries: a systematic review. *Lancet, 365*, 1309–1314.

Felitti, V.J. & Anda, R.F. (2010). The relationship of adverse childhood experiences to adult medical disease, psychiatric disorders and sexual behaviour: implications for healthcare. In: R.A. Lanius, E. Vermetten & C. Pain (Eds.), *The hidden epidemic* (pp. 77–87). New York: Cambridge University Press.

Figley, C.R. (1995). Compassion fatigue as secondary traumatic stress disorder: An overview. In: C.R. Figley (Ed.), *Compassion fatigue: coping with secondary traumatic stress disorder in those who treat the traumatized* (pp. 1–20). New York: Brunner Mazel.

Figley, C.R. & Kiser, L.J. (2013). *Helping traumatized families*. New York: Routledge.

Fjorback, L.O., Arendt, M., Ørnbøl, E., Fink, P., & Walach, H. (2011). Mindfulness-based stress reduction and mindfulness-based cognitive therapy – a systematic review of randomized controlled trials. *Acta Psychatrica Scandinavica, 124*, 102–119. DOI: 10111/j.1600–0477.2011.01704.x.

Foa, E.B. & Kozak, M.J. (1986). Emotional processing of fear: exposure to corrective information. *Psychological Bulletin, 99*, 20–35.

Foa, E.B., Rothbaum, B.O, Riggs, D.S. & Murdock, T.B. (1991). Treatment of posttraumatic stress disorder in rape victims: a comparison between cognitive-behavioral procedures and counseling. *Journal of Consulting and Clinical Psychology, 59*, 715–723.

Foa, E.B., Dancu, C.V., Hembree, E.A., Jaycox, L.H. & Meadows, E.A. (1999). A comparison of exposure therapy, stress inoculation training and their combination for reducing post-traumatic stress disorder in female assault victims. *Journal of Consulting and Clinical Psychology, 67*, 194–200.

Foa, E.B., Gillihan, S.J., & Bryant, R.A. (2013). Challenges and successes in dissemination of evidence-based treatments for posttraumatic stress: lessons learned from prolonged exposure therapy for PTSD. *Psychological Science in the Public Interest, 14*, 65–111. DOI: 10.1177/1529100612468841.

Foa, E.B., Keane, T.M., & Friedman, M.J. (2000). *Effective treatments for PTSD*. New York: Guilford Press.

Foa, E.B., Keane, T.M., Friedman, M.J. & Cohen, J.A. (2009) (Eds.). *Effective treatments for PTSD*, 2nd ed. New York: Guilford Press.

Foa, E.B. & Rothbaum, B.O. (1998). T*reating the trauma of rape: cognitive-behavioral therapy for PTSD*. New York: Guilford Press.

Fonagy, P. & Target, M. (2003). *Psychoanalytic theories. Perspectives from developmental psychopathology*. London: Whurr Publishers.

Ford, J.D., Stockton, P., Kaltman, S. & Green, B.L. (2006). Disorders of extreme stress (DESNOS) symptoms are associated with interpersonal trauma exposure in a sample of healthy young women. *Journal of Interpersonal Violence, 21*, 1399–1416.

Frankl, V.E. (2004). *Man's search for meaning. The classic tribute to hope from the Holocaust*. London: Rider.

Friedman, M. (2003). *Post traumatic stress disorder. The latest assessment and treatment strategies*. Kansas City: Compact Clinicals.

Germer, C.K., Siegel, R.D., & Fulton, P.R. (2005) *Mindfulness and psychotherapy*. New York: Guilford Press.

Gersons, B.P.R. & Olff M. (2005). Kort eclectisch behandelingsprotocol voor de post traumatische stressstoornis (Brief eclectic treatment protocol for PTSD). In: B.P.R. Gersons en M. Olff (Eds.). *Behandelingsstrategieën bij post traumatische stresstoornissen (Treatment strategies for PTSD's)*. Houten: Bohn Stafleu van Loghum.

Gersons, B.P.R., Carlier, I.V.E., Lamberts, R.D., Kolk, B.A. van der (2000). Randomized clinical trial of brief eclectic psychotherapy for police officers with posttraumatic stress disorder. *Journal of Traumatic Stress, 2000, 13*, 333–347.

Gersons, B.P.R., Carlier, I.V.E., & Olff, M. (2004). *Protocol brief eclectic psychotherapy for posttraumatic stress disorder*. Academic Medical Center, University of Amsterdam.

Gewirtz, A., Forgatch, M., & Wieling, E. (2008). Parenting practices as potential mechanisms for child adjustment following mass trauma. *Journal of Marital and Family Therapy, 34*, 177–192.

Giesen-Bloo, J., Dyck, R. van, Spinhoven, P., Tilburg, W. van, Dirksen, C., Asselt, T. van, Kremers, I., Nadort, M., & Arntz, A. (2006). Outpatient psychotherapy for borderline personality disorder: randomized trial of schema-focused therapy versus transference-focused psychotherapy. *Archives of General Psychiatry, 63*, 649–658.

Güzelcan, Y. & Olff, M. (2005). Farmacotherapie bij posttraumatische stressstoornis. [pharmacotherapy in PTSD]. In: B.P.R. Gersons & M. Olff (Eds), *Behandelingsstrategieën bij posttraumatische stressstoornissen [Treatment strategies for PTSDs]* (pp. 61–75). Houten: Bohn Stafleu van Loghum.

Hafkenscheid, A. (2005). Event countertransference and vicarious traumatization: theoretically valid and clinically useful concepts? *European Journal of Psychotherapy, Counselling and Health*, 7, 159–168.

Hamilton, M. (1960). A rating scale for depression. *Journal of Neurology and Neurosurgical Psychiatry, 23*, 56–62.

Hart, O. van der (1992). Het gebruik van mythen en rituelen in de psychotherapie [The use of myths and rituals in therapy]. In: O. van der Hart (Ed.). *Afscheidsrituelen, achterblijven en verder gaan [Farewell rituals, staying behind and continuing]* (pp. 27–48). Amsterdam/Lisse: Swets & Zeitlinger.

Hart, O. van der & Nijenhuis, E.R.S. (2003). Psychotherapie en 'hervonden herinneringen' [Psychotherapy and recovered memories]. In: O. van der Hart (ed.), *Trauma, dissociatie en hypnose [Trauma, dissociation and hypnosis]* 4th edn (pp. 421–447). Lisse: Swets & Zeitlinger.

Hart, O. van der & Nijenhuis, E.R.S. (2007). Fasegerichte behandeling van posttraumatische stress. [Phase-directed treatment of posttraumatic stress]. In: P. Aarts & W. Visser (Eds), *Trauma, diagnostiek en behandeling [Trauma, assessment and treatment]* (pp. 179–192). Houten: Bohn Stafleu van Loghum.

Hart, O. van der, Nijenhuis, E.R.S. & Steele, K. (2006). *The haunted self. Structural dissociation and the treatment of chronic traumatization*. New York: W.W. Norton & Company, Inc.

Hart, O. van der, Dijke, A. van, Son, M. van & Steele, K. (2000). Somatoform dissociation in traumatized World War I combat soldiers: a neglected clinical heritage. *Journal of Trauma and Dissociation, 1*, 4, 33–66.

Hayes, S.C., Strosahl, K.D., & Wilson, K.G. (2003). *Acceptance and commitment therapy: an experiential approach to behavior change*. New York: Guilford Press.

Heesterman, W., Kockman, I., & Wel, B. van (Eds) (2004). *VERS: Vaardigheidstraining, emotie, regulatiestoornis [VERS: training in emotion regulation]*. Groningen/Deventer: GGz Groningen/Adhesie.

Herman, J.L. (1992). *Trauma and recovery: the aftermath of violence – from domestic abuse to political terror*. New York: Basic Books.

Herman, J.L. (2013). PTSD as a shame disorder. *Key-note address at the conference of the European Society of Traumatic Stress Studies, June 6*, Bologna, Italy.

Hermans, D., Eelen, P., & Orlemans, H. (2007). *Inleiding tot de gedragstherapie [Introduction to behavioral therapy]*. Houten: Bohn Stafleu van Loghum.

Holmes, E., James, E., Coode-Bate, T., & Deeprose, C. (2009). Can playing the computer-game 'Tetris' reduce the build-up of flashbacks for trauma? A proposal from cognitive science. *PLoS ONE 4*, 1, e4153.

Hondius, A.J.K., Willigen, L.M. van, Kleijn, W.Chr., & Ploeg, H.M. van der (2000). Post traumatic stress among refugees in the Netherlands. *Journal of Traumatic Stress, 13*, 4, 619–634.

Hornsveld, H. (1996). *Farewell to the hyperventilation syndrome (dissertation)*. Amsterdam: University of Amsterdam.

Horowitz, M.J. (1997). *Stress response syndromes: PTSD, grief, and adjustment disorders*, 3rd edn. New Jersey: Jason Aranson Inc.

Horowitz, M.J., Wilner, N., & Alvarez, W. (1979). Impact of event scale: a measure of subjective stress. *Psychosomatic Medicine, 41*, 209–218.

Hout, M.A. van den & Merkelbach, H. (1993). Over exposure [About exposure]. *Directieve therapie, 3*, 192–203.

Hovens, J.E., Bramsen, I., & Ploeg, H.M. van der (2000). *Handleiding bij de Zelfinventarisatielijst Posttraumatische Stressstoornis (ZIL) [Manual of the Self-rating Inventory for Post-traumatic stress disorder (PTSD)]*. Lisse: Swets Test Publishers.

Hovens, H., Luinge, B.A., & Minnen, A. van (2005). *Klinisch interview PTSS (KIP). [The clinical interview PTSD]*. Amsterdam: Boom test uitgevers.

Huijbregts, K., Veeninga, A., & Hafkenscheid, A. (2008). Getuigenisbehandeling bij child survivors en nakomelingen van oorlogsslachtoffers: een pilot-studie [Testimony therapy in child survivors and off spring of war victims: a pilot study]. *Tijdschrift voor Psychotherapie, 34*, 5, 322–340.

Huizing, W. & Tromp, T. (2007). Werken met levensboeken in de praktijk van de ouderenzorg [Working with life stories in the clinical practice of the elderly]. In: E. Bohlmeijer, L. Mies, & G. Westerhof (Ed.), *De betekenis van levensverhalen, theoretische beschouwingen en toepassingen in onderzoek en praktijk [The significance of life stories, theoretical perspectives and implementation in research and practice]* (pp. 401–414). Houten: Bohn Stafleu van Loghum.

Hummelen, K. (2008). Weg met het concept persoonlijkheidsstoornis. Van symptoom via context naar functiediagnostiek [Out with the concept of personality disorder. From symptome to functional assessment via context]. *Maandblad Geestelijke Volksgezondheid, 63*, 6, 485–495.

Hustinx, A. (1973). Het existentieel emotioneel stress-syndroom. [The existential emotional stress-syndrome]. *Maandblad Geestelijke Volksgezondheid, 28*, 197–206.

IJzendoorn, M.H. van, Bakermans-Kranenburg, M.J., & Sagi-Schwartz, A. (2003). Are children of Holocaust survivors less well-adapted? A meta-analytic investigation of secondary traumatization. *Journal of Traumatic Stress, 16*, 459–469.

Jacobson, E. (1938). *Progressive relaxation*. Chicago: University Press.

Janoff-Bulman, R. (1989). Assumptive worlds and the stress of traumatic events: applications of the schema construct. *Social Cognition, 7*, 113–136.

Janoff-Bulman, R. (1992). *Shattered assumptions. Towards a new psychology of trauma*. New York: Free Press.

Jongedijk, R. (2006). Hoe effectief is medicatie bij posttraumatische stresstoornis? [How effective is medication in PTSD?] *Cogiscope, 6*, 2, 28–31.

Jongedijk, R.A., Carlier, I.V.E., Schreuder, J.N., & Gersons, B.P.R. (1995). Is er een plaats voor de complexe posttraumatische stress stoornis? PTSS en DESNOS nader beschouwd. [Is there room for complex posttraumatic stress disorder? PTSD and DESNOS reconsidered]. *Tijdschrift voor Psychiatrie, 37*, 1, 43–54.

Jongh, A. de & Ten Broeke, E. (2003). *Handboek EMDR: een geprotocolleerde behandelmethode voor de gevolgen van psychotrauma [Handbook EMDR: a protocolized treatment method for the consequences of psychotrauma]*. Lisse: Swets & Zeitlinger.

Kessler, R.C., Sonnega, A., Bromet, E., Hughes, M., & Nelson, C.B. (1995). Posttraumatic stress disorder in the national comorbidity survey. *Archives of General Psychiatry, 52*, 1048–1060.

Kiesler, D.J. (1983). The 1982 Interpersonal Circle: a taxonomy for complementarity in human transactions. *Psychological Review, 90*, 185–214.

Kilpatrick, D.G. (2005). A special section on complex trauma and a few thoughts about the need for more rigorous research on treatment efficacy, effectiveness, and safety. *Journal of Traumatic Stress, 18*, 379–384.

Kleber, R.J. (2007a). *Weg van het trauma [Away from trauma]*. Utrecht: Utrecht University.

Kleber, R.J. (2007b). Trauma en verwerking [Trauma and coping]. In: P. Aarts & W. Visser (Eds), *Trauma, diagnostiek en behandeling [Trauma, assessment and treatment]* (pp. 165–178). Houten: Bohn Stafleu van Loghum.

Kleber, R.J. & Brom, D. (with Defares, P.B.) (1992). *Coping with trauma: theory, prevention and treatment*. Lisse: Swets & Zeitlinger.

Kleijn, W.C, Hovens, J.E., & Rodenburg, J.J. (2001). Posttraumatic stress symptoms in refugees: assessments with the Harvard Trauma Questionnaire and the Hopkins symptom Checklist-25 in different languages. *Psychological Reports, 88*, 527–532.

Kolk, B.A. van der (2005). Developmental trauma disorder: toward a rational diagnosis for children with complex trauma histories. *Psychiatric Annals, 35*, 5, 401–408.

Kolk, B.A. van der, McFarlane, A.C., & Hart, O. van der (1996a). A general approach to treatment of post traumatic stress disorder. In: B. van der Kolk, A.C. McFarlane & L. Weisaeth (Eds), *Traumatic stress, the overwhelming experience on mind, body and society* (pp. 417–440). New York: Guilford Press.

Kolk, B.A. van der, Roth, S., Pelcovitz, D., Sunday, S., & Spinazzola, J. (2005). Disorders of extreme stress: the empirical foundation of a complex adaptation to trauma. *Journal of Traumatic Stress, 18*, 389–399.

Kolk, B.A. van der, Pelcovitz, D., Roth, S., Mandel, F., McFarlane, A. & Herman, J. (1996b). Dissociation, somatization, and affect dysregulation. The complexity of adaptation to trauma. *American Journal of Psychiatry, 153*, 83–93.

Korn, D.L. & Leeds, A.M. (2002). Preliminary evidence of efficacy for EMDR resource development and installation in the stabilization phase of treatment of complex post traumatic stress disorder. *Journal of Clinical Psychology, 59*, 1465–1487.

Korrelboom, K. & Ten Broeke, E. (2004). *Geïntegreerde cognitieve gedragstherapie. Handboek voor theorie en praktijk [Integrated cognitive and behavioral therapy. Handbook for theory and practice]*. Bussum: Uitgeverij Coutinho.

Krakow, B.R., Kellner, D., Pathak, D., & Lambert, L. (1995). Imagery rehearsal treatment for chronic nightmares. *Behaviour Research and Therapy, 33*, 837–843.

Lang, P.J. (1984). Cognition in emotion. Concept and action. In: C. Izard, J. Kagan, & R.B. Zajonc (Eds), *Emotion, cognition and behavior* (pp. 192–226). New York: Cambridge University Press.

Lange, A. (2007). Het verwerken van trauma's door gestructureerd schrijven en imaginaire exposure [Coping with trauma through structured writing and imaginary exposure]. In: P. Aarts & W. Visser (Eds), *Trauma, diagnostiek en behandeling [Trauma, assessment and treatment]* (pp. 273–292). Houten: Bohn Stafleu van Loghum.

Lange, A., Ven, J.P. van de, Schrieken, B., & Emmelkamp, P.M. (2001). Interapy, treatment of posttraumatic stress through the Internet: a controlled trial. *Journal of Behavioral Therapy and Experimental Psychiatry, 32*, 2, 73–90.

Lange, A., Rietdijk, D., Hudcovicova, M., Ven, J.P. van de, Schrieken, B., & Emmelkamp, P.M.G. (2003). Interapy: a controlled randomized trial of the standardized treatment of posttraumatic stress through the internet. *Journal of Consulting and Clinical Psychology, 71*, 5, 901–909.

Lazarus, A.A. (1971). *Behavior therapy and beyond.* New York: McGraw Hill.

Lifton, R.J. (1979). *The broken connection. On death and the continuity of life.* Washington DC: American Psychiatric Press.

Lindauer, R.J.L., Gersons, B., Meijel, E. van, Blom, K., Carlier, I., Vrijlandt, I., & Olff, M. (2005). Effects of brief eclectic psychotherapy in patients with posttraumatic stress disorder: randomized clinical trial. *Journal of Traumatic Stress, 18, 3,* 205–212.

Linehan, M.M. (1993). *Cognitive-behavioral treatment of borderline personality disorder.* New York: Guilford Press.

Liu, R.T., Alloy, L.B., Abramson, K.Y., Iacoviello, B.M., & Whitehouse, W.G. (2009). Emotional maltreatment and depression: prospective prediction of depressive episodes. *Depression and Anxiety, 26*, 174–181.

Livesley, W.J. (2003). *Practical management of personality disorder.* New York: Guilford Press.

Livesley, W.J. (2007). Common elements of effective treatment. In: B. van Luyn, S. Akhtar & W.J. Livesley (Eds), *Severe personality disorders* (pp. 211–223). Cambridge: Cambridge University Press.

Luxenberg, T., Spinazzola, J., & Kolk, B.A. van der (2001). Complex trauma and disorders of extreme stress (DESNOS). Part One: Assessment. *Directions in Psychiatry, 21*, 373–394.

McCann, I.L. & Pearlman, L.A. (1990). Vicarious traumatization: a framework for understanding the psychological effects of working with victims. *Journal of Traumatic Stress, 3*, 131–149.

McFarlane, A.C. (1998) Epidemiological evidence about the relationship between PTSD and alcohol abuse: the nature of the association. *Addictive Behavior, 23,* 813–825.

McGuigan, F.J. (1993). Progressive relaxation: origins, principles, and clinical applications. In: P.M. Lehrer & R.L. Woolfolk (Eds), *Principles and practice of stress management* (pp. 17–52). New York: Guilford Press.

MacLean, P.D. (1990). *The triune brain in evolution: role in paleocerebral functions.* New York: Plenum Press.

McNally, R.J. (2001). On the scientific status of cognitive appraisal models of anxiety disorder. *Behaviour Research and Therapy, 39,* 513–521.

Merkelbach, H. & Hout, M. van den (1993). Classical conditioning: the hegemony is not ubiquitous. *Behavioral and Brain Sciences, 16, 2,* 396–398.

Millon, T., & Everly, G.S. (1985). *Personality and its disorders: a biosocial learning approach.* New York: Wiley.

Minnen, A. van. (2002). Prolonged exposure in PTSD: practical guidelines. *Directions in Rehabilitation Counseling, 13,* 15–24.

Minnen, A. van & Arntz, A. (2005). Behandeling van patienten met een posttraumatische stressstoornis met exposure [Treatment of patients with PTSD with exposure]. In: B.P.R. Gersons & M. Olff (Eds), *Behandelingsstrategieen bij posttraumatische stressstoornissen [Treatment strategies for PTSDs]* (pp. 76–85). Houten: Bohn Stafleu van Loghum.

Minnen, A. van, Kroon, A., & Keijsers, G. (1998). Gevolgen voor therapeuten bij de behandeling van post traumatische stressstoornis (Consequences for therapists in the treatment of PTSD). *Tijdschrift voor Psychotherapie, 24, 4*, 217–230.

Mollica, R.F., Wyshak, G., Marneffe, D. de, Khuon, F. & Lavelle, J. (1987). Indochinese versions of the Hopkins Symptom Checklist-25: a screening instrument for the psychiatric care of refugees. *American Journal of Psychiatry, 144*, 497–500.

Mollica, R.F., Caspi-Yavin, Y., Bollini, P., & Truong, T. (1992). The Harvard Trauma Questionnaire: validating a cross-cultural instrument for measuring torture, trauma, and posttraumatic stress disorder in Indochinese refugees. *Journal of Nervous and Mental Disease, 180*, 111–116.

Mooren, G.T.M. & Kleber, R.J. (2001). The impact of war in Bosnia and Hercegovina: Devastated trust. *International Journal of Mental Health, 30*, 02, 6–21.

Mooren, T. (2001). *The impact of war. Studies of the psychological consequences of war and migration (dissertation)*. Delft: Eburon.

Mooren, T. & Dijk, J. van (2004). Getuigenistherapie bij vluchtelingen, een integratief protocol. [Testimony therapy for refugees, an integrative protocol]. *Tijdschrift voor Psychotherapie, 30*, 359–367.

Mooren, T. & Schoorl, M. (2006). Psycho-educatie aan vluchtelingen en asielzoekers. [Psycho-education to refugees and asylum-seekers]. *Cogiscope, 6*, 2, 5–9.

Mooren, T. & Schoorl, M. (2009). *Beter beginnen, een psycho-educatief programma voor vluchtelingen en asielzoekers [Better start, a psycho-education programme for refugees and asylum-seekers]*. Houten: Bohn Stafleu van Loghum/Utrecht: Cogis.

Mooren, T., Schok, M. & Kleber, R.J. (2009). De zin van ingrijpende gebeurtenissen: een vragenlijst over betekenisgeving na oorlogs- en geweldervaringen. [The significance of disruptive events: a questionnaire on the assignment of meaning after experiences of war and migration]. *Psychologie & Gezondheid, 2*, 49–58.

Moreno, A., Piwowarczyk, L., LaMorte, W., & Grodin, M. (2006). Characteristics and utilization of primary care services in a torture rehabilitation center. *Journal of Immigrant and Minority Health, 8*, 2, 163–171.

Musaph, H. (1973). Het post-concentratiekampsyndroom [The post-concentration camp syndrome]. *Maandblad Geestelijke Volksgezondheid, 28*, 207–217.

Najavits, L.M. (2007). Psychosocial treatments for post traumatic stress disorder. In: P.E. Nathan & J.M. Gorman (Eds), *A guide to treatments that work* (pp. 513–529). Oxford: Oxford University Press.

National Institute for Clinical Excellence (NICE) (2005). *Posttraumatic stress disorder (PTSD). The management of PTSD in adults and children in primary and secondary care*. London: NICE.

National Workinggroup/Trimbos Institute (2008). *Multidisciplinaire richtlijn persoonlijkheidsstoornissen [Multidisciplinary guidelines to personality disorders]*. Utrecht: Trimbos Institute.

Nickerson, A., Bryant, R.A., Brooks, R., Steel, Z., Silove, D., & Chen, J. (2011). The familial influence of loss and trauma on refugee mental health. A multilevel path analysis. *Journal of Traumatic Stress, 24*, 25–33.

Nicolai, N. (2008). Overdracht en tegenoverdracht bij vroegkinderlijke traumatisering. [Transference and counter-transference in early traumatisation]. *Tijdschrift voor Psychotherapie, 34*, 6, 431–449.

Nijdam, M.J., Gersons, B.P.R., Reitsma, J.B., Jongh, A. de, & Olff, M. (2012). Brief eclectic psychotherapy versus eye movement desensitisation and reprocessing therapy for post-traumatic stress disorder: randomised controlled trial. *The British Journal of Psychiatry, 200*, 224–231. DOI: 10.1192/bjp.bp.111.099234.

Ogden, P. & Minton, K. (2000). Sensorimotor psychotherapy: one method for processing traumatic memory. *Traumatology, 6*, 149–173.

Olthof, J. & Vermetten, E. (1994). *De mens als verhaal, narratieve strategieën in psychotherapie van kinderen en volwassenen. [Man as story, narrative strategies in psychotherapy of children and adults]*. Utrecht: de Tijdstroom.

Opler, L.A., Grennan, M.S., & Ford, J.D. (2009). Pharmacotherapy. In: C.A. Courtois & J.D. Ford (Eds), *Treating complex traumatic stress disorders, an evidence-based guide* (pp. 329–350). New York: Guilford Press.

Oppenheim, H.J., Ten Broeke, E., & De Jongh, A. (2008). EMDR bij dissociatieve stoornissen [EMDR in dissociative disorders]. In: E. Ten Broeke, A. De Jongh & H.J. Oppenheim (Eds), *Praktijkboek EMDR [Practitioners Guide EMDR]* (pp. 177–199). Amsterdam: Harcourt Book Publishers.

Orlemans, J.W.G., Eelen, P. & Hermans, D. (1995). *Inleiding tot de gedragstherapie. [Introduction to behavior therapy]*. Houten: Bohn Stafleu van Loghum.

Pelcovitz, D., Kolk, B.A. van der, Roth, S., Mandel, F., Kaplan, S. & Resick, P. (1997). Development of a criteria set and a structured interview for disorders of extreme stress (SIDES). *Journal of Traumatic Stress, 10*, 3–16.

Pelcovitz, D., Kaplan, S.J., DeRosa, R.R., Mandel, F.S., & Salzinger, S. (2000). Psychiatric disorders in adolescents exposed to domestic violence and physical abuse. *The American Journal of Orthopsychiatry, 70*, 360–369.

Pennebaker, J.W. (1982). *The psychology of physical symptoms*. New York: Springer-Verlag. Pennebaker Inventory of Limbic Languidness: http://homepage.psy.utexas.edu/homepage/Faculty/Pennebaker/Questionnaires/QuestionnaireIndex.html (accessed 14 April 2014).

Ramsay, R. W. (1979). Rouwtherapie; de gedragstherapeutisch behandeling van pathologische rouwproblemen [Grief therapy; behavioural treatment of pathological grief problems]. In: *Handboek voor Gedragstherapie [Handbook of Behavioural Therapy], B 4.2*, 1–36. Deventer: Van Loghum-Slaterus.

Reger, M.A. & Gahm, G.A. (2009). A meta-analysis of the effects of internet- and computer-based cognitive-behavioral treatments for anxiety. *Journal of Clinical Psychology, 65*, 53–75.

Rietveld, N. (2009). *De gewetensvolle veteraan. Schuld- en schaamtebeleving bij veteranen van vredesmissies [The conscientious veteran. The experience of guilt and shame in veterans after peace missions] (dissertation)*. Oisterwijk: Uitgeverij Boxpress.

Rijkeboer, M.M. (2005). *Assessment of early maladaptive schemas. On the validity of the Dutch Young Schema-Questionnaire* (doctoral dissertation). Enschede/Amsterdam: PrintPartners Ipskamp.

Rohlof, J.G.B.M. & Scholte, W.F. (2005). Diagnostiek en behandeling van getraumatiseerde vluchtelingen [Assessment and treatment of traumatized refugees]. In: B.P.R. Gersons & M. Olff (Eds), *Behandelingsstrategieën bij posttraumatische stressstoornissen [Treatment strategies for PTSDs]* (pp. 140–155). Houten: Bohn Stafleu van Loghum.

Salcioglu, E., Basoglu, M., & Livanou, M. (2007). Effects of live exposure on symptoms of posttraumatic stress disorder: the role of reduced behavioral avoidance in improvement. *Behaviour Research and Therapy, 45*, 2268–2279.

Sapolsky, R.M. (1998). *Why zebras don't get ulcers: an updated guide to stress, stress-related diseases, and coping*. New York: W.H. Freeman and Company.

Schaal, S., Elbert, T., & Neuner, F. (2009). Narrative exposure therapy versus interpersonal psychotherapy: a pilot randomized controlled trial with Rwandan genocide orphans. *Psychotherapy and Psychosomatics, 78*, 298–306.

Schauer, M., Neuner, F., & Elbert, T. (2005). *Narrative Exposure Therapy (NET). A short term intervention for traumatic stress disorders after war, terror or torture*. Cambridge/Göttingen: Hogrefe & Huber Publishers.

Scheeringa, M.S. & Zeanah, C.H. (2001). A relational perspective on PTSD in early childhood. *Journal of Traumatic Stress, 14*, 799–815.

Schmid, M., Petermann, F., & Fegert, J.M. (2013) Developmental trauma disorder: pros and cons of including formal criteria in the psychiatric diagnostic systems. *BMC Psychiatry, 13, 3*, http://www.biomedcentral.com/1471–244x/13/3 (accessed 14 April 2014).

Schok, M. (2009). *Meaning as a mission: making sense of war and peacekeeping*. (Dissertation.) Delft: Eburon.

Schoorl, M. (2013). *Investigating new process-focused treatments for posttraumatic stress disorder: attentional bias modification and mindfulness-based cognitive therapy (dissertation)*. Leiden: Leiden University.

Schoutrop, M. (2000). *Structured writing in processing traumatic events (dissertation)*. Amsterdam: University of Amsterdam.

Schreuder, B. (1999). Nachtmerries [Nightmares]. *Tijdschrift voor Psychoanalyse, 5*, 2, 71–88.

Schurink, G. (2009). *Mindfulness, een praktische training in het omgaan met gevoelens en gewoonten [Mindfulness, a practical training for coping with feelings and habits]*. Zaltbommel: Uitgeverij Thema.

Scoboria, A., Ford, J., Lin, H., & Frisman, L. (2008). Revision of the Structured Interview for Disorders of Extreme Stress (SIDES): an exploratory and confirmatory factor analytic approach. *Assessment, 15*, 404–425.

Segal, Z.V., Williams, J.M., & Teasdale, J.D. (2002). *Mindfulness based cognitive therapy for depression*. New York: Guilford Press.

Sevinc, F. & Colijn, S. (2009). Psychotherapie en cultuur verschillen [Psychotherapy and culture differences]. In: Colijn, S, H. Snijders, M. Thunissen, S. Bögels & W. Trijsburg (Eds), *Leerboek psychotherapie [Workbook psychotherapy]* (pp. 841–852). Utrecht: de Tijdstroom.

Shapiro, F. (2001). *Eye Movement Desensitization and Reprocessing. Basic principles, protocols, and procedures*. New York: Guilford Press.

Shapiro, F. (2002). Paradigms, processing and personality development. In: F. Shapiro (Ed), *EMDR as an integrative psychotherapy approach: experts of diverse orientations explore the paradigm prism* (pp. 3–26). Washington DC: American Psychological Association.

Shapiro, F. (2012). *Getting past your past. Take control of your life with self-help techniques from EMDR therapy*. New York: Rodale.

Shapiro, F. & Silk Forrest, M. (1997). *The breakthrough 'Eye movement' therapy for overcoming anxiety, stress and trauma*. New York: Basic Books.

Shepard, B. (2000). *The war of nerves*. London: Jonathan Cape.

Sleijpen, M., Mooren, T., & Kleber, R.J. (2009). *Long-term legacies of war*. Oegstgeest: Centrum '45.

Smeijsters, H. (2000). *Handboek creatieve therapie [Handbook of creative therapy]*. Bussum: Coutinho.

Smith, A. (2009). *Listening to trauma. Therapists' countertransference and long-term effects related to trauma work (dissertation).* Nijmegen: Radboud Universiteit Nijmegen.

Smith, A.J.M., Kleijn, W.C., Trijsburg, W., & Hutschemaekers, G.J.M. (2007a). How therapists cope with clients' traumatic experiences. *Torture, 17*, 3, 203–215.

Smith, A.J.M., Kleijn, W.C., & Hutschemaekers, G.J.M. (2007b). Therapist reactions in self-experienced difficult situations: an exploration. *Counselling and Psychotherapy Research, 7*, 34–41.

Smucker. M.R., Dancu, C., Foa, E., & Niederee, J. (1995). Imagery rescripting: a new treatment for survivors of childhood sexual abuse suffering from post traumatic stress. *Journal of Cognitive Psychotherapy, 9(1)*, 3–17.

Sonderen, E. van (1993). *The measurement of social support with the SSQ-I and the SSQ-D. Dutch manual.* Groningen: Noordelijk Centrum voor Gezondheidsvraagstukken.

Spoormaker, V.I. (2005). *Nightmares: assessment, theory, and treatment (dissertation).* Utrecht: Utrecht University.

Sprey, A. (2002). *Praktijkboek persoonlijkheidsstoornissen, diagnostiek, cognitieve gedragstherapie en therapeutische relatie [Handbook personality disorders, assessment, cognitive behavioral therapy and therapeutical relationship].* Houten: Bohn Stafleu van Loghum.

Stöfsel, A.M. (1996). Een ambulante behandeling van herbelevingen bij een Jappenkampslachtoffer [Ambulant treatment of intrusions in a survivor of Japanese camp]. In: A. de Jong (Ed), *Facetten van traumabehandeling [Aspects of trauma treatment]* (pp. 55–66). Assen: Van Gorcum.

Stöfsel. A.M. (1998). Ondergedoken angst [Hidden fear]. In: *Bulletin van de Vereniging voor Gedragstherapie, 31*, 24–38.

Stöfsel, A.M. (2005). EMDR-behandeling in het Sinaï Centrum [EMDR in Sinai Centrum]. *Cogiscope, 1*, 2–9.

Stuyling de Lange, J., Dashorst, P., & Mooren, T. (2009). Trauma en persoonlijkheidsproblematiek, de toepassing van een integratief model. [Trauma and personality, the use of an integrative model]. *Tijdschrift voor Psychotherapie, 35*, 396–412.

Summerfield, D. (1998). Sociocultural dimensions of war, conflict and displacement. In: A. Ager (Ed.), *Refugees' perspectives on the experience of forced migration* (pp. 111–135). London: Pinter.

Summerfield, D. (1999). A critique of seven assumptions behind psychological trauma programmes in war-affected areas. *Social Science and Medicine, 48*, 1449–1462.

Tankink, M. (2009). *Over zwijgen gesproken. Een medisch antropologische studie onder vluchtelingenvrouwen in Nederland, afkomstig uit Afghanistan, Bosnië-Herzegovina en Zuid-Soedan, naar het omgaan met ervaringen van aan oorlog gerelateerd seksueel geweld.* [Talking about silence. A medical-anthropological study among refugee women in the Netherlands, from Afghanistan, Bosnia and Herzegovina and South-Sudan]. Utrecht: Pharos.

Tarrier, N. (2006). *Case formulation in cognitive behaviour therapy. The treatment of challenging and complex cases.* New York: Routledge.

Taylor, S. (2006). *Clinician's guide to PTSD: a cognitive-behavioral approach.* New York: Guilford Press.

Tedeschi R.G. & Calhoun, L.G. (1996). The posttraumatic growth inventory: measuring the positive legacy of trauma. *Journal of Traumatic Stress, 9*, 3, 455–471.

Ten Broeke, E., Jongh, A. de, & Oppenheim, H.J. (Eds) (2008). *Praktijkboek EMDR [Clinical practice book EMDR].* Amsterdam: Harcourt Book Publishers.

Terr, L.C. (1991). Childhood traumas: an outline and overview. *American Journal of Psychiatry, 148*, 10–20.

Tol, W.A., Jordans, M.D., Reis, Ria, & Jong, Joop de (2009). Ecological resilience: working with child-related psychosocial resources in war-affected communities. In: D. Brom, R. Pat-Horenczyk, & J.D. Ford (Eds), (2009). *Treating traumatized children: risk, resilience and recovery* (pp. 164–182). New York: Routledge/Taylor & Francis.

Tomasoa, A. & Appelo, M. (2007). Rationele Rehabilitatie bij de posttraumatische stresss-toornis, een pilot-onderzoek [Rational rehabilitation in posttraumatic stress disorder, a pilot study]. *Tijdschrift voor Psychiatrie, 49*, 8, 529–535.

Veer, G. van der (1998). Counselling and therapy with refugees and victims of trauma. Chichester, UK: Wiley.

Veer, G. van der (2004). Praktische uitgangspunten van psychotherapie met vluchtelingen [Practice based guidelines in psychotherapy with refugees]. *Tijdschrift voor Psychotherapie, 30*, 320–330.

Verhofstadt-Deneve, L., Geert, P. van & Vyt, A. (2003). *Handboek ontwikkelingspsychologie [Handbook of developmental psychology]*. Houten: Bohn Stafleu van Loghum.

Vreeswijk, M. van, Broersen, J., & Nadort, M. (Eds) (2012). *The Wiley/Blackwell handbook of schematherapy: theory, research and practice.* New York: Wiley Blackwell.

Vries, G.J. de & Olff, M. (2009). The lifetime prevalence of traumatic events and posttraumatic stress disorder in the Netherlands. *Journal of Traumatic Stress, 22*, 259–267.

Walsh, F. (2006). *Strengthening family resilience*. New York: Guilford Press.

Weathers, F.W., Keane, T.M., & Davidson, J.R.T. (2001). Clinician-administered PTSD scale: a review of the first ten years of research. *Depression and Anxiety, 13*, 132–156.

Weine, S.M. (2006). *Testimony after catastrophe: narrating the traumas of political violence*. Evanston, IL: Northwestern University Press.

Wel, B. van, Kockmann, I., Blum, N., Pfohl, B., Black, D.W., & Heesterman, W. (2006). STEPPS group treatment for borderline personality disorder in The Netherlands. *Annual Clinical Psychiatry, 18*, 63–67.

Wepster, D. (2003). Over tegenoverdracht en empathie bij overlevingsschuld en overlevingsschaamte [On counter transference and empathy in the case of surivival guilt and shame]. *Tijdschrift voor Psychotherapie, 29*, 2, 115–132.

Wertheim-Cahen, T. (2007). De rol van vaktherapieën bij de behandeling van psychotrauma [The role of non-verbal therapies in psychotrauma]. In: P. Aarts & W. Visser (Eds). *Trauma, diagnostiek en behandeling [Trauma, diagnostics and treatment]*. Houten: Bohn Stafleu van Loghum.

Willigen, L. van (2007). Vluchtelingen en asielzoekers. [Refugees and asylum seekers] In: P. Aarts & W. Visser (Eds), *Trauma, diagnostiek en behandeling* [Trauma, assessment and treatment] (pp. 514–560). Houten: Bohn Stafleu van Loghum.

Wilson, P. (1999). *Het grote boek van de rust [The little book of calm]*. Amsterdam: Uitgeverij Archipel.

Winkel, F.W. (2007). *Post traumatic anger. Missing link in the wheel of misfortune.* Nijmegen: Wolf.

Withuis, J. (2009). De opmars van het slachtoffer. [The rise of the victim]. *Trouw*, 28 November.

WHO (2004). *The World Health Organization Quality of Life (WHOQOL)-BREF*. http://www.who.int/substance_abuse/research_tools/en/english_whoqol.pdf (accessed 14 April 2014).

WHO (2007). *The ICD-10 Classification of Mental and Behavioural Disorders. Diagnostic criteria for research.* Geneva: World Health Organisation. http://apps.who.int/classifications/apps/icd/icd10online (accessed 14 April 2014).

Young, J.E. (2005). Schema-focused cognitive therapy and the case of Ms. S. *Journal of Psychotherapy Integration, 15, 1,* 115–126.

Young, J.E., Klosko, J.S., & Weishaar, M.E. (2003). *Schema therapy: a practitioner's guide.* New York: Guilford Press.

Zlotnick, C., Shea, M.T., Rosen, K., Simpson, E., Mulrenin, K., Begin, A., & Pearlstein, T. (1997). An affect-management group for survivors of sexual abuse with PTSD. *Journal of Traumatic Stress, 10,* 425–436.

Index

Note: 'F' after a page number indicates a figure.